What People Are Saying...

"*Conversations with America's Best Teachers* provides valuable advice and creative methods for dealing with many of the problems teachers face in classrooms all over the country. Every teacher should read this book."

— *Richard Riley*
Former U.S. Secretary of Education

"This is a book you need to read if you want to be—not just a better teacher—but one of the best teachers!"

— *Harry Wong*
Author, The First Days of School

"Towne may not have had America's best teachers in school, but his book provides a national service in helping create more of them. Everyone with an interest in education—and that should include everyone—should read this book and will be glad they did."

— *Milton Chen*
Executive Director, George Lucas Educational Foundation

"You can open Towne's book on any page and find wisdom."

— *Jay Mathews*
Washington Post

"Right out of the mouths of a remarkable collection of teachers. A pleasure to read!"

— *Deborah Meier*
NYU Steinhardt School of Education

"This book renews our faith in the world's most important profession."
— *Dr. Spencer Kagan*
Author, Kagan Cooperative Learning

"A sparkling collection of warm and candid interviews. This book will be of tremendous help to educators everywhere."
— *Jonathan Kozol*
Author, Death at an Early Age

"Fun and interesting. You'll learn something from each of these teachers whether you're a peer or a wonk. Towne has done a remarkable service here."
— *Andrew Rotherham*
Publisher, Education Sector & Eduwonk Blog

"Towne makes an invaluable contribution to the debate over how to provide a quality education to all students, regardless of their backgrounds. It couldn't come at a more propitious time."
— *Walt Gardner*
Education Writer

"*Conversations with America's Best Teachers* makes a tremendously powerful case for teachers as empowered leaders."
— *Virginia B. Edwards*
Editor, Education Week / Teacher Magazine

"The valuable insights of successful teachers in *Conversations with America's Best Teachers* will not only benefit other teachers looking for solutions, but anyone who wants to know the real joys and challenges of the most important work in this country."
— *Michelle Rhee*
Chancellor, District of Columbia Public Schools

"Worthwhile reading for educators, policymakers, and anyone interested in transforming today's public education system."

— *Dennis Van Roekel*
President, National Education Association

"Towne has done a great public service to all those who care about educating our children by highlighting great teachers and the work they do."

— *Randi Weingarten*
President, American Federation of Teachers, AFL-CIO

"I hope this book becomes a primer for teachers in training."

— *Kathleen A. Carpenter*
Editor, TeachersNet Gazette

"These pages will inspire awe, appreciation, and sometimes shock at what is required to excel in the world's most important profession. I hope that every teacher—and every school administrator—reads this book!"

— *Eric Adler*
Co-Founder & Managing Director, The SEED Foundation

"Inspirational! A must read for every teacher and parent. Both new and experienced teachers can benefit from the wisdom of these accomplished educators."

— *Joe Aguerrebere*
President, National Board of Professional Teaching Standards

"*Conversations with America's Best Teachers* is a much needed addition to the education reform literature."

— *Robert Hughes*
President, New Visions for Public Schools

AMERICA'S BEST TEACHERS

MASTERS <small>OF THE</small> CRAFT

The Masters of the Craft series of books is designed to bring together the best voices in various industries, in an effort to inspire and teach others who have an interest in that career path. No matter what career you choose, there will be those before you who spent years mastering it. There is no better way of learning a profession than experience.

Although we can't provide you with years of experience, we will provide you with the wisdom of those who have it. The interviewees in the *Masters of the Craft* series are among the absolute best at what they do, and by agreeing to be interviewed, they are hoping you too will someday become a master of *your* craft.

www.motcbooks.com

CONVERSATIONS WITH

AMERICA'S BEST TEACHERS

TEACHER OF THE YEAR AWARD WINNERS GIVE PRACTICAL ADVICE FOR THE CLASSROOM AND BEYOND

J. WILLIAM TOWNE

With Rita J. Prescott, Editor

First Edition By

Inkster
Publishing

Inkster Publishing, LLC
Los Angeles, CA, U.S.A.
Publishing www.inksterpublishing.com

First Published in the United States of America by Inkster Publishing

Interviews are undertaken with the expectation of publication. In such publication the interviewees alone are responsible for statements of fact, opinions, recommendations, and conclusions expressed. Publication in no way implies approval or endorsement by Inkster Publishing or the book's author.

13-digit ISBN: 978-0-9823244-0-0
10-digit ISBN: 09823244-0-5

Library Congress Control Number: 2009927946

1. Education. 2. Parenting. I. Towne, J. William. II. Prescott, Rita III. Title.

Printed in the United States of America

Edited by Rita J. Prescott
Cover Design by Richard G. Bennett
Interior design and typography by Ghislain Viau

Dedicated to teachers everywhere.
Our future rests in your hands.

Table of Contents

Foreword

When you open this book, prepare to enter a Professional Learning Community with 18 inspirational teachers. Through his interviews, J. William Towne gives voice to *America's Best Teachers*, each of whom was either a National Teacher of the Year Award winner or finalist. The interview format works beautifully, because the authenticity of these teachers' voices jumps off the page, and because Towne asks questions with his readers in mind.

These teachers' practices are as varied as the children they teach. One math teacher encourages his students to use their cell phones to check their work; another uses photography to demonstrate the relevance of math; and a third creates rap songs to reinforce math concepts and, yes, to entertain his students. Some teachers use the aesthetics of their classrooms to engage their students, whether through the creation of a classroom museum, a television station, a poetry coffeehouse or a beach. Storytelling, community service, learning games, and body mapping define the practice of other teachers. A lesson of this book is that there are many roads to heaven.

One teacher, Sharon M. Draper, shares her fourth graders' musings on the definition of a good teacher. Their responses are touching – *A good teacher is soft enough to hug, but too hard to punch;* practical – *A good teacher is not scared of thunder and lightning and knows what to do when the lights go out;* and wise – *A good teacher would be fun to have at your house for dinner, but you'd never want him to come for real.* By the end of this book, the reader knows what good teachers are: those who keep their students at the center of their practice. In reading these interviews, I was struck by three characteristics that define how good teachers manage to do this.

First, they actively foster a sense of shared responsibility. Some teachers expect their students to devise rules for classroom management. As a consequence, the children mostly respect their own rules, and when their peers are out of compliance, they help them toe the line. Good teachers also give their students responsibility for their learning. Ron Poplau learned this lesson when he asked his class, *How come it appears that we do not get along?* They told him that they would listen to him if he would listen to them. His sociology students wanted guest speakers, field trips and community service. Poplau adapted his practice to great results. Other teachers have experimented with self-grading and student choice on assignments.

Second, successful teachers find a way to individualize instruction. Many of these teachers acknowledge that this is the most difficult part of their jobs. They recognize that children come to their classes with varying preparation, varying strengths, varying learning styles, and varying home supports. And they understand that their job is to reach each and every student despite the challenge of being alone in their classrooms most of the time. Nevertheless, you can hear the frustration and the heartache in their voices when they believe they have failed a student.

Third, and perhaps most important, these teachers work hard to develop relationships with each of their students. For me, this is the defining characteristic in each of the portraits. Many teachers confess that relationships come first, before learning. They offer their students unconditional love and kindness. I admire how Tamara Steen accomplishes this. In her words:

Building a relationship means letting a child know that
I SEE him or her, separately, distinctly from all the rest — that

I miss him/her if absent, and that I value that child's contribution to my life. How do I do this? By making sure that there is approval in my eyes whenever I look at them, that I smile with joy for having them present, that I laugh with them and cry with them, that I know their interests and concerns.

Jason Kamras tells a particularly poignant story of relationship-building through Wendall, a child who did not trust Kamras, acted out in class, and was headed for trouble. Kamras visited Wendall's mother, who gave him terrific advice – *make a connection*. Kamras challenged Wendall to play chess, because he knew that Wendall was a talented player. After several knock-out matches in Wendall's favor, Kamras earned Wendall's trust. Over time, Wendall's interest in school matched Kamras' interest in him. Wendall became a good student – so good that he was the 8th grade Valedictorian. It might have been otherwise for Wendall, as it is for so many students.

By design, the ideas shared in this book are for the taking. Keil Hileman advises all teachers to use the C.A.S.E. methodology or Copy and Steal Everything! All teachers, new and experienced, will appreciate the reflections of these talented teachers.

Kathleen McCartney
Dean, Harvard Graduate School of Education

Acknowledgements

I t's important for me to say thank you to a great many people that helped me put this book together from the very beginning. Each and every one of you are a part of this. Aside from the fantastic teachers featured in this book and those who were kind enough to read the book and offer their endorsements, there were many more people who I want to thank, including...

Kendra Beasley, Rita Prescott, Eric Liu, Richard Bennett, Stephen Caldwell Wright, Ghislain Viau, Kathleen McCartney, Taylor Sullivan, Miles J. Towne, Jonathon Towne, Lloyd Soyars, Ryan Blazer, Paola Sueiro, Rae Ellen McKee, Max Schlesinger, Molly Miles, Kris Henigman, Marcia Reed, Mark Norman, Paul Meena, Christen Beasley, Jazmine Carrington, James & Cheryl Carrington, Mark Harris, Bill Crookston, Paul Pearson, and Dottie DeHart.

I also want to thank everyone at William Morris who helped me along the way, including... David Kekst, Karen Ledlow, Josh Pyatt, Jim Wiatt, Jennifer Rudolph Walsh, Mel Berger, Jay Mandel, Bruce Gersh, Charles King, Brad Slater, Michael Cooper, Alicia Gordon, Natalie Hayden, Nicole David, Laurie Pozmantier, Ray Reo, Kim Koser, Jason Hatcher, Eric Zohn, Shannon Mattingly, Amparo Monsod, Anna Jones, Greg Schwartz, Greg Johnson, Kim Verbonitz, Jared Lake, Benjamin Scales, Chris Cate, Montrel McKay, and Drew Welborn.

About the Award

All of the teachers featured in this book were either National Teacher of the Year Award winners or finalists. Every featured teacher was a winner of the Teacher of the Year Award in their own state.

The National Teacher of the Year Program began in 1952 and continues as the oldest, most prestigious national honors program that focuses public attention on excellence in teaching.

The National Teacher of the Year Program, sponsored by ING, is a project of the Council of Chief State School Officers.

The National Teacher of the Year is chosen from among the State Teachers of the Year by a national selection committee representing the major national education organizations. Each April, the National Teacher of the Year is introduced to the American people by the President of the United States.

The National Teacher of the Year is released from classroom duties during the year of recognition to travel nationally and internationally as a spokesperson for the teaching profession. All activities of the National Teacher, and projects involving the State Teachers of the Year, are coordinated through the National Teacher of the Year Program.

For more information visit the CCSSO online at:

http://www.ccsso.org/projects/National_Teacher_of_the_Year

Introduction

"The best way to improve schools is to improve teachers."

I t was this simple quote that led to the creation of this book. But let me back up a moment and tell you my story. It's important because my experiences in grade school were the same that millions of other kids are experiencing right now. But it doesn't have to be like this.

I grew up in the inner-city and was raised by a single, hard-working mother. No one in my family had attended college, and it didn't look like that would change with me. In elementary school my grades were average and they consistently went downhill from there. I honestly cannot remember any of my grade school teachers, as they simply did not stand out. Typically, we were given a textbook, told what chapters to read and memorize, and then tested on those chapters. Everyone in class was given the same book to study, and there was no personal attention at all. By eighth grade, my grades had plummeted, and by high school, I was near failing. I was intelligent enough to have passed, but boredom had overcome me and I saw no real reason to do much of anything in class. It seemed as if the teachers and the administration didn't care, so why should I? By eleventh grade, I basically stopped going to school and dropped out the following year.

After dropping out, I spent years dabbling in part-time jobs and hanging out in the streets with the wrong crowd. I felt as though I had let down my mother, who really valued education. But I also felt like the school system had let me down. Why did school have to be so mundane and boring? Were all teachers like the ones I had, or was there a different breed of teacher out there somewhere that I had just missed out on? The answer came upon a chance meeting with a local community college professor. We were talking, and he told me that in his class the textbook was used for supplemental reading only. He said that his students were given options on the core reading materials and on what they wanted to write about. This was unheard of to me and sounded exciting. I loved to read, but I didn't love to read what the grade schools forced me to read. That professor convinced me to obtain my GED and attend his class. When I did, I was blown away. He was a fantastic teacher who gave his students choices and kept us engaged by using creative methods and instructional games. I got the first A I had seen in years. He then convinced me to enroll full time in college and I did.

Because of this professor, and others like him, I was the first in my family to attend college and it felt really good. I received nearly straight A's that first year of college, which helped me get accepted into the University of Southern California as a transfer student. I was now in one of the elite universities in the country, and the professors there were some of the best I had ever seen. Because of them I was able to graduate *Magna cum Laude* in the top 5% of my class and had a perfect 4.0 GPA in my Public Policy major. It was a long road that did not have to be so long. It was only because I had fantastic teachers that I succeeded in college. If I had encountered fantastic teachers in grade school, it might have saved me years of frustration.

After graduation I asked one of my former professors how to best fix schools and he stated bluntly that, "The best way to improve schools is to improve teachers." He went on to explain how great teachers were able to overcome nearly any educational obstacle, including lack of funding, lack of textbooks, lack of parental involvement, and even the lack of student cooperation. That conversation led me back down memory lane, and it all began to make sense. I knew then that I wanted to do something to help all teachers transform themselves into *great* teachers and become positive influences in the lives of their students. I started my quest by asking as many teachers as I could find what questions they would ask if they had the absolute best teachers sitting in front of them. I got hundreds of different questions, but many of the same ones began to frequently appear, including, among others, questions about parental involvement, classroom management, and how to handle defiant and apathetic students. After singling out the most common questions, I then tracked down as many great teachers as I could in an effort to find out what it was that made them great. How was it that they were able to make students love school and *want* to learn? What practical methods did they use to overcome the many educational obstacles that were reflected in the questions the other teachers were asking? Their answers to these questions are what led to this book.

Conversations with America's Best Teachers is about great teaching strategies implemented by ordinary people who dared to become extraordinary teachers in the lives of children across the nation. The best way to learn great teaching is not through textbooks and theory, but by talking with great teachers. What follows are 18 original interviews with some of the best teachers in America. Not about how they got started, or why they teach, but about practical strategies that can be immediately implemented in nearly any classroom. All of these teachers have either won the National Teacher of the Year Award or were runners-up for that award, and all were winners in their own states. The teachers were all humble and although they don't consider themselves to be the "best" teachers, they take their roles as Teachers of the Year very seriously. They see it as an opportunity to help other teachers learn to master the craft and, consequently, help thousands of students receive a better education. Although a few of these teachers are officially retired, they are all still teaching in one way or another. Even the retirees featured in this book now spend their time teaching other teachers how to improve, either through formal classes or on the speaking circuit. It's not just the awards that make these teachers special though. Their students' standardized test scores are consistently among the very best in their states. They use creative methods to actively engage their students—making them *want* to learn, while concurrently teaching within the required state and federal mandates. And remarkably, they have very few discipline problems in the classroom. It was common to hear a teacher say they had never had to send a student to the principal.

Though they teach a variety of different subjects in various K-12 grades, as I continued interviewing these teachers I started seeing commonalities and patterns develop. I began making a list of the ones that appeared most. Could there be specific methods and attributes that, if combined, would essentially create the perfect teacher? Probably not, I thought. But variations of the same ten methods continued to appear in nearly all of the interviews, whether the teacher taught in a major metropolitan city or a small rural town. These common methods were prevalent if the teachers taught kindergarten or high school, math or social studies, gifted students or special education. Most had never spoken to one another, nor did they have much in common in their personal lives, yet the same ten commonalities emerged time and again. It was so obvious, in fact, that I will go out on the limb and say that *any* teacher who incorporates these methods will, at the very least, become a *better* teacher. You will probably become your students' *favorite* teacher, and once you've mastered these skills you will indeed become a *great* teacher.

Here are the ten commonalities found among nearly all great teachers:

- They solicit student input for planning, implementing, and evaluating assignments.
- They have strong relationships with each of their students as *individuals* and always build on those relationships.
- They focus on educating the "whole child" and not just the academic side, regardless of what the curriculum states.
- They make learning fun by incorporating things like music, art, food, games, and humor.
- They use *hands-on* lessons and projects to reach multiple learning abilities and do very little formal lecturing.
- They actively build effective *teams* with other teachers, administrators, and parents.
- They incorporate technology as a tool to enhance their teaching in various ways.
- They take risks, actively going against the norm to develop new models and programs.
- They write grants and solicit sponsors to help overcome the lack of district and state funding.
- They have mastered their subject matter, yet always continue their professional development.

While these ten commonalities provide a framework of what to do to become great, you will have to develop your own specific methods within it. The forthcoming chapters will show you how great teachers have mastered their craft by using variations of these themes. Inside you will read about a teacher who raps math concepts to middle schoolers, a history teacher who uses 20,000 authentic artifacts to teach with, a reading teacher who dresses up as storybook characters to make the lessons more memorable, and other teachers who use everything from historical simulations, to outdoor learning laboratories, to an in-class television network.

This is a valuable book for classroom teachers, but also for parents—the most important teachers a child will ever have. It's my hope that parents will gain a better understanding of what great teachers do, and use this wisdom and experience to help educate their own children. For classroom teachers, I'm hoping that you will take bits and pieces of each of these interviews, use them to create your own unique systems and methods, and then transform yourself into one of America's best teachers.

J. William Towne
Los Angeles, California

CHAPTER ONE

Alex Kajitani

2009 National Teacher of the Year Finalist
2009 California Teacher of the Year
Mission Middle School
Escondido, California
Math: Grade 8

Alex Kajitani had the hardest time getting his students to grasp math concepts; that is, until he transformed himself into "The Rappin' Mathematician." Since then his students have consistently tested above district averages and now consider math to be fun and exciting. This was no easy task considering Kajitani teaches in one of the lowest-performing schools in his district, in one of the most poverty-stricken areas in his state, and is constantly fighting poverty, gang recruitment, and overall school disinterest.

Kajitani's big change came by connecting with his students on *their* level, using language that they could understand in order to teach them math. The language was hip-hop, and Kajitani began rapping to teach them his math lessons. This was an unorthodox approach, especially for a half-Jewish, half-Japanese teacher. The first rap lesson

7

was a flop, and his students laughed at him. The next day, however, when they had remembered the songs' lyrics and all of the associated lessons, Kajitani knew he was on to something.

Since then, Kajitani's math rapping has transcended his own school and found its way into math classes all over the country, through a series of "Rappin' Mathematician" CDs and workbooks that he created (www.mathraps.com). He has also virtually eliminated discipline problems through a "Routine Rhyme" song that he created to liven up classroom procedures and make them meaningful. When a student breaks a rule, the other students rap part of the song and put the offender back in line. While the rapping has played a big part in Kajitani's success, it's not his only tool. For instance, he often transforms himself into memorable characters like the "Math Magician" and the "Math Mystery Detective."

Kajitani also writes a column offering strategies for teachers on connecting with hard-to-reach students and closing the achievement gap. In addition, he offers a Making Math Cool workshop that provides creative ways to make math more accessible to students. The column and the workshop both help move Kajitani closer to reaching his ultimate goal of closing the achievement gap and providing quality education for all.

Kajitani earned his bachelor's degree from the University of Colorado at Boulder, and his master's from San Diego State University. He lives in Carlsbad, California, with his wife, Megan, and their two children, Senna and Kallan.

TOWNE: Can you talk a little about how the "Rappin' Mathematician" came to be?

KAJITANI: It was my first year of teaching and I was sinking. All that preparation, all those diplomas, and I could not get my middle school students to sit down and pay attention. I felt disrespected and frustrated that I couldn't get them to remember what I had just taught the day before; yet, they could easily remember every word of the new rap song on the radio. Of course, the other problem with this was that they would come in each day singing about violence, drug use, and mistreating women, which frustrated me even more. Then one afternoon, it hit me; instead of turning off their radios, I just needed to offer them a different station. So I went home and made up a rap song about the math we were learning at the time.

TOWNE: What was the lesson?

KAJITANI: It was adding and subtracting decimals, and the song was called "The Itty-Bitty Dot." I practiced it all night, peppered it with clever phrases, and rapped it over an authentic hip-hop beat I'd found online. I remembered my own love of rap in its cleaner youth and imagined how impressed my students would be with my "cool" factor and my way with a rhyme. Early the next morning, when my class came in, I performed it for them...

TOWNE: What did they think about that?

KAJITANI: It was an absolute disaster. They laughed hysterically at me, and I felt anything but cool – more like a complete flop. Now, not only were they not paying attention, but they were laughing at me. Later that day, I trudged off to lunch like a loser from *The Gong Show.* And then it happened. As I walked by the lunch tables, the students were singing my song! The next day, they ran into my classroom, saying things like, "Mr. Kajitani, are you going to rap again? Yesterday was *the best day ever* in math class! Are you going to be on MTV?"

From that moment on, everything shifted. I had connected with my students on *their* level, using language they understood, to get my messages across. I had gotten them laughing – it didn't matter if it was at me, because it meant they were present and comfortable, and that's no small feat in the often dangerous neighborhood my students live in. So by shifting my approach, I had gotten them excited to come to school, excited to learn, and excited to have me as their teacher. The students' behavior improved dramatically, and their test scores began to match, and then outpace, their more affluent counterparts. I began calling myself "The Rappin' Mathematician," and started rapping about all of the math concepts I was teaching and really just let the wacky humor flow. Unlike the songs on the radio, I used language that was positive, and included messages not only about math, but about believing in oneself, making good decisions, and the importance of school. The songs quickly became legendary throughout the school and district and, encouraged by my fellow teachers, I recorded them onto an album one summer so other teachers could use them in their classrooms. One album led to another the next summer, and then a workbook. Now "The Rappin' Mathematician" is teaching lessons in classrooms and homes all over the world.

TOWNE: That's an amazing story. What have the results been like since you've incorporated rapping into your lessons?

KAJITANI: The results have been phenomenal! Over the past two years, my Algebra 1 classes – which include many students whose parents never passed algebra or graduated high school – have scored, on average, in the "Proficient" range. This is a major feat. In my remedial classes, a large number of students enter my class not knowing their times tables, and they leave for high school having scored "Proficient" on their respective 8th grade test.

At our school site, the students have become involved in making Math Rap videos, two of which have won the Innovative Video in Education (iVIE) Award. Here are students, from one of California's poorest neighborhoods, making award-winning videos that are now being viewed in classrooms all over the country, thanks to sites like YouTube. These students are not only learning math, they are also learning valuable technological skills, and their confidence and enthusiasm for school has grown exponentially through this process.

Beyond my classroom and school, my math raps have become a tool for getting students across the country, and even internationally, excited about math. I get phone calls and emails daily from students, teachers, and parents saying that, for the first time ever, math has become something that is "cool" and "hip." What's been great about the raps, too, is that they are being used not only in school lessons, but also are helping integrate math concepts (and positive values) into people's everyday lives. One mother even told me that "*The Rappin' Mathematician*" CDs are the only ones that the entire family can agree on listening to while they're driving in the car together!

TOWNE: In addition to teaching your students, you also frequently give a Making Math Cool workshop. What are some bits of advice from it that teachers can use to make math cool?

KAJITANI: I designed my Making Math Cool workshop to do just that. It is intended to give teachers ideas and games that they can use to liven up the content we're teaching. I have special guests like the "Math Magician" and the "Math-Mystery Detective" that stop by our classroom. Of course, all of my special guests are really just me dressed up in an outfit. Even the "Math Comedian" will stop by to tell jokes about math. Above all, Making Math Cool is really about connecting math to our students' lives – in a language that they understand. Early in the school year I find out what activities they love to do, and then spend the year relating these activities to the math they're learning. A student should never leave our classroom not knowing how he or she will use the information that we've just taught them – and making it fun just seals the deal on getting them to buy into its relevance for them.

TOWNE: A lot of teachers say that they would like to do a lot of fun things in their classrooms, but that their administrators expect them to teach to the test. What advice would you give them?

KAJITANI: Do both! There is no reason why teaching to the test can't be fun. Take the practice test questions and turn answering them into a team competition. I have become a master at turning anything into a game. If we only have five minutes, I'll split the class into two sides, and we'll play a quick game of tic-tac-toe. I write a practice test question on the board, and whoever is called on, and gives the correct answer, gets to place an "X" or an "O" on the grid for their team. The side of the class that wins gets to go to lunch first! It is simple, fun, and also teaching to the test.

The games you play do not have to be fancy or complex. My classes love to play Bingo, Hangman, or toss a beanbag into a bucket for points – all while answering test questions. Break the monotony by splitting the class up into two or more groups, separated by a common theme; such as what season you were born in, or what high school you'll be attending next year, or by mixed ability levels. The same principals that are pushing "teaching to the test" are also most likely the ones pushing "cooperative group work."

Teaching to the test does not necessarily mean sitting in class taking tests all day. It simply means covering the material that will be on the upcoming test. Take this information and find creative ways to present it. Perhaps the most popular *Rappin' Mathematician* song of all-time is called "Test Tiiiiime!!!" I took all of the common test-preparation skills my principal demanded that we teach, such as eliminating wrong answers, and created a rap song about them. Now, the students *demand* that I play the song before every test, and test-taking has become an opportunity for the students to show off their skills, something that is celebrated rather than something they dread.

It is important to understand that principals are under an incredible amount of pressure to raise test scores. Often their jobs depend on it. They are not looking to kill creativity in the classroom, but they are expecting that teachers stay focused on the standards and content that the tests deem most important. As a teacher, when you find a creative way to incorporate a bit of fun into the required material, share the ideas with your school's administration and with other teachers. Tell them about the results you are seeing in your class, and in their test scores. This is a great way to get your administrators and peers on board, and at the same time, get them to trust that what you are doing in your classroom is engaging, effective, and, yes – teaching to the test.

TOWNE: Let's say it's the first day of school with an all-new class. What do you do on that first day to establish authority and control?

KAJITANI: Clear expectations need to be set. On the first day, I firmly communicate to the students how I expect them to behave, when and where I need them to be at all times, and the consequences if they do not fulfill these expectations. This is reinforced in writing, through the use of posters and handouts, and in the organization of my classroom. It's also very important to state the purpose of the class. I begin by saying, "The purpose of this class is to prepare you for high school mathematics." I say it every day thereafter. I want them to know, specifically, why they are in my class, and where they are headed next.

It's crucial, too, on that first day, to present myself personally as someone who is confident, who speaks well, and who is well organized. This really helps to minimize discipline issues.

TOWNE: What about the first week?

KAJITANI: The first week, I continue to reinforce the expectations that I set on the first day. Most students understand that the teachers will come on strong the first few days; however, teachers often get lax in their consistent follow-through when expectations are not met. It's important to follow through on everything you say you will do. Otherwise, students will quickly learn that your expectations, and the consequences, are negotiable. Many a student has said to me at the end of a school year, "Man, I thought you were mean those first weeks of class!" I always say, "Good! That's how I want it to be."

On that note, I think it is also important to say that, although I may get fun and wacky as the semester moves on, I consistently maintain a tone of seriousness and purpose in the first month or so of a class. And, even when we do have more fun after those first weeks, I make sure they always know I am a serious teacher at core. I may be "The Rappin' Mathematician", but I am their teacher, not their peer. I believe in mutual respect between students and teachers, but I also paint clear boundaries, which is critical for effective teaching.

TOWNE: Discipline is a big problem for many teachers, especially at high-poverty schools. You have devised something called the "Routine Rhyme" to help with this. How does that work?

KAJITANI: Walking into class one day, I overheard one student say to another, "Man, we do the same thing in this class every day!" It was then that I realized my students knew the procedures in my class; however, they didn't think of them as anything beneficial.

Since the "math raps" were working so well and making math "cool" to the students, at the suggestion of Harry Wong, I wrote "The Routine Rhyme" to liven up the procedures and make them meaningful. As I reviewed the classroom procedures to my students the next day, and every day for a week, I taught them a rhyme with which to remember each procedure. I kept each rhyme simple and easy to remember and, of course, used a hip beat that students could get into. Each day, the class practiced "The Routine Rhyme," and it only took a few days for them to memorize it—just like they did the rap songs on the radio.

Now, I have very few problems with students being off-task. Whenever a student is not following procedures, another student will rap the line from "Routine Rhyme," telling the off-task student what to do. Thus, the rap song acts as a form of self-correction for the students, and a no-cost, time-saving, classroom management tool! The "Routine Rhyme" has dramatically increased classroom time-on-task and productivity.

TOWNE: How do you draw the line between solving a discipline issue yourself and sending a student to the principal? Can you give an example of how you successfully handled one?

KAJITANI: Export your problem, and you export your power. It has been years since I have sent a student to the principal. The only time I would call for an administrative escort is if a student is posing an immediate danger to another class member, or to myself, such as having a weapon or drugs. Otherwise, I really try to handle everything myself, within my classroom.

I think the key to classroom discipline is preventing problems from happening long before they could develop. Granted, sometimes issues begin at the lunch tables, or at home, and follow our students into the classroom. I see misbehavior as a psychological and sociological issue, and, therefore, apply principles of both to my discipline plan. I use James Wilson and George Kelling's "Broken Windows Theory": Crime is the inevitable result of disorder (which has received much attention in Malcolm

Gladwell's book, *The Tipping Point*). Thus, someone who sees chaos, and sees a system that deals with criminals ineffectively, is more likely to commit a crime himself. The appearance of order prevents crime. Like Rudy Giuliani cleaned up Times Square by cracking down on graffiti and subway turnstile-jumping, I crack down hard in my classroom on the two most visible offenses: chewing gum and being tardy. When students see that they can't even get away with mere gum-chewing, they don't try anything more daring.

My classroom procedures, appearance, and vibe are of orderliness and calm (some colleagues have called it "the Zen classroom"), and I am sure to be consistent and quietly confident in my follow-through at all times. There may be fun in my classroom, but there is no chaos, and there is no yelling. It's the same principle that works with my toddler daughter, whose tantrums are always a direct result of her feeling overwhelmed, frustrated, or insecure; it helps her feel calm and secure, and there are no tantrums. By letting students know what to expect, and know that they are in a safe space where rules are clear and respect reigns, I actually help them relax, which prevents almost all behavior problems in my classroom. Even the most difficult students tend to be calm in my classroom, and I attribute it to this proactive approach.

When behavior issues do occur, it helps to use humor to diffuse situations quickly, and to think about the motivation behind a student's actions. Just the other day a student kept interrupting class by belting out a loud noise, apparently imitating a character from a TV show. I realized he needed some attention, focus, and a release, so instead of reprimanding him, I told him that whenever anyone answered a question correctly, it was his job to make that noise. He and the class loved it. He focused intently on the lesson and got a good laugh from all every time he made his noise (when I wanted him to make the noise, not out of turn) and we got to go on with our learning without further disruption. No one lost face, everyone still felt safe, and order was maintained.

In short, my bottom-line discipline goal is to create ways for my students and for me to feel secure that our classroom is without chaos (no broken windows), and that we have the power to control what happens within this space. When this is accomplished, discipline is rarely an issue, and true learning can happen.

TOWNE: Another popular term often heard in your classroom is "Kajitani Style". What is Kajitani Style?

KAJITANI: Kajitani Style begins each year with the way that I want the students to format their homework paper: for instance, numbering each problem, circling their final answers, etc. The format itself is no different than any other math teacher uses; however, I tell the students that this format is called Kajitani Style. Throughout the school year, it becomes synonymous with doing neat work and staying organized. However, it inevitably becomes an "attitude," and a part of the classroom culture. When a student gets a haircut, I will often mention how good it looks, followed by saying, "Kajitani Style!" When a student says something funny, and the class laughs, another student will often shout out "Kajitani Style!" Young kids often don't question the quirky things we do; rather, they find them entertaining, and a necessary way to break up the boredom. As the year goes on, I insist that they begin to use their own, "(insert last name) Style." They love it!

The true secret to the success of Kajitani Style is being comfortable with who you are. When the students are comfortable with themselves, their confidence soars, and so does their academic achievement!

TOWNE: You often provide advice for teachers on how to connect with hard-to-reach students in your bi-monthly column for RAPSA

(Reaching At-Promise Students Association). What are some of the most effective ways of doing this?

KAJITANI: Hard-to-reach students are often bored or disconnected students. Let's be honest here; in a world of iPods, social networking sites, cell phones, and video games, school *is* boring! Most of us teachers don't allow these particular tech devices in our classrooms. However, we are still in direct competition with them – no matter what kind of school we teach in. Maybe it's not the actual academic content that bores the students — perhaps it's the way we are presenting it to them. Why not, instead of battling these enemy pastimes, use them to our advantage? I try to bring the fast-paced world of the students into the classroom, and show students how each and every one of their technologies relies on the knowledge of math. "So how boring can it be?" I ask. Some tips I've offered fellow teachers in this vein include:

First, capitalize on students' love for video games and internet by using websites and computer programs that teach the subject that we're covering. There are a multitude of programs that offer an alternative to the old pencil-and-paper routine.

Second, use the students' world in your examples. Just the other day, when I related math shortcuts to abbreviations used while text-messaging, such as LOL and BRB, I suddenly had the rapt attention of my entire class.

Pretty much every cell phone has a calculator feature. Imagine if, after doing a math problem, you told your students to whip out their cell phones to check their work. Or, make up word problems about their usage minutes, and how to choose the best plan.

There are songs, like my math raps, on iTunes for pretty much every subject. Students can download them onto their iPods as assignments. Show them that their favorite musical gadget is yours too, and you earn their respect and attention in the process. Of course, allowing the students to use their cell phones or iPods in class requires proper front-loading of what is expected of them. But I've found that the students are so excited about the sanctioned use of their toys that they don't abuse the privilege.

Don't teach alone. Teach the students about the world through real people coming into your classroom. A 15-minute visit is often enough to turn a student's light bulb on. Don't limit it to just doctors, lawyers, and accountants either. Bring in plumbers, construction workers, store clerks, and truck drivers. "Keep it real," as our students say, with people from their surrounding neighborhood, who represent their ethnicity and socioeconomic status.

Finally, make learning a game. One of my favorite activities to pull out on a hard day is called "Stump the Math Professor." Students throw out absolutely any classroom-appropriate topic, and I, as Math Professor, tell them how it relates to math. Soccer? Scores, angles, speed. Pizza? Temperature, cooking time, slices. Get silly, have fun with it.

TOWNE: You have mentioned that your teaching philosophy revolves around two simple words: *Be Real*. Can you talk a little about the three aspects of this?

KAJITANI: I discovered my personal teaching philosophy by experiencing it. Teaching is an art, a science, a passion, and an opportunity to prepare our students, not only for the world as it is, but for the world *as it could be* – to summon the past, examine the present, and shape the future. True teaching takes courage. It takes persistence. It takes honest self-reflection to continuously improve. It requires being real with oneself about what is necessary to be a great teacher. So I summarize my teaching philosophy with two words: ***be real***. And as you mentioned, it can be described as consisting of three aspects of being real.

The first aspect is to be relevant. No subject, especially the mathematics that I teach, can be truly learned if the students do not see the relevance of the information in their everyday lives. I am constantly looking for ways to "meet them where they live." On any given day, I am weaving lessons about the math the students are learning with issues important to them, such as their ethnicity, the internet, and the sports they love. Our projects use real-world themes: analyzing advertisements, investing in the stock market, designing a house, calculating statistics of how many Latinos graduate from college each year. Never will a student leave my class thinking that they will not use the information we have discussed.

The second aspect is to be reliable. My students know what I expect of them well before they enter my classroom each day. My expectations, the procedures in my classroom, and my relaxed, yet firm and consistent manner are all aspects of my teaching that my students rely on. They also count on my creativity and humor helping them to learn. Watching me, my students learn what it takes to be a reliable human being. We cannot demand that our students be organized, focused, and passionate unless we ourselves are all of these.

The final aspect is to be realistic. Living in one of San Diego's poorest neighborhoods, my students constantly deal with severe challenges of violence, racism, and low literacy rates, just to name a few. It is not realistic that each one of my students will show up on the first day proficient in their academic content areas. However, throughout the year, I take students from where they are to where they can be. I believe that every student in my class can learn, improve, and surpass any expectations of them, regardless of where those expectations previously began and ended. Perhaps not every one of my students will graduate from college; however, each and every one of them will someday be a neighbor, a co-worker, and someone who has the potential to make a better world for those who come after them.

This is why I teach, and this is why I love teaching. It is the opportunity for real teaching, and teaching what is real.

TOWNE: One of the things you're most passionate about is closing the infamous "achievement gap." What can an individual teacher do to help close this gap? Is being a good teacher enough?

KAJITANI: Inside our own classrooms, individual teachers can provide a culturally relevant, empowering curriculum. A culturally relevant curriculum is one that considers our students' race, ethnicity, country of origin and socioeconomic status to design engaging, real-world lessons. This means taking into account the politically- and ethnically-charged popular culture our students live within when designing lessons for them. I provide a curriculum that is rigorous and standards-based; however, I adjust it to fit the cultural needs of the students I am teaching. As I've said, I intertwine math lessons with the hip-hop my students love. On a more serious note, when teaching percentages, we often push the textbook aside to examine high school drop-out rates among ethnic minorities. When we graph linear equations, we chart and compare the lifetime earnings of those who do not finish high school versus those who attain university degrees. In both cases, we discuss the consequences and rewards that are associated. As teachers, let's move beyond the discomfort of talking about culture and race, and relate both to the academic content in a way that is challenging and empowering. Let's stop pretending that ethnicity is not an issue, and instead make it an issue that is central to the material that we are teaching.

Being a good teacher is a great start. Staying a good teacher requires a commitment to change, adapt, and have the courage to reflect honestly on one's own teaching. A growing, constantly improving teacher – the best kind, in my book – has the ability to say, "That didn't go very well, I need to change that tomorrow."

TOWNE: What do you wish you had known when you first started teaching that you now know?

KAJITANI: That I am not alone! My first year of teaching, I stayed up late each night designing my own tests, creating my own worksheets, and coming up with my own timetable of what topics to cover, and in what order. One day, toward the end of the school year, I wandered into our department chair's classroom, and to my surprise, she had worksheets and tests that were almost identical, which she had been using for years.

These days, with so many schools restructuring into Professional Learning Communities (PLCs), collaboration is high on the agenda. This year, we have a new teacher who pokes around my classroom whenever she comes in for a meeting and grabs a copy of whatever worksheet I have out. I've also seen her pull out her digital camera and take pictures of projects and ideas on other teachers' walls. My first year, I thought this would be considered "stealing." Now, I realize that when it comes to teaching ideas, "stealing" is what you're supposed to do! I let new teachers know they are welcome to "steal" from me – whatever works to help our students succeed, which is after all our common goal, right?

Another piece of advice I wish I had sooner is that we don't have to go out and spend all of our money on items for our classroom or students. In my first year of teaching I would buy prizes for the students, for getting a good grade on a test or for winning a game we would play in class. One day, after realizing that I had given away my last prize, I told the class that the winning team would get to go to lunch first. They went crazy, and put forth more effort than I had ever seen them do for any of the plastic toys I had been giving away. Since that day, I've gotten very creative in my positive rewards, offering prizes that are significant to the students, and no-cost to me. Some of these prizes include: front-of-the-lunch-line passes, getting to pick the music when we listen during study time, or getting to play a five-minute, non-academic game at the end of class. We often do rap battles in my classes, and, I admit, once it was a hot chili pepper eating contest, which the kids talked about gleefully for months thereafter!

Also, I spent a lot of money on much-needed classroom supplies in my first year of teaching. One day, as I complained about it in the staff lunchroom, a colleague mentioned that whenever she goes to an office supply store, she asks for the manager, introduces herself as a local teacher, and asks if the manager would be willing to donate any of the much-needed supplies. Usually, she said, the managers are more than happy to help! She always follows it up with a thank you card, signed by the class, and keeps the store informed of things going on in the class and at the school. Thus, not only is she getting the much-needed supplies, she is developing bonds between our educational and business communities. This is an idea I have "stolen" with great success.

In recent years, I've expanded this concept, asking other kinds of businesses for donations (the local casino was happy to donate decks of cards for math lessons) and also writing grant applications for larger expenses. Applying for grants doesn't really take that much time once you get the hang of it, and I've been able to get funding for everything from whole-grade field trips to video production equipment just by taking companies up on their offers to submit applications. As teachers, we often forget about how much the public, and businesses, love teachers! People want to help and to feel that they have contributed to educating children, so *let them*. As we often tell our students, you just need to ask.

TOWNE: Finally, are there any books that have had a major impact on you as a teacher?

KAJITANI: Perhaps the single most influential book for me as a teacher is Paolo Freire's *Pedagogy of the Oppressed*. Like Freire, I view education as a way to empower ourselves, in order to make true change in the world. The more oppressed you are, the more you are in need of education. I carry this philosophy with me each day, as I unlock my classroom door and greet students who come to me from homes with no food on the table, or who don't have homes at all. This book reminds us that education is a golden key for these disadvantaged young people, opening doors to opportunities for them to move beyond their circumstances and make a real difference for themselves, their families, and the future of our planet.

Melissa Bartlett

2003 National Teacher of the Year Finalist
2003 North Carolina Teacher of the Year
Statesville High School
Statesville, North Carolina
Language Arts/ESL: Grades 9-12

Current Position: Executive Director, 21ˢᵗ Century Learning

I f there were ever a teacher that epitomized the concept of using student-based input in the classroom, Melissa Bartlett would be that teacher. Nearly every aspect of her teaching revolves around input from her students, including setting class rules, creating lesson plans, and even grading. Bartlett believes that incorporating students into virtually every decision-making process helps them build self-confidence, establishes critical relationships, and provides for unparalleled ownership in their own learning. For over 25 years Bartlett has practiced what she preached, and every year her students flourished, both socially and academically.

Bartlett received her Bachelor's Degree in English from Old Dominion University and her Master's Degree in Teaching English as a Foreign Language (TEFL) from the American University in Cairo, Egypt. She has also earned National Board Certification in Early Adolescent Language Arts from the National Board for Professional Teaching Standards. She has taught all over the world, including stints in Cairo, Egypt, in Lamu, Kenya, and in the U.S. Virgin Islands. During her time abroad, she learned to speak multiple languages including Spanish, Swahili, and Arabic. Since returning to the United States, she has dedicated herself to reforming education policy from a teacher's point of view. In 2005 Bartlett was appointed to the North Carolina State Board of Education where she currently serves as a Member-at-Large. She previously served as the Director of the Center for 21st Century Skills within the North Carolina Business Committee for Education and is currently the Executive Director for 21st Century Learning with Iredell-Statesville Schools.

Her unwavering passion for children has led Bartlett to become a vocal advocate for teachers everywhere and she shows no signs of slowing down. She currently resides in Hickory, North Carolina, with her husband, Walter, and their two sons, Andrew and Matthew.

TOWNE: What is one of the biggest challenges that you've faced as a teacher?

BARTLETT: I moved around a lot as a teacher and didn't stay at the same school for very long. So I would have to say that the biggest challenge I've had, on a personal level, was having to constantly adjust to all the different cultures where I taught. I believe that in order to be a really good teacher, you need to be a part of the community in which you find yourself teaching. You really need to learn all of the cultural mores of the place in order to properly serve your students and their families. I'm not sure if that's a generic challenge that all teachers find, because most teachers that I know stay in the same place.

Now a more generic challenge for me, and the hardest thing about teaching, was to learn what each individual student needed and how best to accommodate those needs. That's a challenge for every teacher, and it always has been.

TOWNE: How did you handle that differentiation challenge in your classroom?

BARTLETT: One of the best ways that I've found to differentiate at all times and in all lessons, is to include a lot of student self-determination and self-directed choice. I always offered more than what was needed so that the students could choose. The kids know what they're most comfortable with and teachers shouldn't underestimate student input. So that's one of the best, and easiest, ways to make sure that you're offering every student what they need, and they get a vested interest by having ownership in the lessons. I always felt that I work for my students. They are my employers and my customers. They own the environment, and it really is their place. To not include them in the decision-making processes would be negligent, as far as I'm concerned. It's our job as teachers to provide students all of the possible decisions that they can choose from and then let them choose.

TOWNE: Did you use any formal pedagogy or systems in your classroom?

BARTLETT: Typically not, at least not the named formal systems that they teach in credentialing programs. I did use *Read 180* in the last year that I taught, as an extra acceleration remediation for some students, and that was their choice. I also used *Paideia Seminar* for the summative activity for reading, where students freely participated and interacted with each other. But the only real systematic approach that I used to organize the learning in my class would be PDSA or Plan, Do, Study, Act. Basically, the students and I are a learning community, and we plan what we're going to do in the class by choosing from all of the possibilities and then do it. We then study what we've done to find out what works and what areas need improvement. We keep what works, and for the areas that need improvement, we brainstorm new plans. PDSA is a method of work, but the most important piece of it is that the students are actually a part of the learning community and they self-direct. I'm very much into fostering the 21st century skills of ownership, responsibility, and self-direction. Those are really the keys to effective teaching.

TOWNE: That gets into my next question about what you do that's different from many teachers. You seem to incorporate the students a lot more in the planning process.

BARTLETT: I incorporate student input into absolutely everything, from the initial planning process all the way through to final grades. That's really been the key to my success as a teacher. In my classroom, students are always the decision-makers, and I act more as a facilitator and a guide.

TOWNE: That seems to be typical of the teachers I interview in this book, but it's far from the norm. In fact, all the teachers I had in grade school had the attitude that it was their way or the highway.

BARTLETT: Teachers like that are afraid of letting go of power, even if it's for a good reason. Not only are they afraid, but they don't know their students well enough to realize that there's nothing to fear. Unfortunately, this top-down approach and unwillingness to share power is far too common, and it's not unique to teachers and schools either. Distributive leadership is a desired form of leadership that is lacking in many organizations, and it's hurting the organization and the clients as well. That means it's really hurting the students in the educational organizations.

TOWNE: You mentioned that you involve your students in the initial planning process. How does that work exactly?

BARTLETT: I'll give you an example. I always made a blank syllabus and listed on it each of the weeks we were in school. Then I would look at how many novels the county and the state expected that particular grade to read each year. I then put a "Must" column on the syllabus. The next step takes some time, but it really is the most successful way of doing this. What I did was make a list of all of the novels my school owned, because capacity can be a real limitation. Resources and facilities are important pieces that cannot be ignored. So once I had listed all of the novels that the school had available, and which fit our state and local mandates, I would then have the kids go to Amazon.com and read the book reviews. If they didn't have access to a computer, I would print out the reviews and bring them in myself. The reviews allowed my students to make more informed decisions on which novels to choose. I then did what I call "light-voting", where the kids would vote on which novels to read. They would vote for their top seven novels out of maybe 21. If the state required them to read four or five, we would choose the top seven and plug those titles into the syllabus, and then the kids would decide the order in which to read them. So those were the minimum requirements and were listed in the "Must" column. We got rid of that column first.

Now we worked on the second column which listed some cool things I could help them do if they were interested. For instance, if they wanted to take a classic piece of literature and turn it into a sock-puppet play and go to an elementary school to entertain the students, then we could do that. There were tons of options here that we could do and this is basically the "nice to do" column. Then the third column is the, "What are you crazy to do, that we can do, that's different?" column. This is the really fun one that gives them a ton of creative input and really makes the lessons entertaining. And that's how we filled out the syllabus. But that kind of choice was a part of everything, even the textbook. For instance, I would take the literature book, open it, and explain to the kids that we have to learn five different genres of poetry or ten short stories or the like. I'd then have them go through the Table of Contents and choose which ones they were interested in studying. They could ask questions about each and then they would make informed decisions. There is nothing that they weren't included in.

TOWNE: So you are essentially giving them ownership even in the "Must" column.

BARTLETT: Within the realm of reality. It's really good training for them to realize that there's a finite amount of resources and that we must always work within those limitations. However, within those limitations, there's no reason that we have to do just what I feel most comfortable with. That's a big mistake a lot of teachers make. They sometimes fall in love with certain pieces of teaching material that they don't want to let go of, insisting on teaching it in every class, with no regard to what the students want. Well, that's not student-centered, that's being an authoritarian, and it's the wrong way to go. You should really aim to tailor the learning for your students and incorporate what they personally like.

TOWNE: I know you are a big proponent of using multiple measures to get a true picture of your students' achievements. What are those measures?

BARTLETT: I graded everything except their breathing! (*laughs*) I laugh, but that's really important. Sometimes I would take a hundred grades per semester, and that's a lot. But this way, if the kid had a bad day, he could afford a little slip up. I know a lot of kids who have failed a class simply because they didn't do something. It wasn't a reflection of them not being able to do it, but rather that they just didn't do it, for whatever reason. Kids usually have a really good reason why they didn't do something, but a lot of people don't get it. Typically, this is because many teachers don't take the time to get to really know their kids and understand where they live and what's going on outside of the classroom.

TOWNE: And how did you handle the actual grading?

BARTLETT: I used what's called formative assessments. I graded every day and always kept the kids involved in that process. That's the whole PDSA thing again as the kids are helping to assess themselves as well as assessing me. I always had them tell me, anonymously, how I was doing so that I could improve. A lot of teachers won't do that and are afraid the kids will just say mean things like they're fat or ugly or whatever. Well, if you don't have a relationship with the students then yeah, they might do that, but if you're a good teacher, and you have already built those relationships, then that's not likely to happen. If a teacher thinks that the kids would only say bad things about them, and not talk about what they're really trying to do, then that pretty much tells the whole story. That means the teacher hasn't taken the time to build those critical relationships, and that they don't trust the kids, and vice versa.

TOWNE: Somehow I knew student input would play a big part of that.

BARTLETT: Absolutely! And it was the same thing with tests. I would often have them make up test questions so that they could see how the process works. A lot of times the kids will know the material but still not do well on an exam because of process issues, not because of content. It's important for them to understand that side of it. So that's the testing piece, but then I always have projects as a big portion and performance measures as well. I did as much performance-based assessment as possible because the students are really into performance. It's public and it's real. I'm talking about public speeches, work that is publicly displayed, and also just everyday performances as well. I would always try to get the students to help me define what "good" was and then they would help me build rubrics to grade the larger performances. I also gave 10% for participation, and that was the enthusiasm piece. It really balanced out and nobody ever failed.

TOWNE: You are truly the master of including student input. I love it.

BARTLETT: I really feel like I'm only there to serve them. You should see their faces the first time I tell them that (*laughs*). They look at me like, "What in the world is she talking about?" It's priceless.

TOWNE: You have said that education should be an "enabling activity," one which enables learners to communicate successfully in real-life situations. Can you talk about what you mean by this?

BARTLETT: Well, there are the big three R's that are espoused by the Bill and Melinda Gates Foundation's work in education: Rigor, Relevance, and Relationships. This is the relevance piece: if you do not make what you're teaching relevant in the real world, to real students, in real time, then you may as well be Charlie Brown's teacher talking gibberish. So the question is, how do you find out what's relevant for each child? My entire career I have used a technique that I've often been criticized for, but that I have found to be extremely effective. It involves the first week of school, which is so important. I don't teach any of the standard course of study that first week of school. Instead, I have my students create interview questions and interview each other. They then present that person to the class and we videotape it. It's a fun activity, but my real *modus operandi* is to get to know these kids, and for them to get to know each other, so that we build community. I believe that you must build that community before you can successfully move on to academics. I agree with the Gates Foundation about it being all about Rigor, Relevance, and Relationships, but with a different order of importance. Relationships should come first, then you teach the relevant subject material that matters to them in real life, and only then, once you know them and know their world, do you introduce the rigor and get some major work out of them.

TOWNE: So other teachers criticized you for using the first week for that?

BARTLETT: They would tell me I was wasting time and ask me how I could afford to do that, and I always ask them, "How can you not?" You don't know anything about the students and they know nothing about you. You've got to get to know each other first, because that makes all the difference in the world. Whenever I mentor young teachers, I remind them that if they reserve the first week for the community activities, then they will always have another week to actually begin the academics. I have always started my school terms this way, from sixth grade through the university level, and it has always worked. The older students might only need three days or so to complete the process, but it really succeeds in forming those crucial relationships and establishes a solid community on which to build. And, for young teachers, it also gives them a breather because that first day of school is just hectic. I remember thinking, "I've got to cover this, I've got to cover that, etc. etc," but you really don't. What you have to do is get to know the kids, figure out what they need, and build a two-way trust between you. I have been very successful in terms of test scores and other formal accountability measures, and I believe it's precisely because I took the time to build community first.

TOWNE: Many teachers say that they would love to do all of the fun and interesting classroom techniques mentioned in this book, but they say they can't because they have to teach to the test. They say that the administration would be all over them if they stray from the standard curriculum. What do you say to them?

BARTLETT: To be honest, they are just wrong. I have never really had a principal give me a hard time. I think some teachers just don't believe that the kids can learn, and that's a big problem. Part of that is because most of these teachers are from different cultures than their students and they don't really know these kids. They get so wrapped up in the material they think they have to cover, that they forget to find out who these kids are and where they come from.

There is also a curricular piece that encourages this misconception, and it is that the American curriculum, in general, is a mile wide and an inch deep. In fact, I've often just completely disregarded it and spent much longer than our pacing guide says on a particular piece of literature or skill that the kids need or want to explore. For instance, rather than barely covering ten novels, I would much prefer to cover three in great depth so that my students can really understand the characters, and the issues at hand, on a much deeper level. What the American education system needs to do is move toward essential standards, similar to what they use in Japan and Singapore. For example, if you look at second grade math classes in those countries, the kids have maybe six or seven objectives that they have to master. Then in the next grade they have six or seven. Some objectives continue on to that next grade, some drop off, and some new ones may be added. But in the United States we have far more objectives than can be realistically mastered in one school year. It's typical, in most states, for second graders to have twenty-one objectives. It's terrible.

TOWNE: What can be done about this?

BARTLETT: Well, I'm on the North Carolina State Board of Education, so I'm intimately involved with the policy side of things. In our state we have put a moratorium on all of our curriculum revisions while our State Department of Public Instruction revamps all of our standards. We are really aiming to move toward that essential standard model and focus on the things that the students absolutely must learn, and learn well. Of course, once that changes at the curriculum level, it changes the tests as well. When that happens, teachers will no longer have that compelling notion that they have to teach twenty-one objectives even though the kids may not have even mastered the first ten.

So the answer is two-fold: part of it is the curriculum, and the other part is the fear that teachers tend to have because of it. That's why I used to get beat up so much. Whenever the other teachers talked about how I was wasting time, I just thought, "You just wait and we'll see how my students do compared to yours." And keep in mind, I always got the at-risk students and the neediest of them all, yet they always did as well, if not better, than those of my critics.

TOWNE: Speaking of at-risk students brings up the issue of classroom management and discipline. These are major problems teachers struggle with and they often cause teachers to quit the profession. How do you handle classroom management?

BARTLETT: I have never really had any serious discipline problems because of these approaches I use. The fact that I have that first week of relationship-building pretty much eliminates all discipline issues. My class is more like a community, or a family, and so they kind of keep themselves in check. I mean, the kids come up with the rules themselves so they aren't likely to break them. One of the first things I do, during that first week of interviews, is to solicit the rules for good behavior and for methods of discipline.

TOWNE: From the students?

BARTLETT: Absolutely. I first have them brainstorm to determine what the characteristics of a good teacher are. And you'll get some silly stuff, like "no homework" or something, and I say, "Would you really consider a teacher to be a good teacher if they never make you work?" Of course they take that off the list. So I do manipulate it to get some of the answers I'm hoping for, but for the most part, the things they come up with are right on target. Once we have the teacher qualities out of the way, it leads me to ask about the characteristics of a good student and they once again come up with a pretty dead-on list. After I get those lists worked out, I move on to classroom behaviors, but I limit them to about three or four and they're typically the same things. It's also the same rules of behavior for the teacher as it is for the students. Finally, they help come up with the consequences, such as how many warnings they should get before sending them out of the room. It usually ends up being three. First is "the look", then it moves to where I stand next to their desk, and the third warning is when I have to actually say something to them. It doesn't usually make it past that third warning though, as the students will typically control one another. So they build the rules, put them on posters, and hang them on the wall along with the consequences. It's all right there and they created it.

Even though I had some really tough kids, I never had any real discipline problems. Some of these kids, especially at the middle-schools, were pretty rough. Some had their probation officers dropping them off at school, and a few came in with bandages from where they were stabbed or shot. These kids could have really messed me up if they wanted to, but they never did.

The relationship was there, the respect was there, and the trust was there. I was their teacher.

TOWNE: In your Teacher of the Year essay you talked about the importance of teachers becoming "joiners" in the community in which they teach. What does that mean?

BARTLETT: It means it's important for teachers to really become a part of their community and not just come in to teach their class each day and go home. If they are not a part of the community, and are ignorant of the culture, then they open themselves up to a lot of unnecessary misunderstandings in communication. I'll give you an example. I taught in Kenya for a while and the students there don't make eye contact with you. And contrary to what we might think, it's not a form of disrespect or a sign that they are not listening. In fact, it's actually a form of respect. But if you're not aware of that, you might misinterpret it and not handle it properly. In some cultures here in the United States, it's the same thing, and I've seen other teachers get angry and yell at kids for that. They say, "You look me in the eye right now!" They misinterpret because they never took the time to understand the cultural differences.

Because I moved around so much in my teaching career, I have had to put real effort into building new community ties each time. The only way to effectively become a part of a community is to become a "joiner", basically joining local organizations, churches, educational classes, fitness classes, and working on local community service events. It's also important to learn the language and customs of the new community. So, for example, in St. Thomas, I learned Rastafarianism and how to read and speak Spanish. In Egypt, I learned to speak Arabic. In Kenya, I learned to speak and read Swahili and learned everything I could about the Islamic law of Shari'a which formed part of the discipline policy of my school. At schools here in the U.S., I joined local church education committees and helped provide Sunday school services. I also joined local chapters of academic organizations such as Phi Delta Kappa and Alpha Delta Kappa. I have sung in local choirs and acted as an advisor on local projects. I also got heavily involved in the local teachers association. I did all of this because I believe that to best serve as a teacher for my community, I must be completely committed to becoming a member of it.

TOWNE: You are a big proponent of using the portfolio approach in assessing teacher accountability. Can you talk about the merits of this approach?

BARTLETT: Just as there must be accountability for my students' achievements, there also needs to be accountability for teachers, and the best way to evaluate this accountability is through the use of multiple measures. Just like I take as many grades as I can for those students, teachers should be graded on many different things as well, and certainly not just on standardized test scores. In my opinion, the best way to achieve this is with a portfolio approach similar to the one they use at the National Board of Professional Teaching Standards. In that system, one piece of your portfolio covers content, one piece covers pedagogy, one piece covers assessment, and one covers community. Within all of these parts of the portfolio, teachers must provide a lot of hard examples of the educational processes that they use. There must be concrete evidence of teaching accomplishments, with samples and analysis of student work, and it should be compiled over time rather than some snapshot. Certainly student achievement on standardized test scores should be a part of the portfolio, but it would only be one aspect of the true picture of a teacher's classroom success and not the whole basis for it. What's so good about the portfolio approach is that it makes teachers really reflect on what it is they're doing. They must take an honest look at everything they do: the good, the bad and the ugly. It makes them look at their practices and find opportunities for improvement, which comes in the 'S' part of the PDSA.

In North Carolina, we did the portfolio approach for two years and then politics got in the way, and the legislature got involved and stopped it. It's really hard, politically, to compel every teacher to make these huge portfolios, so it didn't go over as well as we would have liked. We've more recently adopted a new teacher evaluation instrument, developed by McRel Laboratory, that's a 360° self-assessment checklist. It's not a portfolio, but more of a hybrid system. Teachers have to have their evidence listed, but not compiled like you would in a portfolio, which is a more thorough tool.

TOWNE: What do you wish you had known when you started teaching that you now know?

BARTLETT: I guess how much power teachers have to affect public policy regarding education. If I had known that back then, I would have been dangerous! After winning Teacher of the Year, I traveled around a lot, giving speeches, and I always told teachers that I didn't want to hear, "I'm *just* a teacher." If you have that mentality, then you have already laid down and become some-body's doormat. Teachers have a tremendous amount of power, not just in their classrooms or schools, but on the policy level. Good teachers who know their stuff, simply need to pick up a phone and call their legislators. I have found that they will listen to you; it's just that teachers don't typically call them. I'm the only active practitioner who is on the State Board of Education and probably one of the few in the nation. Most of the educa-tion decisions made in the United States, I'd say 99% of them, are made by people who haven't been in a public school in like

25 years. They are not teachers and many never have been. Teachers simply are not making policy decisions, but they could be if we would just stand up and take charge and refuse to take no for an answer. That's why I have never had a problem with principals, or getting things done that may be considered "out of the ordinary." I gather my data, present it to the principal, and say, "I've got this plan. Give me a chance and let me try it." The data doesn't lie, and enthusiasm goes a long way. Everyone wants what's best for these kids, so administrators aren't likely to deny you a chance for change if you have a good idea and just speak up. Teachers really are the key to school change.

CHAPTER 3

Michael Geisen

2008 National Teacher of the Year
2008 Oregon Teacher of the Year
Crook County Middle School
Prineville, Oregon
Science: Grade 7

Michael Geisen started his career as a professional forester, but soon realized he had a higher calling and found his niche teaching 7th graders to love science. He focuses on teaching main concepts using multiple learning pathways to reach each of his unique students. Humor, movement, music, technology, project-based learning, cooperative groups, art, and theater are some of his tools of choice to make science relevant and engaging for his students.

Geisen graduated *Magna cum Laude* from the University of Washington and went on to earn his Master of Arts in Teaching from Southern Oregon University. After arriving at Crook County Middle School, he wasted no time making a difference. Over the past few years, he and his science department colleagues have successfully helped his students increase their state test scores from 44% (meets or exceeds) to over 80%. And he stays busy outside of the classroom as well. He frequently gives workshops on successful strategies for multiple learning styles, has assisted in a district-wide effort to improve accountability among teachers, and has helped implement a district-wide technology program. He was also critical in the development of a new school-wide grading system that not only offers a better reflection of how students are actually doing, but also helps to improve everything from teacher accountability to parental involvement.

Geisen is also the current Science Department Chair and has led efforts to build a huge rock-climbing wall, and to create an elaborate outdoor learning laboratory. He has recently won the District Exemplary Service Award for his many hours of volunteer and fundraising work and remains heavily involved in community service.

Geisen seeks a balanced, creative and inquisitive life outside of teaching. He is an accomplished photographer, a "mediocre musician", a rock climber, and a mountaineer. He currently resides in Redmond, Oregon, with his wife, Jennifer, and his two children, Aspen and Johanna, whom he considers to be his own greatest teachers.

TOWNE: Many of the teachers I've been talking to have taught for decades, yet you earned the nation's highest teaching honor in a little over seven years. What attributes do you think propelled you to such heights in such a short amount of time?

GEISEN: Well, it pretty much comes down to good looks and charm (*laughs*). Other than that... no, but the reality is, I didn't know anything about the Teacher of the Year program. It was really just me teaching my heart out, pouring myself into my classroom, and just trying to be a good teacher. The rest of it just happened. It kind of found me, and it still seems a bit unreal.

TOWNE: Based on what I've read about you, they made a good decision.

GEISEN: Well thank you, I appreciate that. In terms of what attributes, I think it's my passion for continually innovating in the way that I teach and bringing a lot of creativity into the classroom. I think that's a huge part of it. It was just me incorporating as much fun, art, theatre, music, and technology into teaching science as I could. Of course, I'm not the only one doing these things, which is what's so humbling about the whole thing.

TOWNE: Can you give us an example of how you transform what might have been a boring lecture into something that's memorable to your students?

GEISEN: I try and think about it this way: if I were a seventh grader, how would I want to learn something? Here's an example. One of the current standards here in Oregon is to learn what causes the seasons on Earth. So we could read a chapter in the book and do a couple of labs, but I took it from just giving the students the info and testing them on it, to letting them discover it on their own as if they were detectives.

So it became a two-week journey on what causes the seasons. What we ended up doing was comparing it to a barbecue and a piece of meat. We asked, "Why is it so hot here in the summer in North America?" A lot of the activities we did had to do with this analogy of the barbecue and the piece of meat. We started looking at things like "Are we closer to the sun in the summer or farther away?" We had this campfire prop in the middle of the classroom and we were moving back and forth trying to determine how far away from the sun we were, and we did some measurements and some analysis and were up and moving around. We found data online, graphed it, and learned that, "Hey, there's really not a whole lot of difference between summer and winter in terms of distance. In fact, we're slightly closer to the sun during our winter!" So we were able to dispel some myths like that.

We then started to look at the position of the sun in the sky throughout the year. And for that I used technology because there's software out there now that can show you the sun and simulate a whole day in 30 seconds from anywhere on Earth. They love that. And we do some dancing to show the path of the sun in the sky so that they're tracing out that path with their arms, moving back and forth like a rapper. I also wrote a song about the seasons to help them remember the key concepts. They got a kick out of that.

Another thing I've done some years, if there's time, is have the students use their understanding of the seasons, the position of the sun, and the flow of energy to design and build a passive solar home. They take it all the way from an idea to a blueprint to a physical model that they present to the class. Their peers then evaluate it to determine the home's ability to keep warm in the winter and cool in the summer using only the sun and natural cycles. They come up with some creative solutions and are excited about the possibility of designing their own homes like this someday. Students also get feedback from their peers on their effort and how creative they were with their design. It's a project that really synthesizes so many science concepts into a relevant, fun, and creative project.

But every day is different. What I try to ask myself is, "What can we do as a class that's going to be memorable for these kids and allow them to take something and create something of their own with it?" The more memorable I can make it, the more they tend to learn it.

TOWNE: Do you come up with these ideas when you're creating your lesson plan at the beginning of the year?

GEISEN: Most of the time it just kind of hits me, in the shower or on the way to work or something. I also get an idea, or the seed of an idea from other teachers, and then shape it into something that fits my style. I liken it to planning a menu. I try to make sure the kids are getting not just the meat and the potatoes that they've been getting for the last 100 years in our schools, but a wider variety of healthy foods. I also get the kids involved in the planning process and they come up with ideas on how to learn the concepts. The more the students are part of the actual process the better the outcome will be.

TOWNE: You say that a great teacher is a "unifier of ideas, a unifier of people, and a unifier of ideas with people." Can you talk about what you mean by this?

GEISEN: A unifier of ideas is really getting at the idea that, instead of teaching a bunch of science facts and basic knowledge, it really ought to be about teaching big ideas and then unifying those ideas into a bigger picture of what science is and how to apply it to our lives. For me to best do that, that's where it comes down to creating everything that I do either on my own or locally with the other teachers and the students. So it's really about unifying all of science into a few big concepts as opposed to random facts that don't mean much out of context.

As far as unifying people goes, in my opinion, this is one of the biggest parts of our jobs as teachers, to bring people together. This includes students to students, students to teachers, and teachers to teachers. And then we must unify all of those groups with the larger community as much as possible, which I'm not that great at yet, but I'm really working to improve.

The unifier of ideas with people refers to building an actual community for these ideas as opposed to having a classroom or school with seemingly random thoughts. There don't necessarily have to be strict rules. It's more about figuring out what works best for us as a community. This means involving all community members, including students, teachers, administrators, parents, etc… as much as possible in the actual planning and decision-making processes. It's not enough to just be teachers; we must aim to be unifiers.

TOWNE: Can you give examples of the successful instructional strategies for multiple learning styles that you cover in your workshop? There are so many different learning styles in a classroom and you're only one teacher with a limited amount of time. How do you do that?

GEISEN: This is one of the great challenges of teaching as we've got classrooms full of students that are all different. What I do, as much as I can, is to try and incorporate "project-based learning" into what I'm doing. This way each student, small group, or pair of students, are working on their own individual projects within a much larger concept. Of course, you can't do this every day or even every week, but as much as possible where you have a big concept to get across, it gives students a chance to learn it in a way that best suits their individual learning styles, allows them to be creative, and makes the concept more tangible and real-world.

One of the things I do is to give my students a chance to show what they know to the rest of the class. We call it "Show us what you know!" These are basically open-ended projects the students work on that take one, two, or three days. I just ask them to show the rest of us what they know about a particular concept such as antibiotic resistance, natural selection, or energy transformation. It could be anything, really. The students can show it any way they want.

Some of the students freak out about being given such a blank slate to work with, and these are often the highest achieving students in the class, at least in the traditional sense of achievement. They always want to know exactly what the teacher is looking for, but I don't let them off that easy. It's really an important skill for them because they need the opportunity to develop that creative side that will be so essential in the 21st century. And besides, most real-life problems are open-ended like that, anyway. This is a good chance for them to really synthesize all of the details and the analytical concepts that they've learned, and do something creative with it. They're using both sides of their brain at the same time!

On the other hand, some of the students that are not traditional learners, or who don't do all that well in school, really flourish in this kind of environment. They're like, "Dude, this is cool... I can make a comic strip about that?" And I'm like, "Yeah, you can pretty much do anything you want, as long as it demonstrates your understanding of the concept." So we brainstorm a little bit and decide what kind of things might be good. It could be a comic strip, an advertisement, a video, a song, or whatever. I do give some kids the option to read a chapter in the book and do traditional worksheets, but not many choose that route, and I encourage students to really move beyond that.

These are little projects, but project-based learning in general allows students with different learning levels and styles to be able to be involved in the same lesson at different capacities. Even students with special needs can be successful at getting the main idea of a big concept when approached like this. More important, it gets the kids excited to learn and brings about passion because they actually get to choose the route they take. I do want to stress, though, that it can't be just about the fun. The concept and rigor have to be there. When I assess, I'm looking to see not only if it's artistic, but whether or not it teaches us something. The balance is critical! It can be entertaining, but not just entertainment.

TOWNE: This falls into the secret of your success, your ability to inspire students to *want* to learn.

GEISEN: That's right. My students often learn in the modality that they want to learn in, but only in the framework of what they need to learn. That's why project-based learning is so powerful.

TOWNE: When discussing education and student ability, everyone focuses on the left, analytical side of the brain. But you remind us that the right, creative side is just as important. I agree, but how can we measure the success of the right side well enough to know if what we're teaching is working?

GEISEN: That's a very good question and definitely one of the toughest in education. Since public schools have been around, the focus has been almost entirely on the left side of the child's brain. It's just a lot easier to assess and is much more black and white. The right side is a little more grey, or colorful I should say (*laughs*). There are tools available to measure things like creativity, innovation, collaborative skills, and the ability to synthesize big ideas. These tools are out there but not incredibly well developed, nor are they very well known due to the lack of demand for them. But there are certainly more holistic standards-based tests out there than we are using now. And there are assessment options like portfolios, performance assessment, and other methods that start to really value real-world products and skills.

In my own classroom, it's really just about knowing my students and what each of them is capable of. What is reasonable for a seventh grader to produce in terms of creativity and collaboration with peers? My measurement of their creative aptitude is based on the answer to that question on an individual basis. There's not a whole lot of room in the formal valuation system to measure this, so it's kind of a nebulous act. For some larger projects I've made rubrics that describe a grade scale for this, but for the most part, it's based on my knowledge of the individual student and of what they did compared to what I believe they can do. I'm not sure you can make a standardized test to measure everything, because you can't really standardize creativity and innovation. But you can undoubtedly make the whole process of measuring 21st century skills much more objective, and certainly more valued.

Even though it may not be easy to measure and compare schools on a national scale, these right-brain skills should still be encouraged at that level. Policy-makers need to create an environment in which those things are valued and allowed to grow.

Of course, this concept feeds right into the whole accountability debate, which is a major theme in education these days. The question is, "How can you hold people accountable for something that is measured on an assessment that is less than perfectly objective?" Well, maybe we should come at it from the other way and build up the accountability from within, creating an environment that values that kind of thinking and that kind of teaching and that kind of output from the students. If educators start doing that, I think metrics can be developed which will be more objective.

TOWNE: You've been working on a district-wide effort to improve accountability by having teachers hold one another accountable. Can you talk a little bit about how that works?

GEISEN: I'm just part of a team of people in the district working on this, but the idea is to maintain a 2-way conversation between the teachers and those in the district leadership. Both sides share what they're doing and the results they've found. Most departments in the district are now developing their own assessments for various things. Some of them are modeled after the state assessments, and some are much more performance-oriented. For instance, our state has phased out the requirements to do scientific inquiry labs. Well, our science department didn't think that was such a good idea and believed those labs to be really important. It allowed us to tie concepts into real-world things that the students could grasp better.

We wanted to keep that alive and tweak it a bit, so we developed our own performance assessments that were project-based and kept the students involved in developing their own investigations. And we are really holding one another accountable, looking at data together, and so far, I think it's working pretty good. It's getting teachers out from behind their closed doors, to work in collaboration with other teachers to improve their craft. Some departments feel like it's still too top-down with the administration expecting data and barking orders, but I think most of the teachers feel like it's more bottom-up than it was before and it feels a little bit more grassroots. The expectations are really developed more by the teachers, but we keep that open dialogue with the administration because we know that's important.

There are some efforts around the country that are attempting to base a teacher's salary almost entirely on students' test performances, and I think that's a mistake. But if we are moving toward that model, then teachers need to have a little more say in what we're being held accountable for. It can't just be test scores, because there's so much more to what we do every day. If it comes down to where we're getting graded and paid based on test scores, then you can expect that we're going to move our teachings farther to the left-brain only instruction and less toward building community and relevance and joy into learning. I think this would make a lot of great teachers question why we're teaching, and would start to force us out of the profession, because essentially a machine could do the job for us. There's a great quote by Arthur C. Clarke that says, "Any teacher that can be replaced by a machine, should be." There's a lot of truth in that. If we only put formal value on machine-like qualities, why would we bother?

TOWNE: You've also helped to develop a new and very interesting school-wide grading system. Can you talk about that some?

GEISEN: For many years at our middle school our students have gotten two different grades for each class. There was an academic grade and a citizenship grade. Both grades showed up on their report cards where parents could see them. But the citizenship grade was really pretty nebulous. In reality, it boiled down to how much the teacher liked the student. So if the kid was pretty good, but goofed off a little, she got a B. If he was always helpful then it was an A. A total goof-off got a D. And that's what it ended up being based on. It was basically just "how good is your kid?" Well, we wanted to change it to where the citizenship grade reflected a more objective measure of true citizenship, while the academic grade reflected the true learning of the content that they were supposed to be learning.

So what we did was do a pilot test with the seventh grade class and move to a system where basically all of their academic grade was based on things that actually showed their academic learning: tests, quizzes, and project-based assessment results. The citizenship grade changed a lot. We still kept a component to it that had to do with their behavior, and whether or not the student was a good citizen, but about half of it now reflected their effort on daily work such as homework, in-class labs, and things that were turned in for a grade. These were things that were associated with practicing learned skills, but didn't actually show what they learned. In the previous system these were thrown in with the academic grade, and it just didn't make sense to us. And that's kind of how we broke it down. It was really about trying to tie learning into their academic grade, making their citizenship grade something that was less subjective and a lot more objective.

TOWNE: I think that's a really good idea.

GEISEN: Yeah, it worked pretty well. One of the cool things we did with the behavioral part of their citizenship grade was to ask the students to self-grade their own behavior. Every couple of weeks we would give them a little card that they would go through and put grades on. They would grade themselves on things like respect, focus, preparedness, etc. You'd be surprised at how honest most of them are. One would think they would all just put an A for all of it, but that isn't the case for most of them. In fact, many of them were really hard on themselves! But the idea of self-grading has turned out to work well because it gives the teachers insight into what the kids think of themselves. Some really have no idea how distracting they are and how much they impede the learning of others. When this is the case, it gives the teacher and even their peers, a chance to intervene and work with that child to make it better.

Anyway, because we do this every few weeks, it lets me and the students record the results periodically, and we can see how each of their behaviors has changed over time. Their parents also see the data, and when I speak with them, we can pinpoint problem areas that may be associated with outside influences. Therefore, for instance, if something traumatic happened at home around Thanksgiving, and the student's behavior and grades dropped around that time, we can easily see the correlation.

Since this system worked so well with the seventh graders, we went on and put the whole school on it. There was a little hesitance by some of the eighth grade teachers who thought that it didn't really prepare eighth graders for high school, where there is only one grade and a lot of it is based on homework. So some of them were a little hesitant, but overall, we thought it was a better way of doing it and provided better information to the parents and the students. It's not perfect, but it did better than the traditional system was doing.

TOWNE: No, I think that's very smart. The thought of giving only one grade to a student at any level in K-12 just doesn't make sense.

GEISEN: It really doesn't. The elementary schools have got it down pat. There the students don't get just a grade, they get a full report card that breaks down not just math and reading skills, but a lot of social skills, study skills, and effort. Ideally, this is the way it should be. It's tough. I mean, when you've got an overcrowded classroom already, it just means your job as a teacher is that much harder, but maybe it's worth it. I think the way we do it, with two separate grades, is easy to keep track of and still provides needed information. And with computer grading systems, now it's just a matter of putting the information in and letting the computer sort it all out for you. Eventually I would love to see kids getting three or four grades per class in middle and high school. That way, if a student gets a D, he and his parents won't just assume he's stupid, but can really pinpoint where the problem lies. Maybe he's brilliant or really creative, but just not organized or something. You simply can't determine that with one grade.

The problem is that bad grades have a way of bringing a student to the point of apathy. The student starts to see himself as being stupid and then stops caring. I think we've had a really narrow view of "intelligence" for so long now that it permeates everything we do, without us thinking about it. I think it really affects students, especially as we move into the 21st century when different forms of intelligence, besides just logical reasoning, are going to be so much more important. I think it really is a hindrance to us as a society, but also to individual students, when we basically are telling them, "you're dumb." And in reality, they are probably very gifted in some other way. They could be a successful entrepreneur, a great researcher, or an outstanding mechanic. They might become great social activists, builders, or community leaders, but we're not allowing them to recognize their great strengths! There are so many ways to be intelligent, but unfortunately, we don't value them all.

TOWNE: How were you able to increase your students test scores from 44% to 80% in such a short amount of time?

GEISEN: A lot of schools sort of view the test score as the Holy Grail, and they use all kinds of remediation programs, and drill and kill, and put all their focus on the kids that are right on the cusp of passing to bump them over the line. We haven't really taken that approach at all. Our students are currently only tested in science, at the state level, in the eighth grade. So really sixth, seventh, and eighth grade teachers are all working together to get them ready for the big test. But, again, it was really all about inspiring the students to *want* to learn science. There was nothing really magical about it. If they want to learn, they'll learn. Antoine de Saint Exupery once said, "If you want to build a ship, don't drum up people to gather wood, divide the work, and give orders. Instead, teach them to yearn for the vast and endless sea." That inspiration is what we're aiming for. It takes some courage and a good dose of patience, but it will pay off in the long term, not only with higher scores but also with students who want to keep learning even into their adult lives.

TOWNE: Can you tell us a little about the district-wide technology program you helped implement?

GEISEN: This was interesting. Again, I'm just part of a team, a steering committee if you will, on where to go with this and how to make it work. Last year we got some grants that put a laptop in the hands of every sixth grade student. This was a pretty major step for us as we're just a rural community full of blue-collar workers, mostly cattle ranching, logging, tire manufacturing, things like that. But we're lucky enough to have some real forward-looking people in the district that wanted us to take this to the next century. They wanted to start by putting a laptop in the hands of every sixth grader, and that's now expanded to seventh graders as well. So this is pretty exciting. A huge part of that was organic, professional development for the teachers because we wanted to make sure the laptops were not just fancy pencils and paper, but were actually used to design instruction that's more interactive. We didn't want students just sitting there with headphones on going through learning modules; we wanted them to really create things. Whether they're blogging about what they're doing, publishing data on the web, interacting with people across the globe, or conducting laboratory experiments online, there had to be active learning going on.

In my classroom I try to stay ahead of the curve, or I guess where I'm from it's more like *on* the curve in terms of technology (*laughs*). I've also been using hand-held clickers that students can vote on, which are pretty cool. They're a good way to get feedback on certain things and it makes it fun. We give an occasional comprehensive test on what they learned all the way through middle school, not necessarily for a grade, but just for us so that we can see what we need to work on. We started doing it on these hand-held clickers where the students could take the test at their own pace. It's just a simple multiple-choice test, but the kids come in like "sweet, we get to use the clickers!" And so, even though it's just a standardized test, these kids think that using the clickers is just awesome. We also use them for review games, quick assessments, and for getting student input on how the class is running. They're more than just technological candy; they ensure that each student can have a voice in their learning and in how the classroom community functions.

Finally, this year, as part of the Teacher of the Year program, Smart Technologies gave each of us interactive *SmartBoards*. You basically plug your computer into this thing, and it projects the image up onto this big whiteboard. Then you can touch it and move stuff around, and the kids totally get into it and love drawing on it. So yeah, it's eye candy, but it's much more interactive and physical, and the technology draws students in. Sometimes they don't even realize how much they're actually learning. So I try and incorporate as much technology as I can. It's tough when budgets are as tight as they are, but I think eventually this stuff will be cheap enough to where we all can afford it. We also need to be creative in how we get funds for it in these tight economic times.

But even with the access to technology, there are many days when we don't use it at all and go with old-fashioned note cards, cotton balls, and just miscellaneous junk. A lot of times some of the best teaching you can do is with cardboard boxes, markers, and photos. This is stuff that kids have around their house, and they can go home and show their parents what they've learned. It's real-world and it doesn't take an expensive microscope or fancy toys. I teach photosynthesis using beans and bodies, and it works. Kids actually get into it. You really need to have a mixture of approaches to be successful.

TOWNE: Mentoring is such an important aspect to help new teachers adjust. What would an effective mentoring program look like if you were to design it?

GEISEN: When I first started teaching, I was assigned a mentor. I showed up and it was simply, "Here's your mentor. Here are your textbooks. Good luck." So it was a sink-or-swim kind of thing and luckily I eventually started swimming. My mentor and I didn't really hit it off in terms of teaching styles. I mean he was a nice guy and a good teacher, but we didn't have that chemistry that I think is needed. What really got me through that first year was the fact that I was on an academic team. For instance, at our school the seventh grade is divided into two teams with about 130 students on each. Those 130 students all have the same four core teachers for science, social studies, math, and language arts. So we, the four core teachers, all have the same students and can create or modify their schedules as needed. The four of us meet every day and go over what we're teaching, how we can integrate our projects, and frequently we pull in students or parents with us to discuss how they're doing. This team approach really helped, not just professionally in learning the ropes, but also personally. That first year is a hard year, and just having someone that you can really talk to, and who knows your students, can be a big relief for new teachers.

That being said, having a one-on-one mentor or a master teacher is great too. I think a lot of districts are moving toward a model where they have a specialized coach. So if you're a math teacher there's a district math coach who acts as a kind of mentor. The coach will probably be more for the academic and classroom planning side, and that's good, but I think there needs to be flexibility as well. A lot of times you will just hit it off with a certain teacher. If you're a math teacher you might hit it off with a social studies teacher, and feel like you learned a lot about how to teach. Not necessarily about the curriculum, but about your classroom management or teaching style. It's important to have this flexibility in a mentoring program that allows the mentor and mentee to choose each other and be able to break it off if it's not working out. So if I were to design a mentoring program, it would have a flexible one-on-one mentoring system combined with a strong core teaching team.

TOWNE: What's the most difficult challenge you've faced and how did you overcome it?

GEISEN: Oh, this one is easy. Getting out of bed in the mornings! *(laughs)* I joke about it, but it really can be a big issue for me. Of course, once I get to school, and the first student walks through the door, I'm on 120%. But other than getting out of bed, the most difficult challenge was just getting through that first year. I remember specifically one class I had, my fourth period class. We were on a block schedule then, so we had periods one through four on one day and five through eight the next day. My fourth period class was an hour and a half long right at the end of the day. And I have to tell you, it was just a nightmare. Most of the kids I had in that class were really rough, and honestly, the motivation to do anything for them was very low. I was just overwhelmed by so many issues, and so many of their troubles at home and things outside of my circle of control, that I often felt powerless.

But there was one student in that class who was just awesome. Courtney was intelligent and helpful and always had an upbeat and positive attitude no matter what was going on in there. I remember apologizing to her almost every day, and asking if she wanted to switch classes. But she always said "no" with a smile and wanted to stick it out. Well, that was a huge lesson for me because she always stuck with it and gave me the strength to get through that fourth period class and my whole first year of teaching. So it was one positive student, along with that team of teachers, that made me realize that I'm not in teaching to teach science; I'm in teaching for the people. I'm not teaching concepts; I'm teaching human beings with a wide variety of learning styles, strengths and challenges. It's really all about the people and the relationships. Whether those people are other teachers, students, parents, or other stakeholders, that realization got me through that hard time, and it still gets me through hard times today.

TOWNE: How did that class turn out by year's end?

GEISEN: To be honest, as I look back on that time, I felt like kind of a failure at the end of the year. I wish I could say that the class did a 180-degree turnaround, but they didn't and it bothered me.

I do think a lot of those kids had a mildly good time and might look back on it as at least a positive experience, but unfortunately for a lot of them, that was the best I could do. I would hope now, of course, that if I got that same class, I would be able to handle it a little bit better, but it was a big wake-up call. I grew up in an upper-middle-class environment and hadn't really had much interaction with children of poverty or kids that had such a rough life. At first, I felt sorry for them, but then I felt inspired by them. These are needy students and it's my job to do everything I can to make learning accessible to them and help them feel like they're amazing people, because they are.

Teachers need to remember, it's not about the subject you're teaching; it's about the people you're teaching. It's about building a relationship with those kids and helping them realize how special they really are. The better job we do of making it about them, and meeting their learning needs, the better teachers we become.

CHAPTER 4

Keil Hileman

2004 National Teacher of the Year Finalist
2004 Kansas Teacher of the Year
Monticello Trails Middle School
Shawnee, Kansas
Social Studies/Museum Studies: Grades 6-8

K eil Hileman's classroom credo is "Explore Your World, Empower Yourself and Those Around You, Excel In Everything You Do." Aside from winning the Kansas Teacher of the Year Award, Hileman was also selected as the 2007 Outstanding Teacher of American History by the Daughters of the American Revolution and as the NEA Horace Mann Award winner. He was recently selected by the U.S. Department of Education as one of the first 2009 U.S.D.O.E Teaching Ambassador Fellows.

In addition to his numerous awards, Hileman is most known for his creation of a *Museum Connections* elective, which evolved out of his social studies class. The *Museum* class has amassed an impressive collection of over 20,000 teaching artifacts from various periods of time and from every corner of the world. This "classroom museum" has transformed Hileman's classroom into a magnificent place of wonder that has garnered national attention in the media and within education circles. Aside from this *Museum* class, Hileman also teaches a hands-on Archeology class at Johnson County Community College, a Classroom Museum course for teachers at Mid-America Nazarene College, and a graduate/undergraduate "artifact-supported" history course at UMKC. He has taught every grade from 5ᵗʰ-12ᵗʰ and is known for his innovative techniques, which include having his students create their own textbooks, final exam projects, and just about everything else.

Hileman holds a Bachelor's and Master's Degree in Middle and Secondary Social Studies from the University of Kansas and has taught at the middle school level within the De Soto Unified School District for 17 years. He lives in De Soto, Kansas, with his wife, Amy, and their three children: Lane Claire, Suzanna Caroline, and Katherine Aulana.

TOWNE: Your classroom sounds remarkable and quite awe-inspiring.

HILEMAN: Thank you! It's been a lot of fun and I'm glad to talk with you. As my wife likes to say, "Just because a child isn't sitting in your class, doesn't mean they aren't your responsibility." I take that to heart and do whatever I can to help students everywhere.

TOWNE: Let's talk about that amazing setup you have. If we were to walk into your classroom right now, what would we see?

HILEMAN: You would see a collage of artifacts on bookshelves all the way around the room with pieces of history and magnificent student projects. You would see a 1920s barber chair, a 1898 brass cash register, a 1930s Texaco Fire Chief Gas pump, and several glass display cases filled with random things like cameras and tools. You'd also see a student-made Viking ship, a student-made dragon head and, when you factor in all of the rocks and stamps and things, you would see over 20,000 different artifacts.

TOWNE: That's amazing. And this is a social studies class?

HILEMAN: It started off as one, but then it became a little too popular. Parents of kids who were in other social studies core classes began requesting that their kids be put in my classroom. When I was teaching the regular social studies class, my students were doing all of these exciting things like archeology and working on the museum, whereas kids in the other social studies classes just weren't getting those opportunities at that time. So this heavy demand put pressure on the administration to offer me an opportunity to write an elective class that anyone could sign up for. This led to the *Museum Connections* class which it's currently called.

TOWNE: And now it's being emulated at other middle schools, correct?

HILEMAN: We're the fastest growing school district in Kansas, by percent, and have been for the last ten years. We've opened a new school every couple of years, and we now have two new middle schools in the district. Well, when we opened these two schools, 80% of the kids in them came from my building, and the students and parents put pressure on these schools to provide a similar museum-type class. So now the district has asked me to list everything that's in the museum and divide it three ways. They want to put a classroom museum in both of the new middle schools, along with a new curriculum that anybody can teach. It sounds great, but a lot of the artifacts in my class have come from people who have donated them to me with the understanding that they would remain in my classroom and under my direct supervision. It's the trust that these people have in me that allowed this whole thing to start in the first place. It took me seventeen years to get here, so it's not like we could just snap our fingers and the full class is up and running at another school. It takes time. But I definitely want to expand the concept to *every* school. My Board of Education has recently directed me to work with the administration to implement the *Museum Connections* class in every middle school in our district, so that's a start.

TOWNE: How did your classroom museum come to be?

HILEMAN: In my first year, I was teaching eighth grade and was trying to teach my students about the Civil War. I did all the right things: I had a traditional syllabus, a traditional textbook, and used the traditional curriculum, but I just couldn't get the kids to really understand what it was like back then. It's one thing to read it in a book and memorize dates and stuff, but it's another to empathize with those soldiers who were actually there. So to help them visualize it better, I showed them parts of the movie *Glory* with Denzel Washington. Well, at the end, when the blacks and whites were fighting and dying together, the kids were laughing. They just couldn't believe that one bullet would make a person fly like that and kill you so quick. Needless to say, I was ticked off at their response, so I ended up ordering two real Civil War bullets to show them and that's how the whole thing started.

TOWNE: Two bullets started the entire museum?

HILEMAN: They sure did, just two used bullets. They had been fired and were all scratched up and dented. See that's a trick that I use. I would rather have a historical artifact that is dented and scratched and ruptured and tarnished than one that's pristine, because the dents and the scratches allow for stories, and inspire creativity and wonder about how it got that way. And that's exactly what happened. The kids talked a lot about how they thought these bullets got like that, and we found ways to fit these ideas into the context of the entire war. I also talked about how damaging something like this would be flying towards you at 1,200 feet per second. After a long and engaging discussion about this stuff, I showed them the last fifteen minutes of *Glory* again, and there wasn't a dry eye in the classroom. They really began to understand the power of these things and the damage that could be done in more ways than one. It became real to them. After that my students began bringing in other old artifacts from the Civil War that their parents had in closets and attics. We did the same thing with those and created stories around each of them while putting them in context. These artifacts and the stories that we created around them, ended up teaching my students more about the Civil War than my lesson plan, textbook, and the entire curriculum combined.

TOWNE: Does it all come from donations? And if so, how did you get so many people to donate?

HILEMAN: Seventy percent of everything has come from donations, usually from items found in kids' attics, basements, and homes. Fifteen percent I purchased or got the district to buy, and the rest are student projects. Many of the parents that donated items made me promise never to sell the artifacts that were given to me and to use them only for teaching. Well, that simple credo became my pitch for getting items from others, and it's what led to the 20,000-plus artifacts that I teach with today. And it's not like I have some divine plan for the items that I get. If it works, I use it; if it doesn't work, I modify it. If it still doesn't work, then I don't use it anymore. The fact is, there are enough artifacts out there in attics, basements, and garages that if schools made a room available, promised never to sell these, always to teach with these, and got a teacher in there to use and organize these artifacts, there could be a museum in every public school in the country tomorrow.

TOWNE: You're a big proponent of using primary sources, as opposed to secondary sources, in the classroom. What are primary sources, and why are they so important?

HILEMAN: Well, all of the artifacts that I use are examples of primary sources. Primary sources are just sources that were written or created during the time under study, while secondary sources are things that analyze primary sources, such as textbooks and research papers. When students are reading textbooks and doing worksheets, it disconnects them. I want my kids to build things and feel things and see things that will have a lasting impression on them. The more you can do to connect your kids to whatever you're teaching, the better. Teachers can use artifacts like the ones I use to help connect their students to the real world. You just have to get your hands on one primary source, tell a few interesting stories about it, and suddenly history has come to life. One artifact can be the key to an entire unit. I had one single button from the Revolutionary War that helped teach that whole lesson. I had the kids write all sorts of papers on how they thought that button got bent up, who they thought wore it, what famous figures of that time period may have touched it, and in what circumstances. You can do so much with so little when you use primary sources as opposed to just textbooks and worksheets. That being said, I do sometimes incorporate secondary sources as supplemental material. For instance, I have my students research primary sources and then go and build their own textbooks! Now that's a secondary source worth looking at.

TOWNE: Many of the teachers reading this book may love these ideas, but what if they don't teach history or social studies? How can this benefit teachers of other various subjects, like math?

HILEMAN: It's actually a dream of mine to see a teacher take this concept and make a mathematics museum. Every mathematical concept that is taught has a person that discovered it, invented it, defined it, or created it. So you could put a picture up of each one of them all the way around the room, along with each concept that goes along with it. Every mathematical concept has a tool, a machine, or a device that was used to confirm it. So every time a math teacher needed to introduce a new concept, they could put up a picture of the person who invented it, talk about who that person was, and then show an artifact that the person used to figure it out. This immediately turns a complicated math concept into something real that was designed by a real person. It's not just a bunch of numbers. Do this for each concept and, at the end of the year, you've got a solid timeline in front of you and the kids would have a much better understanding of each concept.

It's not just math either. This museum concept can be used for any subject in school and that's what's so wonderful about it. Not only do teaching artifacts bring history to life, history and these artifacts also bring every other subject to life. Science has had fun toys to use and has been able to blow things up for years, so that could easily fit into the museum format. English and literature have a lot of reading and they could have a few artifacts for each lesson that help bring those stories to life. Using artifacts, and other primary sources, should seriously be considered by every teacher no matter what subject is being taught. Just try it and you'll see the difference.

TOWNE: You put a big emphasis on hands-on learning with student-created projects. Can you talk a little bit about these?

HILEMAN: They are student-chosen and student-created projects. When I wrote the plans for this class, the curriculum director at the time wanted me to use ten multiple-choice questions for each unit as our final exam, basically turning it into the same formula as our state exam. I told him to forget it and that I wouldn't do it. I got in a little trouble, but I didn't care. Instead, I tell my students that I want them to *build* their final project. They can choose anything that we have studied that reflects a culture or a time period that they found interesting. Once I approve the project material, they can then decide how they want to present it. They can produce a PowerPoint presentation, create a movie, a CD, or make a picture book. Their options are virtually unlimited. Once they choose how they want to present it, they have to get approval by me and their parents, and then they design and build it. After this project is complete, they then have to write a one-page paper about it, telling me what it is, how it represents the specific culture, and what they have learned about it. They also have to get up and give an oral presentation on the subject as well. So as you can see, it really covers everything, as they have to research it, build it, write about it and speak about it. It's all the basic skills that they need to be working on and practicing before they get to high school. I can get away with this being a "final exam" only because my class is now an elective, but I think every teacher should consider doing some kind of similar project even if it isn't a final exam. The kids just learn so much from it.

TOWNE: In credentialing programs teachers learn a ton of formal pedagogy and methods. What sort of methods do you rely on that you've found to be effective in your classroom?

HILEMAN: Probably the most powerful thing I use is "the question" and my lack of answers to "the question." It's the Socratic Method, and it works great. You ask the class a question, leave it hanging in the air, and then there's this whole wait time as the students consider possible answers. Then as the students begin tossing out answers, I come back with even more questions, basically forcing them to think critically about the subject and learn to come up with their own answers. I love the idea of Socrates sitting on the steps and asking a bunch of questions and making people think. We actually have oral exams every Friday, like group sessions, and it's just amazing to ask kids things and literally watch them brainstorm and come to these logical, and often correct, conclusions.

Another thing I often use is student choice. There is a lot of power in letting kids choose. The first year I started teaching, I was just freaking out with all the rules and regulations and how I would get in trouble if I didn't do this and that exactly as they wanted. It was more than a little overwhelming. It was even worse dealing with students who didn't seem to want to be there and didn't care about learning or turning in homework. I didn't really know how to deal with them, but then I learned that it all boiled down to giving them choices. If you're a student in my class you can choose to participate and learn. If you choose not to, then that's fine too. I'm just a scorekeeper. I don't give you grades; you earn them. If you want to succeed in a soccer game, and you choose to lie down on the field and start snoring during the game, then you are not going to do very well. If your goal is to be well-rested, then that's great, but if it's to play well and win the game, then you have made an unwise choice. It's the same thing in my classroom. My students will always know what my expectations are of them and all of the various consequences of not meeting them. I make sure that these expectations are quite clear, right up front. Once these are clear, however, it becomes their choice. It seems so simple, yet it takes a great deal of stress and pressure off of you as a teacher.

A final big thing I use is the power of research. Research skills are absolutely imperative. It's far more important to teach someone *how* to find the answer to something than it is to give them the answer. In this day and age it's critical for teachers to teach their students how to find information in various ways. I have read that everything we know as a human race doubles every three to six months. That is an enormous amount of information. We simply cannot memorize everything there is to know about a subject, and we will never be able to again. It's far more important to teach kids how to find information than to have them memorize it; plus it's more like the real world. Let's say I give my students a random topic that they don't know anything about, like General Patton in World War II. Who is he? Tell me about him? What were his major achievements? Find six pictures of him, make me a timeline of his life, and write a one-page paper on him. Well if they can do that, then they can work pretty much anywhere they want. If a manager comes in and asks them for some marketing statistics, they should be able to quickly look them up, print them out, and discuss them. Memorizing them is senseless and a waste of time. Why memorize something that's constantly changing? And even if it didn't, is that really something we want to store in our memory when it's only a few clicks away? It's so much more important to make sure our students have the skills to quickly find legitimate information that relates to whatever the topic may be. This skill will help them succeed in just about anything they want to do, in school as well as the real world.

TOWNE: In the past you've mentioned how isolated teachers can be. Can you elaborate?

HILEMAN: There are certain weaknesses or problems that are built into our job and one of the big ones is isolation. You can literally go into a building and teach in your room for 30 plus years and never have a clue what's happening in the classroom next door. There may be a teacher at the end of the hall that has the perfect solution to a problem you've been having, or how to deal with a certain disruptive student of yours, and you will never know unless there's some happenstance connection. This is because there's so much happening simultaneously and you're on your own, in your own room, and you never consider reaching out and making these connections. And it's not just teachers in your own department that you should reach out to, but teachers from every department. It's not enough to just know the names of other teachers; find out who they are, what their background is and what methods and techniques they use in their classrooms. Spend some time actually observing them teaching. It doesn't take long, maybe just fifteen minutes here and there. Not reaching out to your peers is a huge mistake and one that can be easily corrected. So that's *building* isolation, but there's also *national* isolation.

Teachers sometimes tend to feel like we're all alone. That all the problems that we face in our school, district, city or state, are just our problems and that's just not the case. I never realized that we are all so connected until I had every other state Teacher of the Year together in one room with me. We all started talking amongst ourselves and a lot of it revolved around the challenges that we faced and the breakthroughs that we've come up with to meet those challenges. It was great stuff. And as these teachers were going around the room talking, it hit me that we are all facing the same challenges all over the country. It was really an epiphany for me as I suddenly had this wonderful sense that, "Wow! It's okay. We're all in this together." So yeah, we're isolated as teachers, but we can solve this. First, we have to recognize it, and then we have to take the initiative to change it.

TOWNE: One would think that having a mentor would go a long way toward solving these isolation problems, right?

HILEMAN: Not necessarily. Young teachers need to really network. I know new teachers will, in all likelihood, be given a mentor when they start, but I encourage them to seek out their own mentors. I love the C.A.S.E. methodology: Copy And Steal Everything! We should never waste time reinventing the wheel. The best place to start is by asking the students at the school. The students know exactly which teachers are the best. They know which teachers come in early and which stay late. They know which teachers go above and beyond and love teaching and which ones are just counting down the days until they retire. Ask the students who are the best teachers at the school and seek them out. Go observe these teachers and talk with them. There are great teachers in every school, and it should be a priority to find out who they are and learn all you can from them.

With so much going on in your own classroom with your own students, you're not going to know the most effective ways of handling things without observing and talking to other teachers. At one point, I was trying to figure out a way to organize papers, like what's turned in, what hasn't been graded, what's been graded but not handed back, what's been graded and handed back. It's just a ton of paper. If you're a teacher in a core class and have 125 kids every single day and each of those kids turns in one paper per day, then by the end of the week you will literally be swamped in papers and overwhelmed. These are things that sometimes new teachers don't realize until it's too late. But anyway, I happened to go down to have the Home Economics teacher sew a World War II uniform sleeve for me that had torn, and as she was sewing it, I was looking at her board and she had all of these magnetic plastic boxes stuck to it. And they're labeled first hour through seventh hour and there's a "Turn in" box and a "Return box". I was in shock as the concept was so simple and yet the design and implementation of it was flawless. It worked perfectly. I asked her where she got them and she said she got them for $1.50 each at Office Depot. Another teacher I observed had a file drawer with a file folder for each child. Anytime the kids finished their work, they didn't turn it in, they didn't take it home or put it in their desks; they simply put it in their own file folder. She checked these folders once a week, and if you had your stuff in there, you got points; if you didn't, you got nothing. During parent-teacher conferences she pulled out the folder and showed the parents everything the kid did or didn't do. It was so smart. You really have to reach out to other teachers though. Don't wait for them to come to you. You must be willing to ask for help, and if you aren't, then you will be alone on an island surrounded by a bunch of experts that could have saved you.

TOWNE: You have stated that you have very few discipline problems in your classroom. How are you able to accomplish this?

HILEMAN: I hardly ever have discipline problems. From my experiences, there are two kinds of kids that cause nearly all of the trouble in a classroom and they're completely opposite. The first is the student who already knew everything and understood it all before they ever walked in your door. They're bored, and bored students are some of the worst ones you will ever run across. The second kind of problem student is the one who has trouble learning or is already behind before class even begins. These students are frustrated and don't know how to contain or express this frustration, so they act out. When you have these students in your class, it can easily get out of hand because they're both easily bored and feed off of each other. So the first thing you have to do as a teacher is recognize who these students are and in which of these two categories they likely fit. Figuring this out is half of the battle when dealing with problem students. Once you know what the problem is, then you can put together a plan to correct it.

What I do with the student that has trouble keeping up is to help them achieve whatever they can with me. I give them ownership of the class in certain ways, such as having them do chores, sharpen pencils, use the pointer, or whatever. I make them a teacher's assistant and have them doing all sorts of special jobs.

This makes them feel good and keeps them engaged. They feel like it's their classroom to a certain degree. It gives them a sense of power whereas they had previously felt powerless. Once they have that confidence and respect, they tend to take their studies more seriously and really want to learn. Add that newfound confidence to the fact that they are now too busy to behave badly, and you will have no more problems with this student.

Now for the gifted student who is bored out of her mind. I put these students to work as well, but in a different way. The work I have them do is more related to actual study. For instance, I may have them work as a tutor with some of the other students to help teach them. I may have them do a brand new project for the museum that they can start researching right away. I may have them put together a PowerPoint presentation for the students on an upcoming lesson. This would not only keep them busy and engaged, but it also benefits me, and the other students, as they have essentially created a new teaching resource that I can now use for future classes as well. There's an infinite amount of things they can do to keep busy and that's the trick.

TOWNE: How do you feel about the use of extra credit?

HILEMAN: I absolutely love extra credit! In both of these previous examples you can use extra credit as a selling point, but you should be using it in various ways. It's one of the best tools a teacher has at his or her disposal. The thing you have to remember is that kids in elementary and middle school don't tend to really understand percentages when it comes to grading. So here the trick is to make extra credit worth thousands of points. When I used to give papers that were worth 5 extra credit points, I might get them back on toilet paper or all stained up; that is if I ever got them at all. But when I switched it up and made the papers worth 5,000 points, suddenly every student was doing them and I was getting them back on golden paper with perfect binding, protective layers, and tabs. It was as if it were a sacred document from the President of the United States! They were so excited to get all of those points, even though it was really no different than the 5 points, but with different percentages. I've heard teachers tell their students that there is no extra credit and that they should just do the work given because that's their job. Well the real world doesn't work that way. In reality, the more work you put into something, the more you're going to get out of it.

Using this huge amount of points extends beyond extra credit as well. This is a real trick of the trade and teachers should use it to their advantage. I give my students 100,000 points a day for participation, 500,000 points for tests, and projects are worth over a million points, so you can imagine how good a job they do on those! If it sounds like a lot, they are going to put in a lot. If it doesn't sound like much, then you aren't going to get much in return.

TOWNE: Besides the museum, you're also passionate about the use of technology in the classroom. You use a lot of PowerPoint slides and video clips and things like that, right?

HILEMAN: PowerPoints are awesome and a great way to hook in videos and video clips. Yes, I often show my students clips of various movies that relate to the current lesson and then have them write about what they saw. They write about the conditions of the time and also tell a story about minor characters that were in the clip. For instance, we might see a minor character in a scene where the camera only shows him for a moment and then we never see him again. I would then ask my students to come up with creative ideas about that character. What was his name? What were the conditions that led him to this point? Why did he choose to do what he is doing, or was it a choice at all? So there's a fun writing activity that forces the kids to research the period and the people from that period, yet, at the same time, it's fun and engaging. And with PowerPoint presentations you can tie in pictures, text, links, and all sorts of things. But even so, this is the old way of doing things and now technology has evolved.

I am now a big proponent of using an iPod in the classroom. Not that little one, but the big one that has video capabilities and a ton of storage. Well, this thing has an input on it that allows you to attach a cable; you know the red, white, and yellow cables that you plug into the TV? Well you plug that cable into the bottom of your iPod and the other end to the TV, you hit a button and it shows the movie. I can carry the video clips for every single movie I have ever shown in any class, on that one iPod. I can sort and organize them by clips and I don't have to go through credits or menus. I can carry a ton of music on it as well. I can go into class during a lesson about Japan and have Japanese music playing in the background while I teach them about the country and its culture. I can have every PowerPoint presentation I've ever used stored on this thing and pull it up in a matter of seconds.

Some of the most amazing things are already hitting classrooms as we speak. Just look at Josh Anderson's school, Olathe Northwest, where every student was issued a handheld Palm Pilot and keyboard the moment they got there. These Palm Pilots were essentially their text books, lesson plans, homework assignments, and everything else. The kids would walk into a classroom and aim their Palm Pilot at a little black sphere hanging in the corner and it would instantly beam all of the required reading pages from the textbook. The teacher can assign an article that she wants her class to read by the next day, and all her students have to do is aim their Palm Pilot at the sphere as she hits a button and they all instantly have the article ready to go home. Later, whenever the teacher is ready, the students point the Palm Pilot back at the sphere and it beams them a digital test. They take the test on the Palm Pilot, hit send, and they have just turned it back in. The tests are instantly graded by a computer and downloaded directly into the teacher's grade book. It's fantastic! Just by not buying textbooks, the school saved hundreds of thousands of dollars which allowed them to purchase these Palm Pilots, and the software needed for them, for every kid in the building. This isn't the future I'm talking about. This is actually happening and it's only going to get better.

My last point about technology is about the wonders of the internet. This thing is an absolute goldmine for teachers. There are just so many great websites out there with free stuff that teachers can use. I've recently discovered one called *TeacherTube*, which is kind of like *YouTube*, but for teachers. It's a free internet site that has tens of thousands of videos of teachers teaching real units. So if I needed to do something on volcanoes, for instance, I could go to this site and find actual teachers teaching about it and use it with my kids. Other websites that I love are *Papertoys. com* and *Canon 3D PaperCraft*. These are great sites that every teacher needs to know about. These sites have thousands of free projects on them that you can download and use. All you do is print them, color them, cut them out and build them. There's stuff for virtually every subject: math, science, history, you name it. All of these great internet sites are examples of how things are constantly changing, and we, as teachers, really have to keep up or we will miss out on many opportunities. Any teacher that's still using only textbooks and worksheets needs to have a wakeup call. They are making their lives, and their students' lives, much harder and much more boring than need be. Teaching and learning should be fun for everyone.

CHAPTER 5

Jason Fulmer

2004 National Teacher of the Year Finalist
2004 South Carolina Teacher of the Year
Redcliffe Elementary School
Aiken, South Carolina
All Subjects: Grade 3

Current Position: Program Director, CERRA

"I have the opportunity to give feet to dreams," said Jason Fulmer, summing up the dream-enhancing potential he provided to his third-grade students. "Teachers are in the dream-developing business." Fulmer has always taken pride in his role as an educator and enjoys the satisfaction of helping others reach further than they ever thought they could. When he was named South Carolina Teacher of the Year, he was the first male in 17 years and the 6th in the history of South Carolina. He is the youngest teacher ever to receive the honor.

Fulmer entered his first classroom fired up and ready to inspire. Though it was just a shabby trailer, he made the most of it. After creatively designing the look and feel of it, Fulmer delved right into what would become his modus operandi, building ironclad relationships with each individual student and their parents. To spice up the lessons he incorporated music and movement, which brought the kids happily out of their chairs and into a fun and memorable learning experience. Before long, all of his students were dancing and singing educational songs created entirely by them and their teacher. There was never a dull moment in Fulmer's classroom as even the most apathetic students became actively engaged and learned to love school.

Outside of the classroom, Fulmer remained busy as well. He served as the chairperson of the South Carolina Teacher Forum and spent many hours involved in various community outreach projects. He soon returned to the Aiken County School District to serve as an Elementary Induction Teacher Coach and Title II Coordinator for Professional Development. In 2006, Fulmer joined the staff at South Carolina's Center for Educator Recruitment, Retention, and Advancement (CERRA) to serve as a regional Teacher in Residence, to recruit the brightest and best to the teaching profession. In his current role at CERRA, he leads the development of mentoring and teacher leadership initiatives for South Carolina educators.

Fulmer holds a Bachelor's Degree in Elementary Education from the University of South Carolina Aiken and a Master's Degree in Educational Leadership from Augusta State University. He currently lives in North Augusta, South Carolina.

TOWNE: You put a lot of time and effort into creating an appealing and engaging classroom appearance. Can you talk a little bit about the importance of aesthetics in a teacher's classroom?

FULMER: Before learning begins, you must set the stage for it. The classroom environment plays a big part in the overall learning experience, and it's important for teachers to take a lot of time and be very purposeful in thinking about the way that environment is created. I think back to my first year in the profession and the opportunities that I had. As I walked into my school for the first time, I was excited because I was finally going to have my own trailer to teach in. It was a portable and I was to get Portable #1, the best of the bunch due to it being so close to the building. My school was undergoing a major expansion project that summer and, as I was getting some things together for the class, there was a knock on the door from my principal. She said, "Mr. Fulmer, we've had to do some shifting around and you're not in that portable anymore." And I said, "Wow, I get my very own classroom in the building in my first year?" And she said, "No, they just brought your portable in, and you're going to be in Portable #15." This was the farthest portable from the school. It didn't get any better when I saw it either. I walked in and realized this thing hadn't been painted since the mid-80s or so, and it was in terrible shape. There were all sorts of specimens growing in it and all I could think was, "This is not what I signed up for."

TOWNE: You had your work cut out for you.

FULMER: Oh, I really did. Well, my family and I take beach trip every year, which is one of my favorite places to be, and fortunately that trip was the next week. So while I was at the beach, I decided that I was going to make my classroom my home away from home and that I would build my very own beach house trailer – in Beech Island, South Carolina! Never mind that there wasn't a beach or an island anywhere to be found in this rural area of Aiken County. So I got my principal and family and friends together, and we painted the classroom and really began setting the stage. I thought about that poem *Footprints*, and I knew that as an educator it was my responsibility to give feet to dreams. A lot of thought went into selecting the things that went into my classroom. I had everything from fish hanging in the windows, to seashells, to my very own reading island with beach chairs. It was really decked out and ready for my third graders. After the first day with my students, one of them came up to me and said, "Mr. Fulmer, this place looks like Red Lobster and I'm going to love it!"

TOWNE: That's when you knew you were on to something.

FULMER: Absolutely! The classroom has to be inviting. It has to be a place where children want to be and provide an opportunity for them to be a part of that environment. My classroom wasn't just pleasing to the eye, but really focused on the students. It allowed us to showcase their work, which became just as much a part of the environment as the beach setting. One of my students came back to me the next year and said, "You taught me to dream as big as the ocean."

TOWNE: This is a good point and so often overlooked. I spoke with many teachers about this book, and when I visited a lot of their classrooms, they pretty much all looked the same. They had the usual ABCs and stuff, but there was nothing really unique about them. It seems like such a wasted opportunity.

FULMER: It really is. You have to take advantage of everything you're given when it comes to teaching kids. Leave no stone unturned.

TOWNE: I'd like to run a few hypothetical situations by you. Let's say, a new school year is starting and it's your first few days of class. You're faced with a group of skeptical and apathetic students that are aching to test the limits. What's your game plan for establishing trust, authority, and respect in those first few days?

FULMER: My game plan begins well before I get that group of children. I look to make connections with my students and their parents from the moment I get my class roster. It's critical that I make these connections prior to them arriving in my classroom as that sets the stage for the entire year. This lets the kids get to know me and allows me to talk with them and their parents. I would also send postcards to the families, over the summer, that describe a little bit about what third grade would be like. At pre-open house, I'd have a science fair board with a picture of me on it from when I was in third grade so the kids can see that I was just like them and a part of the same learning process. Take the time to establish these relationships and trust early on, and when your kids come in those first few days, it becomes all about building upon those relationships as opposed to creating new ones. And it tends to go pretty smooth since you already know the kids, they know you, and they know that you know their parents, which is really important. That often used saying, "You have to reach them before you can teach them," is very much the case. After that, it's all about focusing on procedures, procedures, procedures.

TOWNE: That's brilliant. So many teachers have a difficult time in those first few days when kids are nervous and anxious and nobody knows what to expect.

FULMER: This method has worked quite well.

TOWNE: Continuing our hypothetical situation, we move further on in the year and you have a student who's angry and you're not really connecting with him as much as you'd like. Dealing with the parents hasn't worked well because they are unresponsive. What steps do you take to try and reach this child and hopefully build a better relationship with the parents?

FULMER: In every classroom there are hidden gems. Finding those gems and figuring out ways to reach them is critical. You must have persistence and think back to your purpose as an educator before you approach that type of situation. I would really have to examine this situation much further and look for opportunities to connect in other ways. Maybe it's attending their baseball game or their dance recital or something. Maybe it's finding a common ground and meeting with the parents in a place that's not at the schoolhouse. Sometimes parents are a little intimidated at school, but meet them at their house or a restaurant and they tend to be more relaxed. The old way of sending a letter home to the parents as your only form of communication just doesn't work today and, unfortunately, that's the norm many times. Teaching is not just a job, it's a science and an art. It's a professional practice just like a doctor and lawyer. But a teacher's practice is all about his students, and we must use whatever strategies we can conjure up to reach them. Be creative and go against the norms if need be. No matter what, it's not going to be easy, and persistence is the key.

TOWNE: You touched on something I thought was interesting. You said that sending home notes to parents about the child doesn't work anymore. This falls back into what you mentioned earlier about building relationships with parents early on. Basically, you are building the relationships *before* you really need them, which is critically important. All of the great teachers I've spoken with stay in constant contact with parents, not just when there is a problem.

FULMER: That's exactly right. One of the strategies that I use is maintaining a parent log which tracks how many times I've contacted the parents of each child in a variety of ways, be it e-mail, a note, or a phone call. These contacts were all positive and it wasn't just something like, "Nice job," but giving them concrete examples of what their child is learning and doing in the classroom. This goes a long way in establishing those relationships and building that trust. And remember I start all of this before the first day of school.

TOWNE: So because you are reaching out to these parents when their child is good, it makes it easier to get potentially defensive or unruly parents on your side if the child acts up.

FULMER: By then, the parents already feel like they are part of a team and not someone you are coming to for help only when you need it. We're partners in the process.

TOWNE: Back to our hypothetical situation. So now it's moving toward the end of the year and another student is not doing so well academically and it looks like he might fail. Your principal asks you for your thoughts on social promotion versus retention. Neither one is a very good option. Are there other options?

FULMER: Both social promotion and retention are failed policies. They are the equivalent of a coin flip on a kid's life, and the future of a human being is far too important for that. We have to look at better ways to structure our schools from the ground up. We must continuously monitor and adjust to meet the needs of our students, their families, and society. There have to be real choices and options for students that are having academic difficulty, and both multi-age grouping and looping are viable options in this arena. When we begin to look at these alternative options in the structuring of our schools, then a lot of the negatives that we find in social promotion and retention fade away because then our focus is not on stigmatizing a child just because they haven't quite mastered a concept. That's taken out of the equation when you have teams of teachers working with the same students for multiple years or classes with a variety of ages in them. These are good options to start meeting the needs of our students and focus more on the individual needs in that classroom instead of the stigma of being held back or just promoted. Retention leads to higher and higher drop-out rates, and with social promotion...

are we truly preparing them for the work force if we just pass them on? There are other options, and it begins in the structure of the school itself.

TOWNE: Why do you think looping hasn't caught on much in mainstream education circles?

FULMER: People have a tendency to fear and resist change, even positive change. A lot of teachers and principals know the advantages of looping and multi-age classrooms, but it's just like it is with any new concept: there will be some that will be courageous and give new things a try, while some are more likely to sit back and take a "wait and see" approach. Others will just wait forever. But I think looping is so important in those early grades, and multi-age grouping should be seriously considered right through high school.

TOWNE: You mentioned that you must cater your teaching to meet the learning styles of the rich diversity of your students. How can one teacher meet so many different learning styles at the same time? To be truly effective, wouldn't you need a different lesson plan for every student?

FULMER: You don't have to create a lesson plan for each child. You have one master lesson plan, and it's the paths that you take to teach it that vary. It's all about utilizing a variety of different methods of delivering that instruction. Differentiated instruction is really thinking about how you can maximize the learning, over what traditionally happens in a one-size-fits-all approach. You're choosing to maximize what kids learn as opposed to settling for what they could learn. In my classroom, I utilize the multiple intelligences and try to teach the information in a variety of ways. Whether your kids are visual learners, auditory learners, or whatever, you have to work to provide that instruction in ways that meet all of their needs. I utilize grouping to make differentiated instruction more efficient in my classroom. Some folks think that differentiated instruction means that you just put them in groups, but that's not real differentiation. Your groups must be carefully selected and the learning must be customized. These grouping interactions really mirror what we want to see in the workplace, and it's important to provide this opportunity for our kids. Often some of the richest learning occurs peer-to-peer no matter the age.

TOWNE: With the push to maximize test scores and meet standards, the arts are taking a backseat and often disappearing from classrooms altogether. Can you talk about how important it is for you to integrate the arts into your lesson plans?

FULMER: The arts open up numerous opportunities for all of our kids to succeed. I can't imagine functioning in my classroom without music, art, and drama. It's so important, because it makes connections for kids and awakens the creative mind, which is what we need in the 21st century. It allows them to take key concepts and learn them in new and different ways. One of the things I often remind folks of is how we used to learn songs to help us remember things. That still works and hasn't changed. Think about the true power of music. We often identify songs with a particular time in our lives, or feelings that we had about something or someone, and just about anything special to us. Music has a way of connecting all of us and I definitely utilize it as a teaching tool in my classroom.

Many of my life lessons come from my very first teachers – my parents and my grandmother. Long before I learned the power of the arts from studying brain research and analyzing key linkages, my grandmother provided that lesson. We went on a cross-country trip when I was in the fourth grade, and my grandmother had me keep a journal of all the places we visited. Well, as a fourth-grader,

I did not want to write in a journal, so she made a deal with me and we made up little songs to help me remember all of the places we visited.

Fast forwarding many years to my third grade classroom, I used those same techniques. In my first year I was working with my students on rounding numbers to the nearest ten and they were pretty good at it. But one of our standards asked them to round on the number line and they just weren't getting it. So one night I was up late working on a lesson plan and *The Jeffersons* came on TV. I was singing away and then it hit me. If the Jefferson's could "move on up" to the east side, then my class was going to "move on up" the number line. So I went back in the next day and tried that jingle with the kids and they really got into it and started moving on up the number line. They finally began to understand it because we were taking the concept and applying it while moving our bodies. I'm a big fan of body mapping. What you learn with your body you never forget, because you take it with you everywhere you go. It's easy to fuse movement, music, and your body. Music, art, drama, and a variety of other things also help to open up learning possibilities and make it fun for you and your students.

TOWNE: I know kids who know every word to songs on the radio, but can't tell you who the President is or name even half of the states.

FULMER: Yeah, so do I. A little creativity could fix that.

TOWNE: Do you remember how great *School House Rock* was? Talk about a wonderful learning experience!

FULMER: That was fantastic! That's exactly what I'm talking about. Another thing I do is have my students actually write their own verses, and they come up with some of the most amazing and creative things. The best part is, they took their verses and began interacting with children in other classes and teaching the verses to them. They were so excited that they had created these things and they wanted to share them. If your students have ownership in the learning process, it makes a huge difference. I think that's the single biggest thing I've seen that makes students *want* to learn. There was a dramatic increase in my students' level of enthusiasm and their excitement for learning. I had students who had scored below basic on standardized math tests and, once ownership learning principles were applied, they blew the math standards out of the water. It wasn't because of me, but because I gave them ownership in their learning. That's the secret to getting kids to learn. Give them ownership, and it's theirs forever.

TOWNE: You stated in your National Teacher of the Year application that the mark of a successful school is shared leadership. What is shared leadership?

FULMER: Shared leadership is moving beyond the top-down approach. Traditionally school leadership has adopted that top-down approach from business and other organizations and that's unfortunate. It's important that we realize all of the various talents that are within an organization or a school. There is no "i" in the word "leader." It takes every individual in some way, shape, or form to really maximize success. So shared leadership to me is about allowing, enabling, and empowering teachers to be leaders. As teacher-leaders we have to lead not only within our classrooms, but beyond those four walls as well. I think through shared leadership opportunities, an administrator's role changes from simply an authoritative figure to that of a lead learner. Part of administrative leadership is tapping into the expertise that's within their school. But in order for administrators to feel comfortable doing that, teachers have to become leaders outside of their own classrooms. This teacher-leadership concept is often tossed around, but seldom followed. Some folks just don't know what to do with teacher-leaders. Teacher-leaders should be involved in major decision-making processes ahead of time. When everyone is involved, the process becomes much more effective and gives teachers an ownership aspect similar to the student ownership we talked about. Giving the teachers ownership drastically increases the chances of success both in their classroom and the entire school. It's really about having a shared focus and a common goal. What the school reform movement has ignored for so long is the obvious – teachers need to be at the table.

TOWNE: You've been working to better the educational mentoring process since you created the STARS program in your second year of teaching. Can you tell us what that was and how it worked?

FULMER: STARS is an acronym for *Supporting Teachers to Achieve, Reach, and Succeed.* After that first year of teaching I was motivated by my own challenges in the classroom. We all experience those joys and challenges and I had a great mentor, but looking back on those experiences, I was isolated. What I really needed was a chance to connect with other people and discuss different problems and solutions that related to teaching. What was missing was that peer-to-peer camaraderie where all of us, in similar situations, could discuss ideas and problem-solve. The creation of STARS afforded a formal situation where that could happen. This was before we knew what a professional learning community was, although that's certainly a buzz word today. It was clear, though, that STARS was not meant to be a gripe session, but an opportunity for folks to share practical ideas and concepts with one another to help improve our processes. For example, one concept might be classroom management. So your ticket in the door was a technique or strategy that you could share with the group on ways to improve classroom management. Other topics included things like differentiated instruction and various ideas on involving parents.

In my current role I'm serving as Program Director for Mentoring and Teacher Leadership at CERRA, which is the Center for Educator Recruitment, Retention, and Advancement. I'm now working to implement across the state the same kind of ideas that we brainstormed in those STARS sessions. We are working hard on improving our mentoring initiative, because it's so important that schools move beyond the buddy system of support. They need to begin embracing research-based, structured support systems that provide mentors with the tools, strategies, and resources they need to give quality support. For many years the focus of a lot of education discussion has been on recruitment to the profession and too little has been focused on keeping them once we get them. Our goal is not to simply keep new teachers, but to assist in building accomplished teachers who know how to help students succeed. Mentoring and peer-to-peer groups, like STARS, are built as an effort to retain good teachers. The idea is to get them more involved in the processes that shape their teaching and not just the teaching itself. Any teacher can start a program like STARS, and probably should if there isn't already one in place at their school. Just having a mentor often is not enough.

TOWNE: It wasn't long ago that you went through the teacher credentialing program. What didn't the program teach you? How can it be improved?

FULMER: We have to examine all facets of education in terms of our students, whether they're in kindergarten or college. In order to meet the changing needs of society we must constantly review them. I felt as though my teacher credentialing program at USC-Aiken prepared me well to enter the workplace because they allowed me the opportunity to try new things and to not fear risk. In terms of thinking of ways to improve, there should be more professional learning programs where folks are placed early-on in school systems that work hand-in-hand with colleges of education. These work really well as you have professors out there in the field working among pre-service teachers. It also allows for more real-world approaches. We do a disservice to pre-service teachers when we create an ideal setting for them. They need to be exposed to a variety of different situations, and the best way to do that is with the development of these professional learning schools.

TOWNE: One of the problems with the public school system is maintaining a belief in it. Many wealthy and educated people are now taking their children out of public schools and putting them in private schools. Why should they care about public schools if their kids are no longer in them? What's in it for them?

FULMER: Access to public schools is one of the greatest freedoms we have in America. It gives *everyone* the opportunity to learn and that is so important. For many years we've looked at public schools in the wrong light. Too many people are focusing on the costs of public schools when they should be shifting their focus and thinking about them as investments: investments in our children, investments in our society, and investments in our nation's democracy. We have to take the "either or" philosophy out of the equation in terms of thinking about our public schools. I think it's great to offer a plethora of options and choices, but we can do that within the public school system. We must promote more accurate dialogue in the public and in the media so that more rational information can be shared. For instance, a report might say that a school is near the bottom in math scores, but if you dig deeper, you might find that that school also has far higher standards for those scores. You might read a report that says a state is near the bottom in SAT scores, but when you research it, you may find that they allow unrestricted access to the SAT whereas other states are highly restrictive on who can and can't take it. So you really have to look at the ways that we report and examine data. It's important because once you start looking rationally at all of the data, you start to see that public schools are actually performing well in many areas.

We must prepare our students to be creative thinkers and problem-solvers. Our educational focus must shift from preparing students to perform well on a test, to equipping our students with the skills and knowledge necessary to be successful in an ever-changing world.

Why should folks invest or support public schools? Because they have a partnership and a role in helping make the changes that we need to prepare our kids for a global workplace. We're teaching children for jobs that don't yet exist and we, as a society, are ultimately responsible for preparing our children for that world. The other thing is the misconception of some parents that public education doesn't affect their children once they are moved to a private school. The fact is their kids are going to be friends with those public school children. They're going to be their employees and employers. They're going to be their co-students in college and co-workers at the office. You can't successfully live in our society without public education having an impact on it.

TOWNE: I want to come full circle and end with a final hypothetical situation. An outstanding teacher comes to you during her first year and she's considering leaving the profession. You know she's really good, but she's frustrated with the lack of respect she feels and the difficulty of reaching her students. How do you encourage her to keep going?

FULMER: Again, I think it comes back to finding that key role in the concept of a mentor. Many schools focus on providing a mentor for the first year, but if we look at statistics, we lose a great deal of our teachers after the first five years in the profession – approximately 46%. That's an alarming rate, but it can be dramatically reduced by creating those structures of support along the way. Throughout my research and work, one of the things I've looked into is the New Teacher Center at the University of California Santa Cruz. Our mentoring program in South Carolina is actually modeled after their program. One of the key areas that they focus on is attitudinal phases that teachers experience in the profession. At the beginning of our teaching careers we tend to go through an anticipation phase where you have this missionary view and are going to change the world and nothing is going to stop you. But then you soon move into survival mode and reality hits. I remember being the first car in the parking lot in the morning and the last car in the parking lot in the evening, and wondering what in the world was wrong with me. Then you move from that survival phase into disillusionment. And I can't help but think about the song *Rescue Me* by Diana Ross because in this phase you really need someone to offer that sense of encouragement that keeps you going.

So one of the first things I would do is to share this information with that teacher to show her that all of us experience this same thing and that it's perfectly normal. Many of our new teachers can identify all of the negative things that are going on, but it's my job as a mentor and veteran teacher to also show them the positive aspects and to identify some of those key areas where they're doing well. I would also try to get them involved in leadership areas that would expand their functions within the school. We must refrain, as a profession, from new-teacher hazing and not overload a beginning teacher; we must invite the new teacher to the table to engage in meaningful opportunities that can make a difference in our profession. It goes back to what we talked about regarding shared leadership. When new teachers see multiple pathways for advancement and learning, it encourages them to keep moving forward. Ultimately, out of that disillusionment phase comes rejuvenation and reflection, and then it all becomes worthwhile.

CHAPTER 6

Samuel Bennett

2006 National Teacher of the Year Finalist
2006 Florida Teacher of the Year
Garner Elementary School
Winter Haven, Florida
All Subjects: Grade 5

Current Position: Dean of the College of Education,
Southeastern University

Samuel Bennett began his career as a police officer, but soon realized that his heart was elsewhere. "I wanted to help children *before* they ended up on the wrong side of the law," he says. Before long, he was standing in front of a wide-eyed group of elementary students as their teacher. This was his big shot to make a real difference in the lives of children, and he wasn't about to let them down. For the next 20 years Bennett would enthusiastically serve the public schools, including stints in elementary, middle school, community college, and adult education.

Calling himself an "Education Heart Specialist," Bennett's *Aim for the Heart* approach to teaching has allowed him to successfully reach nearly every student he has met, including those that were defiant or apathetic. He accomplishes this by building close relationships with his students and finding ways to put his lessons directly into their hands. He also does everything he can to make learning fun. For instance, he often dresses up as storybook characters to help students visualize their reading, thus making the lesson much more memorable.

Outside of the classroom, Bennett is active on both county and state levels of public and parochial education, serving on the board of the Florida League of Christian Schools and the Education Advisory Council of the Foundation for Excellence in Education. He also serves on the Education Committee with the Winter Haven Chamber of Commerce, is a board member of Noah's Ark of Central Florida, and is the President of the Winter Haven Optimist Club.

Bennett received his bachelor's degree from Toccoa Falls College, his Master's in Elementary Education from Clemson University, and his Doctorate in Organizational Leadership from Nova Southeastern University. As the current Dean of Education at Southeastern University, Bennett spends most of his time recruiting and preparing future educators to become Education Heart Specialists and to "Aim for the Heart" with their students just as he did. He also teaches both undergraduate and graduate courses at Southeastern. Bennett currently lives in Winter Haven, Florida, with his wife, Debbie. They have four children and two grandchildren.

TOWNE: I would like to start by talking about pedagogy. You are now running a teacher-credentialing program where dozens of formal classroom methods are taught. What teaching methods did you use in your grade school classrooms?

BENNETT: I've always believed in working from the "inside out" with my students and helping them to feel good about themselves. Students perform better both academically and socially when this method is used. It's very difficult for students with low self-esteem to achieve and, therefore, my focus has been centered on this method of teaching. I simply call it "Aim for the Heart." In addition, I mix this with a lot of hands-on learning, allowing the students to become actively involved in the learning process. I've used these methods successfully for twenty years in the elementary classroom, and it continues to work today with my college students. The students' needs are basically the same. The material is somewhat different; however, "Aim for the Heart" still prevails. I'm fond of doing this presentation where I become a heart surgeon, coming into the classroom wearing a lab coat bearing a logo saying "Educational Heart Specialist." I then give all my students the prescription for a healthy heart and present them with the five ways of improving.

TOWNE: And what are those five ways of improving?

BENNETT: H.E.A.R.T. is actually an acronym. The H is "Help Others"; the E is "Encourage Others"; the A is "An Attitude That Is Positive and Contagious"; the R is "Respect Others"; and the T is "Tenacity for Life:" in other words, don't quit. The last one is important. You are going to have some tough years as a teacher; however, you have to remember it will not always be like that. You must keep things in perspective. Teachers do not go into teaching for money, which means there is something much more powerful guiding them to it. When things look grim, you have to remind yourself of what that is and why you became a teacher.

TOWNE: For years, you taught the class Advance Methods of Teaching Reading. Can you give us a breakdown of the methods found by your research to be most effective for teaching reading, and specifically reading comprehension, to children?

BENNETT: I think that students need to understand what they are reading before comprehension can take place. They must connect with the text to increase comprehension. The art of teaching pre-, during-, and post-reading strategies seems to initiate and maintain the connection with text. I believe in word study and word fluency; both are important tools in developing better reading comprehension. You have to make sure these tools are in place before comprehension can take place.

TOWNE: How do you feel about Reading Across the Curriculum? There's a lot of debate about this. One argument says that reading should be taught in all subject classes; on the other hand, there are teachers who say they don't have time to teach reading when they barely have time to fully teach their own subject matter. This is especially the case with standardized test prep taking up so much classroom time. Where do you stand on this?

BENNETT: Reading is the foundation for all subject learning, and I fully believe in Reading Across the Curriculum. Reading should be integrated in all subject matter, and I agree with the argument that it's a necessity to improve a child's reading skills, no matter what the subject area. Reading can and should be taught in all subject areas, including math, social studies, science, art, and music. It just stands to reason that since content areas (other than language arts) rely so heavily on reading, teaching reading strategies in those areas makes learning the content more comprehensible. Without that foundation, those other subjects could not exist. The teachers who say they do not have time to also teach reading need to figure out how to integrate it and make it a part of that math or science lesson. They need to open their minds and understand that you can teach a lot of skills within those content areas.

TOWNE: You've been long recognized for using originality in your classroom. For instance, you have been known to dress up as storybook characters in order to bring the reading to life for your students. What other techniques did you find effective in drawing these students into learning?

BENNETT: I still use a lot of those techniques even in the college classroom! I use music too, which has also worked very well. I do this technique I call Karaoke in the Classroom. I take a song and leave the catchy tune but rewrite the words. For instance, I did one the other day called *Secret Teacher Man* for which I rewrote the lyrics to *Secret Agent Man* to fit everything that a teacher does. I also love using Elvis songs and so I'll do *I Can't Help Teaching at This School* instead of *I Can't Help Falling In Love*. With Elvis, I have my scarf, and I put on sunglasses and a giant badge that says, "Secret Teacher Man". I also do Willie Nelson songs where I put on a pigtail and transform myself into him and really have fun with it. I've found that both young students and adults love these presentations. Music and dressing up have always been a staple of my teaching at every level and remain so today. Not only do I dress up; but I also allow my students to dress up and make presentations as well.

I also like to bring lessons to life. When I taught science, I would construct these skeleton models from chicken and turkey bones. Instead of just talking about the skeletal system and other body systems, I would demonstrate them. I would bring a cooler full of whole chickens, and we would dissect them and look at muscles, bones, nerves, tendons and everything else. These chickens would be bought from a public supermarket, and they would turn the class into a real science lesson. This is what I mean by having a hands-on classroom: hands-on teaching and hands-on learning.

When I was hired here at Southeastern University, our president told me two things. He said, "First, don't take yourself too serious", and second, "Have fun." Well, that has always been my philosophy of teaching. You really have to have fun in your classroom. You let the students know that school is serious business but there is plenty of time for fun as well. Therefore, I mixed it up with music, costumes, games, and crazy experiments. The students never really knew what I was going to do from day to day, which created a huge boost in attendance as they just had to see what was coming next. I recommend that teachers really do things that are out of the box, staying far away from the ordinary. Do something different. You'll keep their attention, which keeps them in the classroom, and learning will take place.

TOWNE: And that seems to be the key. If you make it fun, it's going to be more memorable, and the students will *want* to learn it. That's what we were missing in my grade school classes where all they did was lecture and assign textbook readings. There was nothing fun about any of it, and we dreaded even showing up.

BENNETT: I do not do very much lecturing, at least not in the traditional sense. When I do lecture, I try to make it different and exciting. My motto has always been to not just talk about something, but to put your lesson into their hands. I mean literally put it out there in their hands and say, "Here, this is what we're talking about today". For instance, I might give a lecture that is a part of a magic trick or an illusion that I present. Years ago, while I was teaching elementary, I decided to learn magic tricks that I could use for my math and science classes. Believe me, a student won't forget a lecture that comes with a built-in magic trick, no matter what the actual lesson is about. Now that I'm preparing college students to become teachers, I'm actually teaching these tricks to them, as I want them to start off with an exciting classroom that keeps their students intrigued and engaged at all times.

TOWNE: The next set of questions asks about specific research you've been working on over the years. The first is techniques on increasing parental involvement.

BENNETT: I did my dissertation on how to increase parental involvement at Title I elementary schools. When parents get involved, the students will almost always show major improvements, and if you can get the dad onboard too, it becomes even better. The school where I taught was a poverty school with almost 90% free and reduced lunches. A lot of students were either living in single-parent homes or had parents that were incarcerated, so they were living with an aunt, uncle, or a grandparent. I had a lot of those situations where there was not a mom or a dad at home and often there was neither one. There were a couple of things I focused on to increase parental involvement. The first thing was starting early. I always tried to make contact with parents before classes started, either with a home visit or a phone call. I introduce myself and let them see who I am and that I am concerned about their child. That early contact is so important because it's neutral, and you're not calling them with a problem or something bad. That way, if there is a problem later on, you've already broken the ice.

The second focus was on keeping the communication open throughout the year. For this I used classroom journals that went back and forth from home to school every day. I would write something and a parent would write something back. It was almost like a continuous telephone conversation between parent and teacher. The parents always knew if there was homework due, how their student was behaving in class, what would be due soon, and just about anything else they needed to know. I was always aware of what was going on at home that could possibly be affecting the child's performance in my classroom. This method of communication worked very well. I required my students to have that journal signed every night by a parent even if there was nothing written in it for that day. That journaling back and forth was critical in keeping the parents involved. They basically had no choice but to become involved, even if it was only to read a paragraph that I wrote and then sign it.

The third focus was on encouraging extracurricular involvement from the parents. I started a Single Parent Association at Garner because I saw the needs of so many single parents that were struggling with the stress of raising children by themselves. I started the Single Parent Association in order to get those parents involved and get them to the school. We also had All Pro Dad meetings in an effort to get the dads in for a breakfast with their child once a month. That was a big success. For the first meeting, I was hoping for 10 or 12 dads to show up and, instead, 47 came! Grandparents Day proved to be very successful as well. There are numerous ways to get parents to the school; you just have to be a little creative.

TOWNE: You mentioned in a previous interview that you were a big proponent of educational learning communities at schools. Why do you feel they are so important?

BENNETT: It's really all about teacher collaboration. One of the more popular collaborative methods are teacher book clubs where you'll take educational leadership books, or some other current educational books, and read them together and meet once a week to discuss them as a whole faculty. These meetings are very effective and they put everyone on the same page; but, more importantly, they allow each teacher to have their voices heard. When teachers go through a book, they come up with different ideas for things and say, "Hey, let's try this and see if it will work here. If it works, come back and report it and let's see the outcome. How is it working? How can we tweak it to make it better?" This often leads to important changes at the school level, thereby eliciting more teacher buy-in due to the sense of ownership it creates.

TOWNE: What are your thoughts on the effectiveness of pre-service teacher education programs? What don't they teach in these programs that you think is important?

BENNETT: Since I am responsible for a teacher pre-service program, I will gladly answer this one. We're constantly seeking ways to improve our program. Our college has developed a partnership and collaboration with our local school district which is a critical connection for our State Department of Education. I'm constantly trying to think of how to build an even stronger partnership and always ask for feedback from school teachers and administrators throughout the district. We also go to the schools and ask the principals and teachers if they are finding areas where our students are weak. Although we love to hear great things about our school, what we thrive on are the criticisms, because those are what will essentially make us stronger. We actually found a couple of situations last year where our students really had no prior knowledge of "data day" and, furthermore, some of our students ended up working with IEPs (individualized education plans) and didn't have enough knowledge about them. So we came back as a faculty and asked which of our classes would be best for this information? We made some adjustments and have corrected both issues.

Pre-teacher service programs really need to be flexible, adaptable, and always seeking to improve. One thing that is critical for pre-service teachers is field experience, and the sooner the better. Students need to be placed in field experience situations as early as possible even if it's only for observation. In this way, they can see if this is something that they really want to do or not. Some might decide that teaching is not for them and believe me, not everyone is cut out for it. At our school, we have three levels of field experience before they ever do their final internship. I know of a lot of programs where the students barely even see a school classroom until they start their internship, and then the poor souls are like, "Uh Oh, there's children here." It's really the difference between practical knowledge and theoretical knowledge. A good school should be focusing on the practical a lot more than theory. We just started a new practitioner's degree called the Master's in Teaching and Learning. This degree consists of twelve practical courses and no thesis. Instead, the students really learn the nuts and bolts of teaching with a lot of real world examples. So far, it's been a big success.

TOWNE: What are your thoughts on the cooperative learning model and in what ways did you apply it in your classroom?

BENNETT: I am a big fan of cooperative learning and the many models that incorporate it. I did cooperative learning before it had a fancy name. I was doing it back in my early years of teaching and have always used those principles in every classroom I've taught. We had students sorted with a scorekeeper, a timekeeper, and a group leader. Each group was carefully divided, and it brought healthy competition in the classroom. The students really competed and excelled. I love cooperative learning and know for a fact that it works at every level from elementary right up through graduate level college work.

TOWNE: When you broke them into groups, did you break them into specific groups in order to differentiate?

BENNETT: As far as groups go, I tried to have one low, one high, and two moderate levels. They didn't always work out that way, but that was my aim. I changed the group structure once every nine weeks, but never before. I see it as being just like a job. In the working world, most people operate as some part of a broader group of individuals. There aren't too many careers left that are entirely independent and rely on no one else. The students need that group exposure and have to learn how to work issues out among themselves. My students would come up with ideas, debate them, have problems, work them out, stick it out and come up with solutions. In nine weeks the groups change and we do it all over again with a different set of issues. This type of structure better prepares them for the real world even at a very young age.

TOWNE: What are your thoughts on increasing teacher retention and our ability to retain great teachers in low-performing schools?

BENNETT: I have always taught in a low-performing school because that's where I felt the greatest need was. First of all, male elementary school teachers were rare and a lot of those students needed a positive male role model. Many didn't have one at home and some had never even met one. I knew that I was needed at this type of school and that's where I went. I didn't have to be bribed to go there or offered supplemental pay; it's just where I felt I needed to be. Now that's just me. Not everyone feels that way and because of this, I think we do have to work on retention strategies.

Whenever a new teacher came to our school, I always got very involved in the mentoring process. One of the first things I did was to try and plug them into the community and start getting them involved in civic clubs, church events, and things like that. I would also try to get them to buy a house in the area. We were finding that the young teachers coming in would have little apartments somewhere, and when things got difficult, they would just up and leave. The ones who actually bought a house in the area would have much more tenacity and be more likely to stay and work through those difficult times. If you get a great teacher, work with them to establish some roots in the community as much as possible. If the teacher has that buy-in to the community, they are far less likely to leave.

It's really unfortunate, but often the worst teachers are placed in the worst schools, and they don't have a choice. Consequently, the best teachers are placed in elite schools where they aren't really needed. Most of these students are on auto-pilot and they would survive without them. I think we need to really encourage our best teachers to join the efforts of the low-performing schools, even if that means offering pay incentives or other incentives such as flexible schedules. These could even be funded through grants and things like that. It's just so important that we find ways to get the best teachers to commit to the worst schools.

TOWNE: What trends do you see happening in education at the classroom or policy level that you think will have a big effect, either good or bad, on teachers?

BENNETT: High-stakes testing has really become the center of every school's curriculum. In Florida, we have the FCAT which determines grade promotion and graduation. It's the main test instrument used to decide a child's future. Now I'm not against accountability and testing, but I would like to see students judged in more areas and with more than just one instrument. I've had students in my classroom that had been poor test-takers, yet they made a ton of progress in social or behavior skills. Even with all of that progress, in their eyes they were a failure because they could not pass the FCAT. Say you have a child who shows major improvement in these social and behavioral skills; those students are tremendously successful, but FCAT comes along and basically tells them they're failures. The trend is that more and more teachers seem to only be preparing students to take the next test, whether it's the actual state exam or a practice test for the exam. I was talking to some teachers the other day who said they were testing for an FCAT practice test. It was basically a test they were taking that was a prep test for the FCAT *practice* test!

Therefore, pretty much the entire year is being spent in preparing students for this test.

You simply cannot have one instrument that judges the success or failure of a child; it's just not fair. While academic progress is certainly important, students also should be assessed in areas of social improvement and character development.

TOWNE: What were some of the biggest challenges you've faced as a teacher, and how did you overcome them?

BENNETT: Probably, the biggest challenge that I've always had is working with seriously apathetic students, because I'm so passionate about education and about life. I want them to be just as passionate, but often it's hard to get past that apathy. I seem to be drawn to those students though, and I use that "Aim for the Heart" method to help them develop the attitude that they do care and they do want to be better. Again, when you make students feel better about who they are, they will, in turn, do better and perform better in the classroom.

I see students doing things now that many people said they would never do. For instance, Steven was a little Haitian boy I had in my fifth grade class years ago who has become my unofficial adopted son. He's in high school now and just made Honor Roll with five A's and one B. His dad died when his mother was pregnant with him and he had a real tough life up to the point of being in my class. I was really drawn to him during class and used that same "Aim for the Heart" method that I always do. When I won Teacher of the Year, they interviewed all of my students, and Steven made this statement that has lived with me forever. He looked at them and said, "I wish he was my dad." Since then he has basically become my son. I took him to church with me, took him to a Buccaneers game, and just a lot of different places. I try to stay involved in his life and want badly to see this young man succeed. On his first day of middle school, he did one of those papers that was kind of a bio sheet and one of the questions asked him what the happiest day of his life was. Steven wrote that the happiest day of his life was when his fifth grade teacher told him that he made Honor Roll for the very first time. That's the kind of impact a teacher can have on students, and that's why we do it.

TOWNE: What do you wish you had known when you started teaching that you now know?

BENNETT: I wish I would have known a lot earlier how much influence I had in the lives of my students. When I first started teaching, I was always so concerned with following lesson plans and teaching toward tests, and not concerned enough with the needs of the students. Eventually, I came to understand how important everything else is. I realized there's a lot more to teaching than just helping students learn reading, writing, and arithmetic. That's just one function of being a teacher. There are students in your classroom that need somebody to really encourage them and give them guidance and direction that they may never get from anyone else. Somebody said once that children are like wet cement because they are so impressionable. Well, that's very true, and I didn't really understand the depth of that as a new teacher. Looking back, I can see that the level of influence I had on my students was downright scary. I remember parents telling me that their child would come home and would be at the supper table and their parents would say something and the child would disagree and say, "Oh no, no, no, that's not right." And the parents would be like, "What do you mean it's not right?" The child would say, "No, no, no, Mr. Bennett said this" (*laughs*). This kind of thing happened all the time. No matter what I said in class to these students, it was absolute gospel and no one could tell them different. That's a bit eerie.

I wish I had known earlier how much power I had. I hope that all of the teachers reading this book don't take that power for granted and understand that every word you say to students sinks right in and stays there, often forever. I hope teachers will use that power for good and aim to make a positive difference in the lives of their students. I've certainly tried my best.

TOWNE: I hear that you're in the process of writing a book. May I ask what the book is called and what it's about?

BENNETT: It's called *The Edutainer* and it's basically my life story. It talks about how I went from being a student who didn't think he could ever go to college, to eventually becoming the dean of a College of Education. It was a long ride and I hope to inspire others who may not believe they can succeed. I talk about my years as a police officer and how I realized that my passion was really teaching children. My partner on the force told me over and over that I had a real knack for children and that I was way too nice to be a policeman. I eventually listened and gave it a shot. The book talks about how that transformation came about; it discusses how I went on to receive my bachelor's, master's, and doctorate degrees and went from a 5th grade teacher all the way up to the dean of Southeastern. Of course, I get into a lot of detail on the classroom methods that I've used along the way and how "Aim for the Heart" works. I also talk about all the fun things that I've incorporated over the years as well.

TOWNE: That sounds like a great book. When can we read it?

BENNETT: I've been working on it for years, but I've been slacking.

TOWNE: You know people are going to want to read that, so you've got to get it done (*laughs*).

BENNETT: I will have it done!

CHAPTER 7

Joshua Anderson

2007 National Teacher of the Year Finalist
2007 Kansas Teacher of the Year
Olathe Northwest High School
Olathe, Kansas
Speech/Debate/Language Arts: Grades 9-12

J osh Anderson loves to read, but he's not too fond of textbooks. In
fact, he was a big factor in his school nearly getting rid of them
altogether. Instead, Anderson and his colleagues decided to be
innovative and step into the 21st century. Laptops and PDA's have
virtually replaced textbooks in many of the classrooms at Olathe
Northwest High School, which recently earned Anderson the "Top
100 Wired Schools" Facilitator Award. His efficient use of technology
in the classroom has garnered national attention and has gotten him
recognized by the New York Times, Harvard University, and many
other major organizations, as one of the most innovative educators
in America. But Anderson was just getting started. He also helped
design the nation's first virtual charter school, which has thus far been
a tremendous success.

If one were contemplating debating the importance of technology with Anderson, one might want to reconsider, as he also heads his school's debate and forensics team which recently won the State Championship and was runner-up the year before. In 2007, he won the Kansas Debate Coach of the Year Award, and every one of his senior debaters on that team was accepted into an Ivy-league college. Anderson feels that the skills and lessons from activities like debate carry over into the real world and help students become better listeners, learners, and leaders.

Anderson earned his Bachelor of Science Degree in Education from Emporia State University and his Master of Arts Degree in School Leadership from Baker University. Aside from being named Kansas Teacher of the Year, he has also won the Outstanding Graduate Student Award from Baker, the Diamond Key Excellence in Education Award from the National Forensics League, and has been inducted into both the Mid-American Educational Hall of Fame and the Baker University Educational Hall of Fame.

Since helping to open the doors of Olathe High, more than 97% of his students have passed the Kansas Reading and Writing Assessments. Anderson works with each of his students to provide them with the advanced skills of innovation, creativity, and design – skills that he feels are critical for a global economy in the 21st Century.

In his free time, Anderson enjoys reading, spending time with his friends and family, and working on his blog. He currently lives in Overland Park, Kansas.

TOWNE: Probably 95% of the teachers I've had in school followed this ritual: lecture as the students take notes, expect the students to memorize a lot of facts and figures, and then test them on those facts and figures. What's missing?

ANDERSON: What's missing is that our students are not learning the skills that they will need to succeed in the 21st century, skills that they didn't necessarily need in the 20th century. These include innovation, creativity, design, etc. All of these skills are least acquirable through the traditional lecture method, so I think change is needed.

TOWNE: What do great teachers do differently?

ANDERSON: I think what makes teachers great, at least in the eyes of their students, comes down to the relationships that are formed with those students. I know a lot of phenomenal teachers that don't connect with their students, so it's difficult to call them phenomenal teachers.

TOWNE: That's interesting. In fact, earlier today I asked a 13 year-old who she thought was the best teacher she ever had and why. She named a teacher from two years ago and said the reason was that he actually listened to them and that they had a great relationship.

ANDERSON: There's really no magic. It's just a matter of taking that time to build it.

TOWNE: There are three simple questions posed by Rick DuFour in a wonderful book he wrote on education called *Getting Started*. You referenced these questions in your Teacher of the Year application as being extremely important for all teachers to entertain and seek to answer. I would now like to pose these questions to you.

ANDERSON: Okay.

TOWNE: What do we want students to learn?

ANDERSON: Nationally, I think we need to clarify our focus as a national school system. I'm a big advocate of national standards for a bunch of different reasons that we may or may not get into. But we really need to clarify, as a nation, what we want our students to learn. I think that the answer must be defined in part by job skills that are needed for the 21st century. In some part it's defined by local needs, but that's less important than it was fifty years ago. And I think we should continually be revamping our classrooms to reflect the changing needs of the futures that our students will face.

TOWNE: How will we know if our students have learned it or not?

ANDERSON: Well in part, if we are producing students that are consistent with the needs of the labor market, then we know we did our job, but in the current situation it's a little too late for that. So now, how are we doing it? I think that's where No Child Left Behind is doing a good job. It's helping us to measure basic skills, but we need to do a better job of measuring advanced skills. Or rather, we need to *start* measuring advanced skills. The way it's designed now we are not doing that at all because it's so difficult to quantify.

TOWNE: What do we do if our students have not learned it?

ANDERSON: That's where our schools need the biggest change. We spend a lot of money on something that we call differentiated instruction, but only about 10% of what we call differentiated instruction is actual differentiated instruction. The rest of it is probably a lot more like remediation for kids who have fallen behind. And if we're going to keep the system that we have now then we're going to have to keep spending a lot of money, resources, and time on remediation, whether we call it remediation or differentiated instruction. But the truth is that our students aren't learning in the way that we need them to, and, of course it's our fault, not theirs. And so we've got to do a better job of designing a national school system that guides local entities in adopting sound systems that work for both students that do well and students that don't do well. Right now, with the factory model that exists, it's only working for the students that were already doing well.

TOWNE: Your principal has talked about your outstanding ability to empower students. Can you talk a little about how you're able to empower your students, especially those that are not already motivated to learn?

ANDERSON: I have a somewhat unique method. Well, it's not really unique, but in my English class for example, they are tested on the state assessment. In fact we just finished our state reading assessment. So it is something between a convenience and a luxury that I can walk in on the first day of school and explain to them the positive consequences and the negative consequences of not doing well on the state assessment. When I can have that conversation with them, suddenly I stop being the authoritarian, and I start being the mentor who can guide them on their journey. They are then all very motivated to do well on the assessment. Once I started teaching like that, about six years ago, I started noticing that if I would get off track, it was my students who would say, "Hey, come on let's go. We've got to learn such and such." And so those are good conversations that I have with the kids. And it's unfortunate that the state assessment has become the carrot or the stick in that situation. But that forms a powerful motivation for kids, knowing that they will be held accountable. That's something that hasn't happened before in the school system.

TOWNE: You and several other Teachers of the Year mention the importance of educating the "whole child." What do you mean by that, and why is this so important?

ANDERSON: Well, that's a great question. A lot of times "whole child" is defined however the user wants to define it. But I think the message there is that we have to go beyond basic skills. We must be providing not only basic skills, but also a civic education, a social education, and a cultural education. We're inducting students into our culture, and it is not enough for them to just have a 2400 on the SAT. They also need to be able to interact with others and raise a family and have a social consciousness. They need to have political views, opinions on the environment, and a strong ethical base. I think that's where educating the whole child comes in. The learning must go beyond that which can be measured on any standardized test.

TOWNE: As important as a good curriculum is to a teacher, you mention that it is "the culture and the climate that really determine success." Can you explain what you mean by this and give an example of how you try to create an ideal culture and climate in your classroom?

ANDERSON: In part that goes back to relationships. It is starting to become trite to talk about relevance, relationships, and rigor, but they really are the best three terms for what our classrooms need. It's not enough to have two of the three; you need to have all three. The climate is the attitude with which you teach and the students learn, and in which we interact with one another. The culture includes the expectations involved. What do the students expect of me and what do I expect of them? How articulate can we be in terms of expressing these expectations?

In my classroom the expectations are very clear right up front and so the rigor is there. For preparing them for the 21st century, the relevance is there. And with the relationships – we just have fun all day long. We laugh and we clap spontaneously and have a good time and cheer for each other. It's not something that I tell them to do. I don't say, "Okay, now we're going to cheer for this student." That's pretty artificial, but when you establish a culture of taking risks and being aggressive about pursuing your own education, I think that kind of empathy for each other comes out as a result.

TOWNE: At one point students with disabilities were 20% of your student population, yet you were able to teach these at-risk students so successfully that they scored as high as many of the gifted students on tests. How do you accomplish this?

ANDERSON: It kind of comes down to this. I have to do a lot of teaching "the test" and I'm sure not ashamed to say that, because the standardized assessments in Kansas are so closely aligned with the curriculum. We have 16 well-defined curriculum indicators, and we know that every state assessment that students will take will have between four and eight questions on each indicator. So we can be very precise about what we teach and what the students need to learn in my classroom. The students at every learning level know exactly what's going to be on the test, and they're very familiar with the test format itself. A skill that we need our students to know is how to take a standardized test. Many of us had to learn it the hard way, which is why only 18% of our students go on to get a four-year degree in this nation. We just don't usually teach people that skill, and we should. This is a skill that we cover extensively in my class, and by the time my students take that test, there are no real surprises.

I genuinely believe that for many of the students I have, this is probably their first brush with success, especially when they've been identified with any number of disabilities or labels or whatever you want to call them. It's difficult today for them to have success, or for their parents to have success, and I think that the students see something in themselves that they didn't see until they were in this culture and climate.

TOWNE: You said that the most effective and active classrooms in schools today are those that encourage collaboration among parents, teachers, support staff members, administrators, and the students themselves. If you were teaching at a school or district that had no collaboration, what would you do to start the process?

ANDERSON: I would take advantage of technology, because that's where I have found the most success in terms of collaboration. I'll break it down for you. Every Sunday morning I send out a two-page newsletter that contains every bit of information you can think of about the class. This includes specific homework assignments, an explanation of what we did last week, what we're going to do this coming week, tests and projects that are coming up, information about the ACT deadline, basically everything they would need to know on two pages. And I do that not because I have nothing to do, but because that kind of forces me to do my lesson plans. I'm just lazy enough that I will try and wing it and if I don't commit to a solid set of lesson plans every week, then things go awfully wrong. So that newsletter is e-mailed to anyone that would be interested in the class, including guidance counselors, social workers, other teachers, parents, coaches, department chairs, you name it. And what that does, is it clarifies for everyone what's happening in Mr. Anderson's class this upcoming week.

We also have an electronic grade book that allows me to email out progress reports. So what I do is send those out maybe once or twice a week and I can build into the system exactly who I want those reports to go to. So if little Suzy is struggling, then maybe her mom gets a progress report and her dad who lives on the other side of town gets a progress report, and her social worker, case manager, probation officer, and anyone else who might be relevant gets a copy too. And so what ends up happening is that rather than saying "How was school today?" Suzy now has ten people asking her if she studied for her vocabulary test. Teachers just don't do good enough jobs of empowering the parents to become secondary teachers at home, and this really makes a big difference.

So it's the combination of those that work for me. The grade reports are based on how the student has already done, and the newsletter forecasts what's coming up. So everybody who has an interest in one or more of the kids in my classroom gets a lot of communication each week. I think that's something 95% of schools can accomplish. E-mail is now available in every school, and there are a lot of grade books that can be found online that you can use to automatically send out progress reports as often as you wish.

TOWNE: You mention that one of the most threatening things to our public school system is the nature of the debates surrounding it as opposed to the debates themselves. In your application for Teacher of the Year you used an analogy of blind men and an elephant and compared it to what's happening at the policy level. Can you talk about that and give an example of how we might find common ground among stakeholders?

ANDERSON: Well, I have to tell you that my application packet was written in the state of Kansas about two years ago. And if my memory serves me correctly, we made national headlines when our Board of Education decided that the biggest and most important issues were Darwin, dinosaurs, and creationism. Our application process for state Teacher of the Year includes many of the same questions that are used on the national application. So what ended up happening, unintentionally, was that I had answered that question on the essay specifically for the state of Kansas. But they send that same application on to the Nationals. So it wasn't really meant to have national implications, but it was meant as an indictment of the way we were handling things in our state. I felt that we were overly concerned with the science standards and, really at the end of the day, who cares whether it's creationism or evolution? I mean, with respect to all of the other problems that we're struggling with in schools, that should not be priority number one. So that essay was meant to be my take on an important issue, which was that we are spending so much time bickering that we are getting nothing else done in the way of making progress.

TOWNE: And that's not just Kansas. A lot of states have that same issue where things like standing up for the pledge of allegiance and vending machine contents seem to be the biggest problem in education. Never mind that a quarter of their students are failing.

ANDERSON: And in some ways I understand why that is. Those are issues that the public and the media can wrap their heads around. They can't wrap their heads around No Child Left Behind, because it's all second-hand information. So anyway, that was the message I had sent to our state Board of Education and, interestingly enough, when I received the award, that was the speech that I read with all of the state board members sitting right in front of me. It was actually kind of awesome to tell you the truth. I do think that when it comes to all of the disagreements, we're talking about 5% of the big picture. And, unfortunately, we don't often take enough time to clarify the 95% of things we do agree upon.

TOWNE: I know you're a big proponent of incorporating technology into the classroom, and we spoke a little about how you use it for your newsletter and grade books. In what other ways has technology helped transform your classroom?

ANDERSON: I think technology is very important, not only because it offers the opportunity to enrich delivery of instruction, but it also has the ability to improve the quality of what the student is provided, including things like lessons and projects. Unfortunately, this is a big struggle for a lot of schools. We're quickly becoming a have versus have-not country and the achievement gap is not being helped with schools that lack technology. So I would say technology is a critical piece in the classrooms that can afford to have it and afford to maintain it. Luckily, the price of technology is dropping, so hopefully more schools will be able to incorporate it.

Another big piece is that students need to learn how to use technology. We take that for granted, but I have to tell you that my students can get online and play *World of Warcraft*, they can assemble and disassemble an X-Box 360, they can text all day long, and we just assume that they have computer skills. But honestly, they can't do a simple Excel spreadsheet or format a document properly in Word. So when we talk about technology in the classroom, sometimes we make the mistake of assuming that we mean technology in the hands of teachers or we mean a laptop in the hands of every student. What we really ought to be talking about is whether the student knows how to create and format basic documents, whether they know how to deal with networks and how to problem-solve. Technology for students is great, but we need to make sure they learn the practical applications of that technology and not just use it for entertainment.

TOWNE: You helped found one of the first virtual charter schools and have said that online courses can often be an adequate substitute for the classroom. Can you talk about this?

ANDERSON: There are certain subject matters that lend themselves more readily to online instruction. And there are divisions within subject matters, specifically basic skills, that are sometimes a lot easier to tackle online. The idea is that if a student can spend part of their day online taking classes and part in the classroom interacting with others, then it's entirely possible that the student can make a quicker advancement than just a traditional classroom could offer. It's much more self-paced and allows for flexibility to a greater degree.

TOWNE: And is that virtual charter school still around?

ANDERSON: Absolutely. We had 65 students our first year and now there are over 400.

TOWNE: That's great. Let's talk a little about the success of your debate teams. How are they consistently so good? Why would getting students involved in something like debate help?

ANDERSON: They are good because we have an excellent school system. And to be completely honest with you, the kids that I inherit on the first day of debate are already highly talented. They were already going to go on to great things, but I think they will all tell you that debate raised them to a higher level. It took them from potentially going to good colleges to being accepted into great colleges.

Debate gives students that extra push, but more important, it gives them a context for all of the other classes that they take. When they're in debate, they're using math and science and literature, and they're using everything that they've learned and applying it immediately. And so rather than us having conversations about when they get into the real-world, we can have a conversation about what they will debate that weekend which is always very real-world.

TOWNE: What words of advice or support do you have for pre-service and new teachers?

ANDERSON: First of all I would read Harry Wong's book, *The First Days of School*. That's a classic and a tremendous help for any new teacher. That book helped me in the beginning as much as anything else.

In a very short period of time our nation will be crying out for young educators to step up and take leadership roles. And so for new teachers, while on the one hand they're not even sure what they're going to do that afternoon, let alone five years from now, there is a rock-solid home for these folks in the world of education. The good news is that we have found out most of the problems, but we are just starting to find the solutions. And so new teachers, in this day and age, will be part of the solution generation and can spend their time articulating those solutions rather than articulating just the problems.

Speaking of solutions, have you read a book called *Tough Choices or Tough Times* written by the National Center on Education and the Economy?

TOWNE: No I haven't read that, but I've heard a lot of good things about it.

ANDERSON: I have to tell you that this book absolutely changed my life. What it does is lay out an entirely brand new national school system, and it's getting a lot of attention from policy makers. It hasn't made as much of a dent in actual education as it has on the policy level yet, but every educator that reads it just falls in love with it. The ideas in this book became the center piece of my message as Teacher of the Year. There's a free 28-page Executive Summary online in a PDF file so teachers should at the very least check that out and if they want to read more, go out and get that book.

CHAPTER 8

Dennis Griner

2004 National Teacher of the Year Finalist
2004 Washington Teacher of the Year
Garfield-Palouse High School
Palouse, Washington
Social Studies/Multimedia Studies: Grades 11-12

eloved by students and colleagues alike, Dennis Griner was
raised in a rural, somewhat remote, logging community in
central Idaho. He knew from a young age that he wanted
to teach and found several significant mentors who helped him get
there. He began his teaching career in the small Idaho town of Deary,
having no idea that, 37 years later, he would be considered one of the
best teachers in the country.

Griner began by teaching social studies and physical education
and later added an elective called Audio/Video Communications. It's
this latter class that played a significant role in thrusting him into
the national teaching spotlight. Since the class began, Griner has
built it into an impressive audio/visual program that is equivalent to
an entire television station, but based entirely out of his classroom.

This classroom television network has the capability to broadcast programming for any Garfield-Palouse game, or event, anywhere at nearly anytime, including on television or the internet. With money being an issue, Griner used his exceptional grant-writing skills to successfully secure funding for virtually every aspect of the program. Today, other schools and districts have sought his expertise on creating similar classes.

Griner earned both his Bachelor's Degree in Education and his Master's of Arts in Teaching Degree from the University of Idaho. He has been honored with multiple awards, including being named Washington State Teacher of the Year, the National Society of the Daughters of American Revolution's Washington State's American History Teacher of the Year, and a finalist for the National Teacher of the Year. He has also been awarded the Christa McAuliffe Award for Excellence in Education. Despite his many awards, Griner has continued his professional development, and in 2005, he earned his National Board Certification from the National Board of Professional Teaching Standards.

Today Griner continues to teach and is as passionate as ever. He frequently gives presentations to districts and education conferences about technology use and its integration into the classroom. He resides in Palouse, Washington, with his wife and soul mate, Vickie.

TOWNE: What is the biggest teaching challenge you have faced?

GRINER: When I started teaching, things were a little different than they are now. In my present situation, I think the challenge is dealing with a different type of student than I did 35 years ago. Students now often come from households without a structured family unit, and I must find ways to educate children who face problems and concerns outside the classroom that make issues of homework pale in comparison. For these students it's more about security and survival. Some of the students don't even have a permanent place to live, so you can imagine the difficulty of trying to convince them that math or history lessons are really that important.

TOWNE: How can a teacher overcome such a hurdle?

GRINER: One of the major elements of my teaching is focusing on the well-being of my students, which in turn influences their learning. To do this, I work hard at developing and maintaining relationships with them. This means taking time to get to know them outside of the classroom, taking a sincere interest in their lives, and gaining their trust. I spend as much time with some students working on issues of self-esteem and self-confidence as I do with academic issues. I often go to student events, athletic competitions, concerts, plays, and non-school events, in which my students are involved. When you actively seek to make connections with your students' lives outside of the classroom, you become the part of their extended social life. You have a connection that can be used to relate the importance of learning while improving their academic standing in the classroom. A positive comment about their lives beyond the classroom can make a major difference in how they perform in the classroom.

TOWNE: One of your greatest contributions as a teacher is your ability to motivate and instill students with the desire to learn. How do you do this with defiant or apathetic students?

GRINER: Effective teachers must get past the confrontational mode which sometimes happens with apathetic and defiant students. You must get down to where it's one-on-one with a student. I primarily deal with juniors and seniors. They are looking at going out into the world, which for too many students is an uncertain future at best. It can be a real challenge, especially if students don't have the skills or economic security to keep their lives afloat. They don't know where they're going to be a year from now, and that's scary. What I attempt to do with those students is, again, get to a personal level and become an informal counselor to them, talking with them one on one. To be effective using this approach requires consistency over time. I *listen* to their plans and encourage them to pursue their dreams. I'm a firm believer that a compliment works far better than confrontation. As far as the carrot/stick approach goes, the carrot beats the stick hands down. You need students to understand that as a teacher you are there to provide them with opportunities to learn and with knowledge that will help them succeed in life. Most students really understand that. They know there are things students have to do to be successful. They need to be reminded that you, as a teacher, are there to help them accomplish the things they need to succeed. When you reach that point of sincere understanding with your students, the learning environment in the classroom changes.

TOWNE: It sounds like you become a lot more than just a teacher. You also become a mentor, a friend, and a guidance counselor.

GRINER: That's probably true. It's especially true in most small schools where you have a student population that you've known for many years before they ever step foot in your classroom. The students have seen you outside the classroom as a community member, a neighbor, and possibly as a volunteer in youth activities. You, in turn, have watched them grow up. You and your students are not strangers, and they have a good idea of what they're getting into before they ever walk into your classroom. I also teach Drivers Education, which is a big plus. Every student in my school who has a driver's license has taken Drivers-Ed from me. They know who I am and I know who they are. We've sat in a car together for at least six hours, which is valuable one-on-one time. Learning to drive is a stressful experience, and I am able to establish a positive relationship with my students before they ever step into my academic classes. This gives me a better handle on each of them. This has worked well and I would highly recommend teachers find outlets they can get involved in that would provide similar one-on-one scenarios, such as coaching, class advisors, or community youth work.

TOWNE: There are dozens of different formal teaching methods and pedagogy for teachers to choose from. Which ones do you use in your classroom?

GRINER: I garner ideas from the pedagogical methodologies and education philosophies and blend them with my personality to create my own teaching style. Most teachers will tell you that there are very few new teaching strategies. Many of the new strategies are just a repackaging of traditional methods that have been given new names. I do, however, use several philosophies that I've found to be very effective. For structure in my class I use a system that's loosely based on Madeline Hunter's ITIP (*Instructional Theory into Practice)* model. This provides a systematic order of daily and long-term planning. Students are provided detailed weekly lesson plans with the grading rubrics for major assignments included. I say "loosely based" though because I don't tightly hold to the ITIP structure. In fact, I heavily rely on the TESA (*Teacher Expectation and Student Achievement*) model of class discussion by blending questioning and redirection methodologies with the *Bloom Taxonomy Model.* The ITIP model is basically structuring class time and sequencing content presentations while TESA is the manner in which it's done. I also do a lot of *Writing across the Curriculum* because I teach in the social sciences and my students do a lot of writing. I use group work, independent research, peer teaching, and a variety of other approaches as well. In designing my units I have always started with setting the goals and then systematically organizing the content to reach the stated goals. The term used today for that approach is *Understanding by Design*.

I have on my bulletin board the old tried and true *Bloom's Taxonomy Model*. My students also have a copy of that in their folders. They understand that the goal of learning is to have a firm grasp of the basic material and then move toward functioning at the higher levels of learning and questioning. There are different levels of learning, from just basic rote memorization to evaluation of current events and, of course, the learning goal is to get students to function well at the higher levels of learning. With the *Bloom Taxonomy Model* I always tell my students that we're trying to get to the top of that ladder and provide more in-depth thoughts. But to get there, they have to have a basic knowledge of the material before we can hit those evaluation stages. It's a concept that I think they understand and thereby understand the rationality that lies behind each assignment. This is really an important aspect of teaching today. Years ago, you didn't have to persuade students that an assignment was valuable or justify why you're giving it, but that's changed. The just "do as you're told" argument does not carry an effective message any longer. I have to say I think it's a change for the better. I have found that telling students why something is important undeniably increases their performance. If they see real value in the assignment and they see the rationale behind why it's being given, they are much more likely to pay attention and want to learn it. To reinforce the value of each assignment, I also make sure my students are aware, every step of the way, of how the assignment fits into our strategies for achieving our end goals.

TOWNE: You stated that the basic concept of your teaching is that you teach to individual students and not to a class, but at the same time you incorporate cooperative models and group projects. How are you able to successfully balance the two?

GRINER: Each new class takes an online test of multiple intelligences and a test on learning styles. This provides feedback to my students and to me on their skills and learning styles. I would never attempt to use only one teaching strategy when I know I have multiple learning styles in my classroom. So in order to best implement multiple teaching strategies, I design my student study units with several common elements regardless of the content. One of those elements is in the organization of the unit. I design the unit to involve the entire class to work in groups with each individual responsible for specific elements. I can still remember being put into some really non-functioning groups in grade school where someone ends up carrying the load for somebody else, so I try not to do that with my students. I follow the cooperative learning model and part of that deals with that no-hitchhiking aspect.

I always make my learning groups of just three or four students with each individual assigned a task that will challenge his or her ability. The tasks require the students to stretch beyond their learning comfort zone. Within each group I have the students choose individuals to serve as group leader, group presenter, group organizer, and group recorder. As each member of the group has a role to play, each member also has a responsibility to the group, to the class as a whole, and to me. At any time I may call up all of the recorders, leaders, presenters, or organizers from the different groups to give me a progress report. This makes each person within the group responsible for understanding the assignment and knowing their group's progress. When the time comes for a grade, even though they all worked on the same project, the effectiveness of each student in handling their assigned role determines their grade. When my students complete these projects, they have been challenged to go beyond their level of knowledge and skill while becoming actively involved with the entire project.

TOWNE: Student-centered hands-on learning is a major theme in your teaching style. Can you share an example of how you use that?

GRINER: Sure, I'll tell you about the current one we're working on. All the projects that I design have a major community service element to them. I'm on several outside-of-school committees, one of them being with the town Mayor, some City Councilmen and other citizens. The committee is currently looking at a "Brownfield" site. (An EPA identified pollution site that can be reused after cleanup). It is the site of an old service station. Gas, oil, and other contaminants have leaked into the soil. It borders the river that runs through our community. The city is considering taking that property on, rehabilitating it, and then selling it to a business that would then use the site as a commercial venture. I wanted to involve my students in this, and have organized the plan into a total-school project involving the whole staff and the student body. I submitted a grant that outlined this involvement. My Current World Issues students would do the research on similar "Brownfield" projects and the environmental issues surrounding this project. The science classes would actually do site environmental evaluation studies on the pollutants in the soil and water, the vocational agricultural classes would do a plant survey and evaluation of the site with an emphasis on soil restoration, the REAL classes will complete a formal site evaluation for future use by working with the local business community, the art and music classes will work with the multimedia classes to produce informational public service announcements, the history classes would do research on this and other sites nearby as to their historical use in our community, and so on. Eventually, every class in our school would embed one or more aspects of this project into the curriculum. The final report would be created in the multimedia lab and placed on DVD with video, historic still pictures, charts, graphs, and student projects included. So the entire school will be involved in one project. When the project is done, students will have worked with individuals from the EPA, state environmental groups, two state water quality committees, the Mayor and city council, and numerous professional experts. These same individuals will also speak in their classes at the school. The students will have those experiences of working with real people and that's the hands-on concept. It works well and student buy-in is high because we're providing real-life situations that have an actual purpose and value in the community in which they live.

TOWNE: So you take what you're trying to teach them and apply it to real-world topics.

GRINER: Linking the classroom to life is a central theme of mine. I look for whatever happens to be a hot topic at the moment and evaluate the potential for a classroom application of it. If it is a viable topic, I pull all the kids in and ask them what we can do about it. Students get involved at the ground level of the unit: planning, dividing the unit into manageable sub sections, and so on. Rather than doing some textbook chapter that was published for general consumption, I hope to bring the lessons alive with real-world application. I attempt to keep the application local so that the students have a vested interest in it. The greatest asset that this approach has in the learning process is that all students can participate and learn regardless of their academic standing. They could be an A student or a D student. There will always be a role for them where they can participate and be successful.

TOWNE: You mentioned that you are in the process of writing a grant for that project. One of the major problems teachers and schools face is the lack of adequate funding for important educational needs. You have been very successful in writing grants to overcome this obstacle. How important is it for teachers to learn grant writing?

GRINER: It's one of the most important skills a teacher can acquire, especially teachers in public schools where funds are limited. It's really about taking the time to learn how it's done and then actually doing it. There are not as many grants as there used to be, but there are still plenty out there. If teachers really want to get the extra material they need for their classrooms, they need to seriously look at grant writing as an option. The State and school districts just don't have the resources. Education is expensive and to do it right is more expensive than people are presently willing to fund. If you want to go that extra mile and provide that extra incentive for your students in the classroom, you're going to have to come up with that money somehow: either out of your own pocket if it's relatively inexpensive or, if it's more expensive, you need to seek a grant. I didn't take a grant-writing course, but I did seek out one of the grant writers at our local university. I gave him a grant proposal I was hoping to submit. He looked it over, called me back, and mentored me through the grant writing process. From that point on, I never stopped writing them. Most of the technology and software in my multimedia classroom was purchased through grants. The district is pleased, as well, to have all this equipment that has been acquired without school district financing.

TOWNE: This is so important, because I have run across teachers who use lack of funding as a major reason they can't get things done. You're a perfect example of how someone who really wants to get something done, will get it done.

GRINER: It's going to take some time and effort, but it can be done and the results are well worth it.

TOWNE: It also helped that you had a grant-writing mentor who taught you, I'll bet.

GRINER: Absolutely. Every university and most junior colleges have someone there who writes grants. I strongly encourage teachers to visit these schools and find out who gets the money for various departments. You can track down the main person who writes grants for that department and just ask for help. Many of these folks are professional grant writers. Any advice can only make you that much better at writing grants. I was very fortunate that my first four grants were all accepted, but that was unusual. I have also put in a lot of hours and energy into grants that were never funded. If it is a good idea, another funding source will come along and I just touch up the grant application and resubmit it. I have been able to eventually find funding for these projects, allowing me to purchase the materials needed to promote student learning in my classes. Seeing your students successfully completing a funded project is what offsets the time/energy component of the process. So find a mentor and practice, practice, practice. Keep on writing and applying, no matter how many rejections you get. As a teacher, I feel obligated to provide the best education for my students, and in order to do that it takes hard work, patience, and hopefully, somebody else's money.

TOWNE: Another skill that you excel at is integrating technology into education. Can you talk a little about the multimedia technology model that you helped develop and tell us how other schools and teachers might be able to benefit from such a program?

GRINER: I teach Current World Issues, U.S. History, and A/V Technology. That last class sort of grew out of what the kids wanted to do. Years ago, our district used to have what was called the "gifted and talented" program. I talked with the administration and they agreed to offer something similar to that program for all students regardless of their academic ability. I started this class and asked the students what they wanted to do and where they wanted to go. They really wanted to go into television broadcasting and commercials. I wrote the grant, got the funds, and we implemented a local educational cable television broadcasting system at our school. That was years ago, and now it's grown so much that we broadcast all of our home basketball and volleyball games and even concerts. We can do time-delay broadcasts on anything that we tape, and it's worked out wonderfully. We have video editing equipment and sound mixers and pretty much everything that a regular small television station would need. All of this is done right out of my regular classroom so that equipment is available for all my other students as well. Students in my classes can use this equipment to create anything they like. The room is open before school, lunch time, after school and for a ninety minute block during the school day for individuals who have approved projects they wish to work on.

We also have all the software there that is needed for student production. In my U.S. History class, I use the equipment to print newspapers with stories from time periods we happen to be studying. For instance, if we're on the Civil War, I'll ask them to create a newspaper dated the day after the Battle of Antietam. I divide the class in half. One half of the class writes from the Northern perspective and the other half of the class writes from the Southern perspective. Their final newspaper accounts make the learning experience rewarding while providing students lessons in "historical perspective" and interpretation of historical "facts." All students have their own computer, software, and internet access. Student work can also be displayed on our two cable channels and/or broadcast over our internet broadcasting station.

TOWNE: And now other schools are beginning to copy those models?

GRINER: We've actually had our broadcasting model copied and implemented in several of the other districts around us. They send teachers and students to watch us "do our thing" and then incorporate our model into their own schools. It does make a major difference in getting students involved. When you can motivate students that are not currently involved in any school activities to become dedicated to working in multimedia, you have succeeded in making a difference in their lives. A major transformation can take place. They start to see value in being at school. Other students comment on their work. In the process of carrying out the daily expectations of audio-video production, students learn skills that carry over into other aspects of life – leadership, team work, problem solving. For a normal broadcast to be seen live on our cable channel, and on the internet, requires several hours of work: pre and post broadcast, and the broadcast itself. Students are expected to master many different skills: wiring, sound setup, video camera operation, announcing, audio and video mixing, character generator operations, digital capturing to computer, and digital editing. The students have pride in their work. It is this self-motivation that enforces student learning. Many of the students involved in the program have little other extra-curricular connection with the school. In our school and others that I have visited, this program fills the needs of students on several levels. Students do the design work, the setup, broadcasting the program, set the tape delay broadcasts, edit and burn the program to DVD, and all the while they are learning life skills in the process. As student knowledge is passed down from student to student, they expand the program. This is why other schools are looking at our model. I have only positive comments concerning this program of student-driven learning. It has proven to be highly successful.

TOWNE: I think that's great. And it also teaches the kids skills that they could actually use after high school if they wanted to.

GRINER: Yeah, some of my students have gone on to professional careers in broadcasting. The goal, however, is not to produce professionals in the field but to teach students leadership, teamwork, self-reliance, responsibility, accountability, and work ethic.

TOWNE: I'd like to talk a little about parental involvement. It's such a vital part of a child's education. How do you encourage it?

GRINER: Many parents have left the total education of their children in the hands of the public school. They want the school to teach the kids to read, write, be polite, and do math. But if public schools are to thrive, parents must be brought in as active partners in the system. The parents' role must expand and the schools must change. This means all areas of concern, including curriculum design, school day design, textbook adoption, and other major issues that affect their children's education, and by extension, their future, must have increasing parental involvement.

I encourage parental involvement both directly and indirectly. One of the things that I do is invite parental input. In my U.S. History class, one of my students' research projects is to do an oral history. The students interview the elder members of their families as the project actually involves them in the "homework". Because of this, the family becomes more involved in the school life of their children. Also in my Current World Issues classes, I require survey work. Students are encouraged to ask their parents about issues discussed in class, and in some instances, we complete formal surveys. For example, I have a water unit I use in my Current World Issues class. Water is an important issue here in the Inland Northwest. There's a major concern about not only the amount of water available but also the quality of water. Our aquifer and the demands placed upon it are major concerns. Articles dealing with these water issues are in our local papers nearly every day. My students are required to complete a home survey of water use: simple things, like whether the water is left running when they brush their teeth, the length of their showers, watering the lawn, etc. The students go home and talk with their parents and they come back to school and share the information they gathered and their parents' input. So indirectly parents are always getting involved. But I also take a direct approach and go out and talk to the parents as well. Last night, I went to the home basketball games and talked with six or seven parents. Parents feel free to stop and talk. I encourage it; in fact, I go out of my way to make it happen. So whether it's at school activities, a casual conversation on the street, or a more formal meeting, I always keep the parents involved.

TOWNE: You have stated that student academic progress should not be used as a measure of teacher accountability because there are so many variables outside of the teacher's control. What other types of evaluation methods might be worth exploring?

GRINER: Well, I don't know the most effective way. I do, however, know an ideal way, and that's peer evaluation. Unfortunately, it is unlikely to become a reality. Ideally, it should be done through a panel of teachers who are your peers. There would probably be an administrator to oversee it, but many administrators have not been in the classroom as a teacher for a long time. Administrators have a lot more duties than just teaching. Their role is fundamentally different than that of a teacher, yet they're given the responsibility of being an effective evaluator of those who teach. Well, for those who haven't been in the classroom for the past 10 or 15 years, the classroom has changed and so have the students. Administrators invariably lose contact with these changes through their extended roles. That's not anything negative against the administration, that's just how it is. You really need to be in the classroom to understand the dynamics of what's going on if you're the one responsible for evaluating it. Having someone not familiar with current classroom dynamics evaluating that classroom just doesn't seem to be the most logical means of doing so. Most teachers are going to know their subject matter very well, so it's not a question of whether a teacher knows the information. Teachers know most of the teaching pedagogies, so they know how things should be done. Therefore, the evaluation should be focused on how well teachers are effectively carrying out the task of promoting student learning. This attribute is better recognized by their peers than by an administrator.

TOWNE: What do you wish you had known when you started teaching that you now know?

GRINER: Well, I feel like I waited too long to start applying the methodologies and techniques I currently use. I held back because I was waiting for more experienced colleagues to show me the ropes. If I had "gotten it together" earlier in my career, I could have been a more effective teacher. My advice to other teachers is to aggressively pursue excellence in teaching. If you know something could be done better, then step up and make that change. Take risks. If you believe you can make an impact and affect your students in a positive manner by changing your teaching style, then change it. Many highly qualified teachers have unique methods and systems designed to meet student needs. At one point in their careers, each of them took the initiative to try new techniques to improve their teaching effectiveness. This is what makes great teachers. Never be satisfied with your approach to teaching. Work to improve your skills with each lesson. Each time you step forward to improve the classroom environment or your teaching style, students benefit.

CHAPTER 9

Philip Bigler

1998 National Teacher of the Year
1998 Virginia Teacher of the Year
1999 Milken National Educator
Thomas Jefferson High School
Alexandria, Virginia
Humanities/History: Grades 9-12

Current Position: Director, James Madison Center

"Good teachers are zealots. They are totally committed and they don't give up," says veteran educator, Philip Bigler. Having taught history and humanities in the public school system for over 23 years, he certainly knows a thing or two about commitment. He has been committed to students, in one fashion or another, for decades and is widely recognized for his creativity in the classroom and his innovative methods. "My job is to bring history to life," Bigler says. He does this primarily through the use of interactive historical simulations, the core of each class he has taught. Whatever or whenever the lesson may be, his students become a part of it. One week they may be members of a Greek *polis*, debating important issues of the day. The next week they may argue constitutional law before a mock Supreme Court. His students also frequently write letters to one another as if they were living in a certain time period.

Bigler's methods have worked and he has been extraordinarily successful as a teacher and as a historian. Aside from winning National Teacher of the Year, Bigler has also won numerous other awards, including the Washington Post Agnes Meyer Outstanding Teacher Award, the Hodgson Award for Outstanding Teaching of Social Studies, the Norma Dektor Award for Most Influential Teacher, and the United States Capitol Historical Society's Outstanding Teacher/ Historian Award.

As Director of the James Madison Center at James Madison University (JMU), Bigler works closely with K-12 educators and pre-service teachers. Each year, the Center co-sponsors the Virginia Teachers of Promise Institute, which pairs award-winning educators with novice teachers to provide a high quality in-service experience. He continues to teach courses at JMU in both history and teacher education. Bigler has recently completed his sixth book, *Liberty and Learning: the Essential James Madison*. In 2006, he co-authored *Be a Teacher: You Can Make a Difference*, which is intended to help new teachers make the transition from college to the real world of the classroom.

Bigler holds both a Bachelor's and a Master's degree in Education from JMU as well as a master's degree from the College of William and Mary. When not working or teaching, he enjoys photography, boating, fishing, snorkeling, and especially spending time with his wife, Linda, who is also an educator. They live in Bethesda, Maryland.

TOWNE: I'd like to start with a common theme in most classrooms today: lecture, assign textbook readings, quiz and test. This is what most classroom teachers do, from my recollection. What's missing? What do great teachers do differently?

BIGLER: Well, my sense is that nobody would read a textbook if they didn't have to. I know I wouldn't (*laughs*). The problem with most textbooks today is that they're written for such a low common denominator that it takes the magic out of the subject. So it's the teacher who has to add that magic, making the classroom exciting and giving the kids a sense of why they should be taking your class. A lot of teachers who become textbook-dependent are generally not comfortable enough with their subject matter. They need to be able to go beyond the textbook and breathe life into the subject. There needs to be a lot of activities that involve the students, making the learning memorable for them. Lecture is certainly a valid teaching tool. I do it occasionally, but it's not something that you would expect teenage kids to sit through for an hour and a half each day. Teachers really need to get the kids involved and get them out of their seats and interested in the subject at hand.

TOWNE: When I had teachers rehashing boring textbook readings, I did all I could to try and stay awake. Often it didn't work.

BIGLER: Yeah, I can imagine. I found that when you ask kids why they like a particular subject it almost inevitably goes back to who they had as a teacher. In other words, if it were a great teacher, then they're going to say that they loved that subject, regardless of what it is. And if they hate the subject then very often it's for the same reason — that the teacher didn't bring the magic into it. By the time the kids get to college they will already know what subjects they like and don't like, but invariably it is because of the teachers that taught them.

TOWNE: Are there any recent trends that you see in teaching, either within the classroom or at the administration or policy level?

BIGLER: What's really encouraging to me is that I'm seeing a lot of young people going into administration and starting assistant principalships or principalships. These are really talented teachers that have been successful in the classroom, but want to raise their level of influence by becoming an assistant principal or a principal. They seem to have a real sense of enthusiasm and excitement which is what is needed. This youth movement is very exciting in education because these people have a lot of good ideas. They tend to be innovative and are willing to try different things. So to me that's something that's exciting. The other thing is the technology component. It's so amazing today what you can do in a classroom with technology. When I started out teaching in 1975, we were pretty much dependent upon whatever materials we were given by the textbook manufacturers. Now, with the internet and all of these other enormous resources, we have the ability to communicate between educators and get different lesson plans and different ideas. You're no longer isolated in the classroom by yourself. So I think all of those things are really encouraging, and it's probably the most exciting time in the world to be a teacher.

TOWNE: How do you immediately establish authority and respect in your classroom?

BIGLER: The first thing is that you don't waste time. It's very important that when kids come into your class they are engaged throughout the period and that means at the very start of the class. Statistics show that more kids get into trouble in the first five minutes or the last five minutes of class than any other time. A lot of times that's because the teacher either doesn't begin class on time or doesn't finish class on time. So it's really important that you show your students, just as soon as they get into the classroom, that you have meaningful things for them. As far as authority goes, I think that basically comes from being a good role model and really knowing your subject matter. If students respect you, it goes a long way in establishing that authority. That respect is usually given to teachers who are serious, know their subject matter, and know what they're doing. That not only builds respect, but also eliminates pretty much all of your discipline problems.

TOWNE: And if you keep them engaged, then they will respect you even more because now they love what they're learning.

BIGLER: Exactly. I always say to the kids, when they come into my classroom, that what we learn in this period will be the most important thing they are going to learn the entire day. Of course, I expect that to happen in their next classroom as well (*laughs*). But really, I think you invariably see that approach in good teaching and good educators.

TOWNE: Can you talk a little about how your teaching has changed over the years and what you've incorporated in recent years?

BIGLER: My belief is that you can't be the same teacher the first day of class as you are the last day of your career. You really have to continuously develop and look for ways to do things better. So even if I taught the same subject matter year end and year out, I would always try and look at different and more effective ways of teaching it. I think good teachers are always on the lookout for good ideas, always willing to try new ideas, and always willing to listen to other people's ideas. For me, it was the use of technology that was the biggest change in my career. We basically went from calculators to web pages and that's pretty dramatic. I don't fight change, I embrace it. Every change along the way has made me a better teacher. Right now we're faced with an information overload in our society which is really the first time that's ever happened in history. We actually have *too much* information. So that means that our new goal as educators is to take all of this information and transfer it into meaningful knowledge. This means helping kids understand that not everything on the internet is worth looking at, nor should it all be accepted at face value. They have to understand that the information out there has to have some meaning and background, because anyone can post anything on the internet and call it a fact.

We really went from a time when we didn't have a whole lot of information, or a whole lot of material for the classroom, to an opportunity to basically pick and choose from a huge variety of things. So the revolution has been in technology and having access to primary resources, archives, and museums from all around the world. All of that is now only a couple of mouse clicks away. But I never do blind internet searches with students. We don't just go to the library and say, "research the middle ages." We look for very specific things and in very specific places for those things.

By now, all teachers should have a webpage, not only to access information, but also to provide information to parents about what's happening in the classroom. It also gives students an opportunity to know what's expected of them and allows you to pre-select some of the more worthwhile websites that might be available. So it was that switch to the information-overload society that has been the biggest change and actually the most exciting.

TOWNE: I think this is especially important for veteran teachers who have been teaching for a long time and are maybe a little bit hesitant to incorporate different things.

BIGLER: It's funny because you'll hear some people say, "I've only got five more years, why do I need to learn that?" Well, my argument would be that you should try to learn something new every year and strive to improve. If you have the opportunity to be a better teacher your last five years, then you should take advantage of that. Quite frankly, the kids today have a higher expectation of using technology in the classroom, and this just gives you so much more opportunity to reach students than you've had in the past. Learning can now be a 24 hour process if used correctly. Students can go home and access material and continue to learn outside of the classroom, far more than they could before.

TOWNE: What formal pedagogy or systems did you use in your classroom, and why did you choose them?

BIGLER: I tried to do something fairly different every day. My goal was to always do different things and never allow a day to become routine. That being said, I guess what I have been best known for doing are historical simulations in class. I found this to be a very powerful tool where the kids actually role-played or became part of an historical event. I did a lot of those. You can do all different types depending on what you're studying, but what I like to do is give kids the opportunity to actually learn on their own, but with the guidance of the simulation. These simulations became very successful for me and they were also extremely content-rich. A lot of times people will use the state standards as an excuse to be a bad teacher, saying things like, "I would be a great teacher, except that I now have to cover 50 Greek philosophers." So they give the students a list and have them memorize it. Well, no kid is going to understand why that's important, and they're not going to learn it particularly well either. So you must place these things in context and make it come alive. We used to do an historical simulation on the Greeks. The kids were all part of Greek city states, and they knew the difference between Athens and Sparta and Corinth and Megara and so forth. And they understood why Pericles was significant because they actually participated in a simulation where he became real. So those were certainly the most popular things I did, but I also did mock trials along with a wide variety of other activities.

TOWNE: Did any simulation stand out more than others?

BIGLER: Well, I've done so many over the course of the year. I used to do one on the My Lai massacre trial which was really fascinating. It was the story of Lt. William Calley, and it basically brought into question our entire Vietnam policy. This was an extraordinarily rich activity where the students became lawyers and discussed nearly every major aspect of the Vietnam War. They then contemplated the question about what happened at My Lai in 1968. The kids actually became very well-versed and understood that whole period. My goal is that the kids become critical scholars of the period. I don't tell them my personal views one way or the other. I don't tell them whether the Vietnam War was justified or not; I just ask them questions and they come to their own conclusions. That's been the case of virtually all of my simulations. The beauty of history is that there are a lot of opinions, and I want my students to be able to develop their own opinions so long as they're based on facts.

The first simulation I ever did was called Grand Illusion. It was a simulation that I bought out of my own pocket and it was about a mythical peace conference where the students tried to work out the issues of World War I. So the kids got all involved in it and everybody was a different country or a different state and they all had different goals. But ultimately what would always happen was that they would end up in war because their goals were so contradictory to one another that they felt they had no choice. Interestingly, 25 years later, I was walking into this trophy store and there was this young man there who was from that very first class of mine. And the first thing he said to me was, "You know I was Bosnia Herzegovina during the Grand Illusion simulation," and then he says, "What's going on in the Balkans right now is a lot like 1914." I thought it was pretty stunning that here's a kid that didn't go to college, is working in a trophy store, and

25 years after the class, that simulation was so content-rich that he could still tell you the basic issues in the Balkans in 1914 and find parallels to the 1990s. That was really amazing.

TOWNE: That's when you know the way you're teaching is working.

BIGLER: I think that said a lot about the power of simulations. But you can also have that kind of impact with other methods. I do a lot of field trips and those are incredibly rich activities as well. Kids may not remember what you do day to day in the classroom, but you can bet they're going to remember those field trips. There was one I would do where I took the kids to Gettysburg. We'd go up there after having read the book *The Killer Angels* and then look up info on Joshua Chambers and other people involved in the Battle of Gettysburg. At first, it was just my class. Then all of the teachers wanted to get in on it because other students were getting jealous, and it soon became a school-wide field trip. It was really cool the way we divided the trip up. What we did was to divide the buses the students were on into Army Corps. Each bus was symbolic of a corps that had been in the Union army during the Battle of Gettysburg. We would have the corps badges and you were either a circle, a shamrock, or whatever. So the students had to study to see what that corps had done at the Battle of Gettysburg and they all wore those corps badges so we could identify them. Once they got off the buses, we taught them how to march and how to fire cannons and all of these really cool things. It's the active way we go about learning these issues that makes it so extraordinarily powerful, and usually the kids come away fundamentally changed.

TOWNE: Wow, the field trips I remember from grade school weren't like that. The teachers basically just took us somewhere, dumped us off with a worksheet and told us to meet back at a certain time. That doesn't sound like your kind of field trip.

BIGLER: That's exactly how you should *not* conduct a field trip. A properly-done field trip should be rich and content-oriented. The teacher must make it come alive. There should be a clear theme, and it should be as fun and as interesting as it is instructional.

TOWNE: Students are now inundated with technology from video games, cell phones, the internet, and a host of other things. How do you keep their attention?

BIGLER: Well that's certainly a big challenge. One thing that really frustrates me is that a lot of times we don't have these kids read enough. Part of the problem is that we need to give them books that are worth reading. In my class we use our textbook more like an encyclopedia. Instead, I find outside reading material that's more powerful, more meaningful, and something the kids can better relate to. These could be books or anything else I can find that can bring the subject matter to life.

We also can use visuals to our advantage. Kids are really into visuals, so why not have them make movies or do some photography or something? In our class the students go out and do sepia tone photography that makes things look like they are from the civil war or the turn of the century or something. Sometimes they make videos and work on various other visual activities. Instead of fighting technology, it's better to embrace it and give the kids opportunities to use it constructively. But keep in mind, it's not about teaching them how to use a video camera or digital camera; it's about teaching them how to effectively convey information to communicate and educate. Technology is just the tool.

TOWNE: If one of your students is falling behind and you know there are personal issues outside of your control causing it, what can you do about it? Can you help them inside the classroom with problems that are occurring outside of it?

BIGLER: You have to take the kids as they are. You can't change who their parents are or their economic situation, but what you can do in the classroom is to give them a caring and safe place for a few hours in the day. The reality is that a number of these students come to school every day with an enormous amount of problems and you, as a teacher, may be the only positive adult figure in their lives. Teachers must strive to be role models for these kids. You must show them that you care about them, are interested in them, and that you value them in your classroom. One of the things we always did in class was to give our students a birthday certificate on their birthday. I have a program that I would run and it was basically "your day in history". So every day I would bring all of my birthday children to the front of the class to be acknowledged. This may be the only time a kid will be in front of the class in their entire year without any type of grade or something on the line, so they're very safe at this point and really look forward to it. All I'm really saying to them by doing this is that we value them as a person and we're glad that they're a part of our classroom. Even with our weaker students this is always one of the highlights of their year. As simple a thing as this is, it means so much to them and lets them know you care. The truth is, there's really only so much you can do. I wish we could take all the kids and give them that safe and productive environment outside of the classroom, but we can't. Therefore, we must focus on what we can do, and it's the smallest things that sometimes make all the difference.

TOWNE: What things do you do to encourage parental involvement?

BIGLER: I really see parents as our allies, and, unfortunately, one of the biggest changes I've seen in education in the last 25 years is the degeneration of the relationship between teachers and parents. Part of that is because of our legal system. When I first started teaching, parents would conference and ask things like what they can do to help the kid and ask what the kid did wrong. But then it became more like, "Here's my lawyer," and "Why isn't the school doing this or that?" So there has been an unfortunate change in that relationship. But we do have to realize that parents, when they give their child to us, are entrusting their greatest treasure to us. They're saying, "Here's my child. Please help me educate him." So first we have to respect that and really listen to their concerns. Sometimes we don't do that so well. We also need to respect what their goals and aspirations are for their children. When all of that respect and caring comes through to parents, as it should, then you will have them as allies and they will be much more likely to be involved.

Back-to-school night is also a critical time. That's the day when you showcase your class and it's really the first impression that the parents are going to have of you. I think it's vital to make sure that it's a positive experience. I've seen a lot of teachers use their ten minutes basically just reading curriculum. What I do is a PowerPoint slideshow of what we did in class, and I tell the parents what we're going to do. I also give them information about our website so that the parents can find out more and know exactly what's going on at any given time. I don't think there should be any surprises for parents, including what you're reading in class or what your expectations are. So, for instance, if you have a list of outside reading for your students, it should be posted on the website for parents to access. And as far as outside readings go, you should really try and give your students, and their parents, a chance to have a choice in what's read. So, in other words, if there are five books on your list, the child and his parents should be able to choose from those five books. This will give them some control and keep them engaged in the process itself. A simple thing like that can really empower them, and they are much more likely to make sure the kid reads the book because they actually chose it.

TOWNE: What's your philosophy on discipline in the classroom and how do you implement it?

BIGLER: The issue of discipline is probably the hardest issue for any teacher because it's usually seen as a negative. But if you have an overall positive classroom environment, then discipline should really just be an extension of that. So rather than focusing on "Thou Shall Not," we focus on the kinds of respect that we are going to show in our classroom community at all times. The absolute worse discipline is yelling and screaming; you're going to lose those battles every time. And even if you think you've won that battle, you've lost the war because now the students know your weakness. When you get mad and upset, you lose.

When my students do something wrong, I correct them, but I also forgive them. A lot of times kids think that if they do something wrong and are corrected for it, then you are going to harbor some kind of grudge against them and be angry forever. It's important to let them know that isn't the case. Tell them that you expect them never to commit that offense again, but that you will not hold a grudge and that you are not angry. I would much rather have my students fear my disappointment than my anger. What I would hope is that students would respect me, and what I'm doing in the classroom, to such a degree that what they would fear most is that I would not be happy with them because they didn't put forth their best efforts.

What this really boils down to is relationship-building. The most effective discipline is only accomplished once you have a solid relationship with the student. Just as with the parents, the relationships with your students are fostered by the little things. You should know who is in your class and use their first names.

It would be good to practice what we call "wayside teaching" which means that you interact with the kids in the hallways and cafeteria and you go to some of their activities. When you have enough knowledge of your students as individuals, you will earn their respect and trust, and classroom discipline problems will become exceedingly rare.

TOWNE: Usually, there's such a wide variety of learning abilities in a single classroom, from gifted to special education. How are you able to successfully keep them engaged while concurrently preparing them for state standards?

BIGLER: Wow. If I get this one right, then I should be the Secretary of Education! (*laughs*) That's a tough question. You really have to look at where each student is individually. Some kids are going to have higher aspirations than others and that's okay. My goal is to help them become successful in my classroom, however that success is defined in terms of ability. I think it's really important, especially with kids with learning disabilities, to have a very clear idea of what your expectations are. We need to make sure that we meet those kids' needs and follow through with their guidance counselors, and that's a huge job. There are a lot of IEP's (individualized education plans) in the world today, and we need to make sure that we're honoring those in helping these children become successful.

What I try to do in my classroom is give the kids a variety of opportunities. For instance, in my simulations there are a lot of different things to do. In the My Lai trial, for instance, we had roles that were lawyers and they were going to need to be pretty strong students to pull that off. But at the same time we had judges. It was a military tribunal, so the judges would be there to ask questions and to consult with one another, which did not require quite as much preparation. So you try to match a student's ability to a role that fits them, which gives them a real chance of success. The kids that may not have been up to the task of preparing a legal brief were still successful as judges.

Today, with our standard-based education I will sometimes hear a teacher saying, "I don't have time to do simulations. I have standards to meet." My argument to them is that a good simulation is content-rich and *supports* the standards, thereby allowing you to teach the standards even better. You really have to teach content in context.

TOWNE: What can teachers, as individuals, do to raise the prestige of the profession and earn the respect they deserve? Is being a good teacher really enough?

BIGLER: First of all, we have to stop complaining. I think that's one of our biggest problems as educators. We tend to complain too much. It's okay to have concerns about our profession, but if that's all anyone ever hears coming from us, then teaching will forever be looked down upon. One of my colleagues at the university was telling me that he thought about becoming a teacher until he went into the teacher's lounge and heard nothing but complaints. He asked me why, if they're all so miserable, are they in this profession? It was a fairly big epiphany for him, but it was also horrifying that this could be the case. There are a lot of positives about teaching, and it would be nice to start talking more about those and a little less about all the things we don't like.

It's also important that we take ownership for our profession and be constantly looking for ways of improving instruction. This means going to professional conferences, going to in-services, and being advocates for the profession. I'm not talking politically, but in terms of advocating and encouraging young people to go into teaching as a career. At the university I'm at now, I feel blessed because I'm getting to work with a lot of young teachers who are so excited to be starting their careers. One of my most important goals right now is to validate this choice in their lives.

Another thing we have to understand is that teaching is a talent and is not something that most people can do. When people ask us what we do in our lives, we need to say, "I'm a teacher!" with enthusiasm and pride. We shouldn't bow our heads as though we've committed some kind of atrocity. We are professionals, just like doctors and lawyers, and we should think of ourselves as such. Most people can't motivate kids on a daily basis. I used to bring these lawyers from Washington D.C. into the classroom, and these people make like $500 an hour, but they couldn't talk to a sixteen year-old. So that's something we should take pride in, because it really is hard to motivate kids every day. I have the utmost respect for elementary school teachers because they work so hard, and they're absolute magicians at doing this.

Your second question was whether or not being a good teacher is enough. And the answer is no, it isn't. It used to be okay to be what we call a "foxhole teacher" where you close the door and that was your kingdom. Back then, if you were a good teacher in the classroom, that's all that really mattered, but today I don't believe that's the case. Now it's really about creating and maintaining effective teams. Parents, teachers, administrators, and staff are all your teammates. And you're still a team even if you aren't all on the gym floor at the same time. That means you have to be a good colleague and understand that all of your teammates are trying to accomplish the same thing, and that's to educate children. So it's not enough to be a good foxhole teacher anymore. These days it's about having respect for your teammates and creating a learning community. It really takes all of us to effectively educate a child.

CHAPTER 10

Susan Barnard

2006 National Teacher of the Year Finalist
2006 Washington Teacher of the Year
CHOICE Alternative High School
Shelton, Washington
Language Arts/Biology: Grades 9-12

Traditional teachers would not allow their students to write about "gross things," much less use controversial language to do so. Luckily for her students, Susan Barnard is not your traditional teacher. Barnard has spent the majority of her 15 teaching years helping seriously at-risk students learn to love reading and writing. Not an easy job, considering she deals on a daily basis with children impacted by poverty, drugs, teen pregnancy, homelessness, and violence. Nevertheless, Barnard constantly finds ways into their hearts by building trust through one-on-one relationships, thus opening the door for successful learning. As Barnard puts it, "I love the challenge of facing kids who hate to read—and really hate to write. I love the satisfaction of seeing them change their minds." To do this, she isn't afraid to use nontraditional means. Some might see her methods as controversial, but few can deny their effectiveness, as they consistently help her students overcome overwhelming obstacles and finish school.

Barnard received her bachelor's degree from Pomona College and her Master's in Education Degree from the University of Washington. She knew she wanted to work in a helping profession and was all set for medical school. She was passionate about becoming a doctor, but things changed and soon the teaching bug had bitten. She began teaching elementary school in Colorado and then returned to Washington where she found a home at CHOICE Alternative High School. After sharing her passion for reading with struggling students, and seeing firsthand how it changed their lives, she knew that she had found her calling.

Outside of the classroom Barnard remains active as well. At the district level, she heads up the Literacy Team and acts as the Language Arts Curriculum leader. She also serves on the district Coaching Cadre and the District Improvement Leadership Team. She remains heavily involved in community service as well, and has spent years volunteering with her local Habitat for Humanity affiliate and serving on its board. When not teaching, Barnard can frequently be found playing with her grandchildren, reading, gardening, traveling, boating, walking, or off learning something new and exciting. She currently lives with her husband, Mike, in Shelton, Washington.

TOWNE: A lot of people might not know much about alternative schools. Can you describe how your school works?

BARNARD: Alternative schools vary a lot. In our regular day program, we teach standard classes where the students attend all day and have courses much along the lines of a traditional school. There's also another component to our school for students that are very close to graduation. These students work on a contract basis and only have to come into our building five hours a week, and the rest they do at home. Then there's another component that is a home partnership program where students just work on computers and theoretically are being helped at home by a parent.

I teach in the regular day program. We have six-week terms, and I believe this helps our students succeed, as they might not be able to hold it together for a full semester. On the flip side, if they have a bad six-week term, it really only destroys that part, and they can easily pick it up again and have a decent term right after that.

TOWNE: What lessons about teaching at-risk students can traditional schools learn from schools like yours?

BARNARD: I think seeing them as real people rather than seeing them as the kids with blue hair and piercings or judging them because they wear baggy jeans and shades. If a traditional school chooses those things as battles, then they have already put a wall up between them and those students. We try hard to be non-judgmental and see each of our kids as individuals with real value from the time they walk in the door. Many of these kids have already been labeled as "trouble makers" and have often been kicked out of school because of these things. These kids hide under their hats and hoods and shades because they're shy or they don't feel like they fit in. We understand that and accept them for who they are, and all of them eventually lower their guards and come to feel pretty good about themselves. Schools that make judgments based on outward appearances have already lost half of the battle.

We really value our school community and we try to help the kids understand that being a citizen of our community is preparing them for the wider community. It's also more like a family and that's very important. So we're building that culture all the time and sometimes that takes a little silliness and sometimes it takes a firm voice, lots of second chances, and lots of love and compassion.

TOWNE: You're a big proponent of educating the whole child. With standardized exams becoming the focus point of education now, how do teachers balance the need to build relationships and educate the whole child with the expectation of teaching to the test?

BARNARD: In my school this is not balanced. The absolute priority is to build relationships, assess the needs, teach the student at his or her level, and then push like crazy to raise those levels. When assessing the needs, we often find that survival issues come ahead of the academic. So we don't balance. We work on the whole child first and attempt to bring them up to speed academically second. We have some students who have no intention of graduating: they are 18, have 2 credits, are at risk of being homeless (parents have said at 18 you are out), and need to find a job. Our work is not to prepare them for passing the 10th grade WASL, required for graduation. Our job is to quickly try to prepare them for transition into the real world: assess skills, improve skills to pass a GED, maybe, help them create a resume, a budget, a plan, and other things that might serve their needs better than the test. However, I must add that the skills required to pass the state test are the same skills needed to function in the real world—so we teach the skills regardless of whether they will be "tested" by the state or in real life.

TOWNE: What's a typical day like in your classroom?

BARNARD: There aren't very many! (*laughs*) No, but I think the kids would recognize that there are typical days. My morning reading class really has a solid system to it. The program that I use is called *Read-Right Systems* and I've used that for a long time, although the way I use it has evolved over the years. Anyway, my students come in, get their work out and work individually in their own little spot of the room. My assistant and I move around and work one on one with them. It can get a bit noisy with all of this happening at once, but everybody is working and reading at their own level and working on their own material, so it's worth it. It might not look like a typical class, but it's certainly an effective one.

TOWNE: Sounds like a lot of differentiation happening in that setup.

BARNARD: Absolutely! It's tremendous because everyone is working at their own pace. There may be some working on second grade material while others are working on eighth grade material. We try to get at least to tenth grade independent reading so that they can pass the state test. Besides my two reading classes, I also have an advisory class which meets for ten minutes every day except Tuesday, when it's a half hour. And this class has the students that I nag about whether or not they're keeping up. Here we build culture and share rules, although they're not really rules but more like mutual agreements.

TOWNE: What about unusual strategies that you've found effective?

BARNARD: Well, the goal is to always keep my students a little off-balance. I change my activities often enough so that they can never predict what we might be doing on any particular day. For instance, in my English classes we do a lot of writing—on occasion they write for an entire period (on-demand writing.) Equally often, they might write only for the last five minutes, and that piece (usually drawing a conclusion on something they learned that period) becomes their ticket out the door. But on any given day, the students rarely know if we are going to discuss, do small groups, read, do a simulation, or write.

Perhaps as part of keeping them off-balance, I change the furniture arrangement for the purpose. If I am going to have a large group discussion, we put all the tables together and sit around the outside (creating an oblong or oval.) This way I can see each student, and they can see each other. It's difficult for them to avoid participating. My reason to keep them off-balance is to stay at least one step ahead of them. If they can predict what's going to happen that day, their whining takes on significance. If I change things up, there still might be whining, but it just doesn't gain steam—they can't possibly say, "We *always* do that."

TOWNE: You stated that you love the challenge of teaching kids who hate to read and write and that you love seeing them change their minds. How do you change their minds?

BARNARD: Trickery! (*laughs*) Not really. With writing, most kids feel they cannot write. In fact, many of them have heard from former teachers that they are miserable writers. So they come into my class with old bruises and zero confidence. Most are afraid to write because they don't spell well, they cannot remember grammar conventions, their handwriting is terrible, etc. I tell them that I don't care about that. I do care that they put words on the paper. We may start off with outlandish assignments—describe the grossest thing you know. Or use all the cusswords you know. It shocks them. We do lots and lots of writing before I ever deal with errors. The only feedback they receive is positive, encouraging them to tell me more, helping them develop their voices. Next thing I know, I have students showing me pages of work. Only after I have them believing they can write, do I talk about quality. Often the practice alone brings huge improvement.

TOWNE: A teacher who lets students write cusswords and discuss gross things. That's something you don't see every day, yet I can see it working well.

BARNARD: It really does! I do that early on and it shocks them. "You mean you're not going to turn me in?" And I say, "No, this is what I want to hear from you today. It doesn't mean I'm going to read it all. It doesn't mean you're going to get graded on it and it sure won't be shown to the principal or your parents." But I really want to see them fill the page with some words. So if I don't shock them a little, use humor and do some silly things, then I can't hook them like I need to. It's all about finding ways to engage them.

TOWNE: What about those who hate to read?

BARNARD: Well it's a similar approach with reading. They say, "I'm here, but I'm not going to read," or "If I do read, I'm not going to like it." I've had years of experience as a reading tutor and the trick is to just find ways to begin. Find something off-the-wall to read about, something weird or crazy and then work together with them. Typically, within five minutes you can celebrate some small success and then build from there. I've had students who would only remain in the room for ten minutes, but I made sure that we read for five. As they began to trust me more, we worked longer. Some were amazed when the period was over. It's trickery. It's an art. And it comes from lots of practice. Humor and kindness are necessary elements as well.

Once students have had a little one-on-one attention, they like it. So if they refuse to cooperate, I have been known to call their bluff and go to work with other students who want my help. After a day or two, they'll do just about anything for me. At that point, I cannot rub it in; I must just matter-of-factly sit down and get to work. We celebrate the good day and expect to continue the next. I am firm and consistent, and once they understand the parameters, then we're off and running.

So yes, I love to see them change their minds. But it's only after we have built a solid relationship that I can tease, "I told you so." We also have reading parties where I give awards and heap on the praise. I have students who have "graduated" out of the program who ask to come to the parties; they speak about their success in the program and inspire the others to work harder.

TOWNE: I think you're on to something. If you can't beat them, join them. But do so in a way that builds trust and inspires further learning.

BARNARD: Most of our kids feel that teachers are just authority, and they want nothing to do with authority. Part of my job is to show them that teachers are much more than that. Once in awhile, for the kids that have earned their credit and are on track, we have a lock-in where they spend the night and the teachers are there and everybody stays up all night; we play games, eat pizza, and just have fun. This allows them to see teachers as people who play and are real human beings. We also have a lot of little clubs that the kids belong to, and it's great because these are kids that don't typically belong to anything. They never played on soccer teams or in Little League. They don't typically play an instrument or have any of the opportunities that other kids have. But they find homes in these little clubs and have a good time.

TOWNE: Who comes up with the ideas for these clubs?

BARNARD: Mostly the kids, and it's great because then they have a sense of ownership in them. Sometimes a teacher will come up with a club idea based on whatever they're passionate about. My club, one of the oldest, is a literary magazine that the kids actually raise money for and get together and produce. We use the money from it to go to art museums or to see great plays and things like that. There's also an outdoor club that went skiing yesterday and another that goes backpacking each year. One of our teachers is extremely passionate about music, so he formed a rock band with many of the kids and they drum and play guitar and really have a blast. I'm also part of a team of teachers who take a group of kids up to the Olympic Peninsula for a science camp, and we do that for three days. So we try to provide opportunities that the kids don't typically get. We really want to help them develop a passion for something.

TOWNE: What is a typical first day of school like for you? I would imagine that's a time when new kids would feel the need to really test limits.

BARNARD: We actually have two first days of school. On the very first day, we have an orientation that includes all of the first-timers, and we try to find out who they are, introduce the culture of the school to them, and do a few assessments so that we have a sense of where to place them. We meet in the auditorium and split the kids into groups with advisors that we have chosen. We then go on to some activities called ropes courses. These are personal development and team building activities that are just invaluable. The kids do a lot of group challenges together where they have to solve various problems. Most of them are physical in nature, like getting across a log or climbing a wall and getting everybody over. Obviously, these are not extreme physical challenges, but there are real problems that they have to solve as a group and after each one we debrief them and discuss it. "What did you have to do?" and "How did you have to help each other?" So we do these on the very first day, and it helps to ease tensions and enables the kids to get to know us and each other. On the second day, we have a low-key picnic where the kids get together and play softball and Frisbee and things like that. This offers teachers and administrators a chance to work, both before and after the picnic, on getting the kids lined up in their class schedules. The *real* first day comes on the third day when we actually start classes. By this point, everyone has pretty much met one another and the stress of the "first day of school" has been contained.

As far as rules go, I have group meetings and class meetings and set very clear expectations right up front. My class and I brainstorm rules and go through them to determine which ones we will follow and which are not that important. I might say something like, "We don't really have to worry about that one," or "That one comes under our *respect* rule." Because they are given ownership in the creation of these rules, they start getting a sense that this is a little bit different than what they're familiar with. They're certainly not used to having teachers ask them their opinions on classroom management.

After we get the rules down, I usually start with some kind of activity like a game, a simulation, or something similar that's very hands-on, fun, and group-oriented. Then the kids have to process it all and talk and ask themselves what they need to do to make it all work. It's wild and a little chaotic, but it's fun and a lot of learning is taking place. However, as fun as it is, I do get tested from time to time. I'm pretty firm though and I just keep reminding them of what the expectations are and the rules we all agreed on. Typically, it doesn't take much, as the rules were set by them in the first place. Ownership circumvents most discipline issues.

TOWNE: Classroom management is a major problem that teachers often struggle with, especially new teachers. How do you handle discipline issues in your classroom?

BARNARD: To begin with, I treat my students with respect. Our school mantra is: respect yourself and the rights of others. Our school has four school-wide agreements: mutual respect, attentive listening, the right to participate or to pass, and appreciations with its reverse—no put-downs. So, the expectations that I set up revolve around mutual respect and, as I mentioned, the kids have a role in determining these expectations and rules.

At the beginning of the year, or each new term with new students, I review our agreed-upon expectations. Often, I have the students who have been in my class share the expectations with the new arrivals; they do a great job. They also share what the kids can expect to see from my behavior.

I choose my battles carefully. There are some behaviors that I can accept, which might not be accepted in another school and these are important trade-offs. The students recognize that if I overlook the little things, then they'd better pay attention to the issues that I hold the line on. I'm firm. I refer back to our mutual agreements, which catch almost every infraction. If a student calls me out in front of the entire class, I do have to deal with it, possibly with a referral to the office. But the next day I make sure to act as if nothing happened and the student is welcomed back into the class. There are times when we have to revisit the event in a conversation, but they seem to know that my goal is to have them remain in the room and complete the work. Often it's new students who have to test this, but they usually only have to do it once. If there are particular combinations of students who spur each other to act out and the problem persists, often our staff finds a solution—maybe changing a schedule for one or two of the students. In our setting, we are able to do this rather easily.

TOWNE: Here's a hypothetical situation. You're writing on the chalk-board at the front of the class and suddenly a paper airplane or pencil comes flying up and hits you. The kids laugh. What do you do?

BARNARD: Well if it's a paper airplane I would comment on whether it was aerodynamic or not and I'd have them fly it again and say, "Wow, that was a great one" or "That one sucked and you better work on that skill because you obviously don't have it." If a pencil is thrown, I tell them how awfully disappointed I am because we have to supply a lot of pencils to students who don't bring them (*laughs*). This doesn't happen often, especially after the joke is turned back on the one who threw it.

TOWNE: That's brilliant! You are not only taking the wind out of their sails, but using their own boat against them.

BARNARD: Yeah, the trick is to go against the grain and handle these types of situations in ways they don't expect.

TOWNE: How do you handle students who act out or try to show out in class?

BARNARD: With arguing and acting out, I really choose my battles carefully, often letting the behavior go. There have been plenty of times when I have refused to let a student ruin my day or destroy my class. Usually, a student realizes that I'm not going to escalate the issue and the behavior stops. Let me give you an example of a recent situation that happened at the beginning of the year. I had this new student who decided he was going to test me. In our class we always go by our first names, but he was really pushing it saying, "Oh, Sue, I love you," and other crazy things just to get a class reaction. Now I didn't do this at that moment, because I believe waiting a bit is one of the most effective things you can do in situations like this. But ten minutes later I quietly called him to the back of the room and asked him why he was doing that. He didn't know. He was really just doing it for attention and approval from the class. I told him, "We just don't do those kind of things here," and then I talked with him for a few minutes and said, "Here's the deal. I'm not going to treat you any differently and I'm not going to say what we talked about back here. If you choose to do that, that's your problem, but I'm not going to say anything about it; we're just going to do business as usual." We walked back out, and I have never had a moment of trouble with him since. The whole thing took maybe two minutes. It was really just me letting him know that I'm not fighting this battle and we're not going to turn this into a big deal. I think he understood that it was really about us showing a mutual respect for each other.

TOWNE: How about a student that has a blow-out or meltdown and is so angry that they are nearly in tears?

BARNARD: There's a natural tendency to leave the room when you're that upset, and I usually let them go. We have a solution center where students may go if they're having a bad moment—or a worse day. A staff member attempts to help the student devise a plan to resolve the issue. When the temper has subsided, I talk with the student. Often when kids blow up it's because he or she is in some kind of trouble or something important is going on in their lives outside of the classroom. If I know about it or suspect that might be the case, then I will follow them out and talk to them about it. Not about the classroom outburst, but about the underlying problem. Usually they are very honest and tell me what's going on. It could be that they didn't get much sleep last night or that a family member is in the hospital or any number of things. If it's something temporary, then I kind of just let it happen and continue talking to them.

How I ultimately handle it really depends. If they're just angry, as long as they didn't call me something really bad on their way out the door, then I just let them leave and settle down. If they do call me something and it's under their breath I will probably let it go as well, because that's not a battle worth fighting. But if they say something loud in front of the class and put me on the spot, then I have to let the class know that at least I'm speaking to the kid, but again I don't make a big deal out of it. Sometimes I have to write it up, but that's rare. One trick that I use is coming up with a code or signal for them. So if they're storming out of the room they give me a predetermined signal that tells me that they just need time to get it together and it's nothing personal. I use this kind of secret code with a number of kids and it works great. They go out, get some water or air, come back in a little later and we pick up where we left off. This has worked so well that I think every teacher should consider something similar with certain students. Not only does it allow for better communication with that student, but it also builds a trust and respect between you both that is invaluable.

I also give my students multiple second-chances and this is especially important for at-risk students. If she misses a deadline, I extend it. If he chooses not to participate one day, I may give an alternative assignment so he can earn credit. I give many, many reminders that an assignment is missing and that she needs the grade or the points in order to earn credit. They don't have to be around me long to realize that I'm never going to give up—so they might as well do the work. Finally, humor is always used liberally in my class. Of course, there are situations that aren't the least bit funny, but if I keep the mood in the room light, I can avoid all kinds of issues before they ever develop.

TOWNE: What is a major challenge you've faced during your teaching career and how were you able to overcome it?

BARNARD: One challenge that has been with me the entire time I have served at CHOICE, is balance. If I don't keep my personal life in balance with my professional life, I am no good to my students. Likewise, if I don't take care of my own emotional health, it is too easy to get caught up in the emotional chaos of my students' lives. I do want to "save" all my students—not, however, at the risk of my own mental health. I work hard every day to meet my students' needs and I certainly bring my students home with me in my head every night. All good teachers do—they continue to solve problems in their minds, to try different approaches the next day. But I have learned that I must take care of my own health in order to be of any value to my students. What this really means for teachers is that they need to find out what they're passionate about outside of the classroom and make an effort to spend time doing it. It could be writing, photography, sewing, rock climbing, you name it. We need to share these passions with our students as well. Passion is contagious and will rub off on many of them. You plant that little seed and you may not see it grow right away, but when you do, it's truly amazing.

TOWNE: You have held many leadership roles throughout your teaching career, including being the leader of the district Literacy Team. What did you learn most from these roles?

BARNARD: To not teach in isolation. Learn what standards are being taught in the grade levels below and above your own. Learn what practices are being used in other classrooms, in other buildings, and at other grade levels. The greatest accomplishment of the district Literacy Team has been to open up the lines of communication among teachers to improve instructional practices, to look at student work, to examine data, and to design ways to coordinate efforts to make our instruction more effective. The bottom line has to be student achievement.

TOWNE: There's an old saying, "I wish I had known then what I know now." What do you wish you had known when you first started teaching that you now know?

BARNARD: How real the effects of poverty are. When I entered the teaching profession, I was motivated to serve people—that motivation has never left me. However, I had very little real-life experience with poverty. What I know now, I have learned from my students—seeing and hearing how resourceful they have had to be. I have learned about the weight of the burdens they bring to school and the crises they need to manage on any particular day before they can focus on schoolwork. As a teacher I have learned that serving people does not mean "doing for" but does mean "struggling alongside."

I believe that teachers have some sort of intrinsic natural core that makes them a teacher. Even with all the training in the world you can't do this job right unless you love kids. There is an internal core that makes you a teacher. That passion for kids must be there, and if it is, then the sky is the limit on what you can teach them.

CHAPTER 11

Kathleen Mellor

2004 National Teacher of the Year
2004 Rhode Island Teacher of the Year
Davisville Middle School
North Kingstown, Rhode Island
ESL: Grades 6-8

Kathleen Mellor is an ESL teacher with 29 years in the field. She has taught ESL at all grades: K through college and adult. Most of her time has been at the middle and elementary levels in North Kingstown, Rhode Island, where she passionately teaches English to the children of families from many different countries. She was the first person from Rhode Island to ever win the National Teacher of the Year Award as well as the first ESL teacher to have done so. In 2004, she also won the U.S. Department of Education's Award for Excellence in ELL Education.

Mellor was instrumental in creating a Collaborative ESL program from scratch. Before she arrived in North Kingstown, students of various ages and abilities were bused to the same school and taught in the same classroom. Mellor knew there had to be a better way. She worked with other teachers and administrators to create a new program that has since proven to be highly successful.

One of her secrets to success has been her commitment to families. When Mellor realized that her students were learning English, but their mothers weren't, she started the Ladybugs, an ESL program for mothers. Once a year, she invites families of the ESL students and former students to attend an annual international picnic at the school. Parents bring various dishes from their homelands and share stories among themselves and the staff in celebration of another successful year. All of this helps to build trust and the camaraderie needed to get parents active in their child's learning process.

Mellor received her Bachelor's Degree in Elementary Education and a Master of Science Degree in Education from Rhode Island College. After becoming certified in ESL, she went on to receive a Master's of Arts Degree in ESL and Cross Cultural Studies from Brown University. She is currently pursuing her Doctorate in Educational Leadership at Johnson & Wales University, and lives with her husband, David, in South Kingstown, Rhode Island.

TOWNE: What was a difficult challenge that you've faced while teaching and how did you overcome it?

MELLOR: I think the most difficult challenge was when I was new in North Kingstown. English as a Second Language and I arrived about the same time. Nobody had a clear vision of what needed to be done. Many teachers felt I should do it all until the children were proficient enough that the other teachers would be able to teach them as comfortably as all other children. While I understood their angst, I didn't feel capable of teaching all subjects to three grades, five teams, and all different proficiency and reading levels. There were too many variables. I knew I needed to get them to buy in. I have found that honesty and humor are a big help in most situations. I explained that I had taken three years of German to avoid one year of chemistry and that nobody would want me even attempting to teach science, besides which, I wasn't certified to teach anything else other than English. The humor and the honesty brought them on board. We all worked hard, and we all learned together what worked for us.

TOWNE: Here's a hypothetical situation. It's your first day teaching a new class. How do you take control of the classroom and establish authority and respect right away?

MELLOR: This is not so much of an issue after 25 years in the classroom because I have had so many brothers, sisters and even parents of children. However, I continue to do what I always have done. I go over my role as a teacher and what I would like to accomplish during the course of the year. I welcome students into a classroom that has high standards, is peaceful, productive, and safe. I try to create an atmosphere where they can be themselves, validating who they are, where they come from, and how much they can accomplish. I explain what my job is as the teacher as well as how crucial it is for them to do their job as good students. I explain that I take my job very seriously and know that my success depends on their success and that we will all be successful. I try to convey that they can all be good students. I acknowledge all their efforts and am careful not to dismiss anything they offer, raising the bar when I feel they are ready. My goal is to encourage them to feel worthwhile and secure in their attempts so that they will buy into the learning process, develop confidence in themselves as students, and become responsible for their own learning. I assure them that they will be given ample opportunity and time to develop the skills and abilities necessary to do well.

Many children don't have the self-confidence or background skills necessary to do well. Informing them that they are starting with a clean slate is motivating. Over time, the skills do develop and improve. For some, it becomes self-rewarding. For some it becomes so rewarding that it becomes self-perpetuating.

My two major concerns are where they have been and where they are going after their time with me, in addition to what we must do together to get there. We discuss all of this the first day. I remind them that I have not forgotten what it was like to be a kid, a student, and to sit on the other side of the desk. I tell them my grading policy, reminding them that their grades reflect what they give to me. Then we discuss and decide upon rules for our classroom and post them. This all sounds so idyllic. You have to know when to go by the book and when not to, or when to look the other way.

One year, as I was writing their behavior suggestions on the board, one girl from a tough background used a ruler to shoot a wad of paper across the room at another student. "What a long year this will be," I thought! But instead of sending her to the office on the very first day, I suggested it might be better for her to have lunch detention with me rather than highlight her inappropriate behavior so soon. We had lunch together and talked. She was never a behavior problem again in my room and made significant gains in her classwork. This worked with her, but another technique might have been called for with another student.

TOWNE: That's fantastic. I'm sure most teachers would have immediately considered punishment or some other form of discipline and you said, no, I'm going to do the opposite. And it worked.

MELLOR: One lunch, and I had no more problems with her.

TOWNE: Let's talk more about what happens in your classroom. What specific methods do you use, particularly regarding homework and grading?

MELLOR: To encourage completion of homework, we go over all of it and I keep track of assignments done. At the end of a quarter, the percent of homework done counts as a test grade. Quiz grade averages also count as a test grade. Both the homework average and the quiz average are then included as separate tests in the test average toward the quarterly grade. Children are more apt to do homework if it counts toward something. The homework is important to me as a reinforcement of what I have taught and as a source of information as to whether they "got it" or not, or if I have to re-teach something another way. This method is also good because it enables a student who may not test well to get a few high grades just by doing homework.

TOWNE: What about unusual methods or strategies that you incorporate in your classroom that may be different than what most teachers do?

MELLOR: About twice a month, to encourage reluctant readers and to build and strengthen reading comprehension in all students, I devised a comprehension game using a short, usually non-fiction reading passage, which I pass out to the class on a Monday. The students are asked to prepare for the game on Friday by reading it on their own. They quickly learn that multiple readings on their part insure deeper and more complete comprehension, enhancing both literal and inferential comprehension. To play the game, I wear some sort of a silly hat representing the month, holiday or time of the year, such as a witch's hat in October. In unison they chant "Witchy, Witchy, give me some gold" (This can be Pumpkin, Princess, Leprechaun, Bunny Rabbit, etc. depending on my hat). I respond. "Yes, I will—when an answer, I'm told." Then, I call out the question. Students use different small devices to signal their knowing the answer to the question. If they are correct, they get a little fake disc of gold. If they are wrong, one other student may try. At the end of the game, all students can redeem their gold discs for school-wide incentive Gold Cards, with 2 discs equaling one Gold Card which can be used to buy school supplies at the school store. The kids absolutely love this game. It is very effective with most students, even those who don't usually read much on their own. It gives everyone a chance to shine and win something, and the play of it takes the pressure off. As children get more skilled at the game, I up the ante by increasing the reading level of the passages. I sometimes let the winner select the next reading. It's fun and effective, but does require a certain level of maturity. If a group tends to be too silly, it isn't fun.

TOWNE: You mentioned that a strong reward system is embodied in your classroom to reinforce important behaviors. Can you describe it?

MELLOR: In Rhode Island, we have a reading standard of 25 books a year, which averages out to 6 or 7 a quarter. While this can seem a daunting task to kids, I have them design a plaque with their name on it. For every book they complete, whether it is one we read as a group or one that they self-select, I attach a 3 inch star with the title of the book and the author on it. Books over 200 hundred pages can earn 2 or more stars. The visual of seeing the string of stars keeps kids apprised of where they are compared to the others and toward the standard. I previously mentioned the school-wide Gold Cards which are reinforcement and incentives and can be used as money in our school store. I give my kids Gold Cards for any grade that is 80% or above, in any class. I also give them when I catch someone being particularly kind or good. I call home frequently with praise about how a child did on a project or how they handled a particular situation. We also have culminating "pizza lunches" when we successfully complete a unit or move to a higher level.

TOWNE: You described your teaching style as being eclectic with part of it being in the traditional teaching style and the other part being more holistic. Can you describe this holistic part and give us some examples?

MELLOR: While there are a lot of teacher-directed lessons, developmental language, and developmental reading lessons, I also encourage students to self-select a good portion of their reading material toward the 25 book standard mentioned previously. They are more apt to enjoy reading topics and authors of their own choice. Being an ESL teacher, I also encourage reading in their native language to maintain their first language literacy skills.

For children who are beginners or advanced beginners, we write dialogue journals back and forth to each other. The letters flow freely, in small notebooks as they would with a pen-pal or friend, and the students get over their fear of the empty page. I get to see the language issues I need to address in class, as well as their growth over time. We both get to see each other outside the role of teacher and student. I think the personalization wards off a lot of behavior issues as well.

For all students, we write response journals which are also part of the RI English Language Arts standards. Response journals follow a simple format similar to a book report. The requirements are three-paragraph responses with the first paragraph giving the title, author, major characters (if applicable), setting and the problem. The second paragraph is a brief summary, approximately 10 sentences, of the book. The third paragraph is their opinion of the work, in which they must support their opinion with examples, details or facts and make a text-to-text, text-to-self or text-to-world connection. Each response is graded for quality, but quantity counts for the quarter. Quantity grades are 8=A, 7=B, 6=C and are averaged with each student's quality grade. They are not required to write a response on every book they read, which could possibly take the pleasure out of all the reading. Instead, they can choose which ones to respond to in writing. When we do stylistic writing or academic writing, I do a lot of modeling before they are expected to write.

For writing assignments, the students always pick their topic or draw upon something they know from their background. I think student choice within the defined parameters set in the classroom is more effective. It's so hard to write about something you don't truly know.

TOWNE: You have stressed the importance of establishing a team approach of teaching where teachers and districts work together to support one another. Can you talk a little about how you work within a team and how, if you were a new teacher, you might go about developing a team-based approach at a school or district that does not have one?

MELLOR: There is more power in teamwork. I think so much more can be accomplished when people of all levels work together. Using the analogy of sports, all teammates have a distinct job to do to win and all must cooperate with each other to work toward the same goal to succeed. In my opinion, everyone within a school district has a function to perform on the same team with the mutual goal being the education of the students. Everyone must respect each other as well as what the other's role is, no matter what the position is. They must all know the give-and-take process of coordination and collaboration within a team and who the leader, the captain or the boss is. Likewise, the leader or boss must value all of his or her staff, their role on the team, and must treat them respectfully.

My perspective, work, and success have been greatly enhanced by the perspective, work, and success of those around me. As an

ESL teacher, I have to work with different teachers in different grades, on different teams and in different disciplines. Each team has its own personality and dynamic. Each teacher has their own style. Each discipline has its own needs. By meeting, talking, and keeping each other informed, we can coordinate our work and everyone can be more effective. While I may have a preference on the way one teacher or one team works, I learned to be flexible enough to work with all in order to be effective myself.

While PLCs (professional learning communities) may seem to be one of the latest buzz words, if I were a new teacher, I would seek out other teachers who taught my grade or my subject to create an informal group that met at least once a month to discuss ideas, common concerns, and effective solutions. I am part of a few such groups by choice. We accomplish a great deal, and it is so validating to be heard, listened to and to learn from others. It's easy to get together with those who share a common cause. Please note that I said by *choice*. I don't think such meetings or groups are as effective when they are forced upon participants. I think the key is the willing participation of those with a common interest or cause.

TOWNE: Being an ESL teacher gives you greater insight in dealing with children from different cultures and backgrounds. In your opinion, where should the line be drawn between maintaining diversity and the need for cultural assimilation?

MELLOR: I don't feel it is my place, or anyone else's, to draw any line regarding how much diversity is maintained and when assimilation must be expected. In fact, I don't think it can be dictated. So much is up to the individual person, and their readiness. It involves a combination of the individual, and the time and circumstances in which people find themselves. I firmly believe that the diversity of the United States is what has made it such a strong country. Historically, those who left jobs, security, and family in their homelands to come here for a better life were the strongest of the strong. I have so much respect for those who faced that challenge. It is not easy.

In time, maybe over generations, assimilation occurs quite naturally as people grow, experience American life, and evolve. I am not really sure though, that we ever fully assimilate, nor should we. Just ask ten people how they celebrate Thanksgiving, and you'll find much of their own cultural heritage reflected in their celebration of this truly American holiday. Cultures are not stagnant entities either. They are vibrant, evolving forces themselves. I think that has always been a good thing. Cultures that don't evolve remain a stagnant part of history. Now, as technology and the world have changed, so must we, as individuals and as a culture, if we are to benefit and survive. Thomas Jefferson, in discussing the institutions of society, likened them to a coat a little boy would wear. While perfectly functional for the child that same coat would no longer serve the grown man. While he did not advocate frequent or senseless change for the sake of changing, he realized that some change is an inevitable function of growth.

TOWNE: How do you encourage and maintain parental involvement with busy or disinterested parents?

MELLOR: By being positive, proactive, and inviting them as partners on "the team" needed for their child to succeed. I contact parents early and frequently, with the positive as much as with any concern. I feel most parents want what is best for their children, which is why they moved here. Having had 3 kids of my own, I know that some have to work harder to juggle schedules or work longer to provide basic necessities. So any actual involvement may not be possible. I try not to judge any of them, but continue to call and invite their assistance, their opinions, and their involvement.

We have a parent advisory group called SOL-PAC, Speakers of Other Languages-Parent Advisory Committee. In addition to the phone calls, emails or communication booklets mentioned earlier, we have four pot-luck dinner meetings a year. I think having the meeting at dinner time, with everyone contributing, is attractive to parents because there is a social aspect to it. It's fun! Although we do not get 100%, they are very well-attended. We eat and visit in a relaxed, non-threatening atmosphere where the parents set the tone and not the teachers. Parents generate their concerns, set the agenda, so to speak, and we address them in future meetings. However, we also use this as a time to inform parents of upcoming events at school, on teams, or in the district, and then we advocate different techniques they can use to support us and their children at home. For years another colleague and I have offered free English classes once a week. Although intended to serve the parents, the classes break down real or imagined barriers between home and school. They serve as a vehicle for parents to ask questions or voice concerns. Frequent contact in a safe, non-judgmental atmosphere works, just as it does with students.

TOWNE: In what ways do you handle a defiant child?

MELLOR: Even though the students are part of setting the rules every year, the rules are usually basically the same regarding being on time, being prepared, and being respectful of all in our room. Kids know what is appropriate for school. The rules are always very clear and fair because they set them. Once set, I am consistent about enforcement. It usually only takes a reminder. I have had defiant children and the defiance usually comes from modeled behavior outside the classroom or a lack of trust, a self-protection mechanism that they have learned to use to shelter themselves. With such kids, I give them time to come around, and then I "kill them with kindness." I remember being a kid and know, for sure, that many deal with much more than I ever had to outside of school.

TOWNE: How about motivating an apathetic student?

MELLOR: Much the same thing for an apathetic student. Most kids want to do well, want to learn, want to be the best they can be, and be valued, but their past experiences can really dampen or thwart their interest in things academic. Time, kindness, encouragement, building on strengths and interests are all helpful. I try to enable them to see the value of a good education and the purpose behind all that we do. However, some kids have so much to deal with at home or in life, that basic survival and security are more on their minds than school. I really feel we have to start where a student is, no matter where they are academically, emotionally, or behaviorally. They come in at all differing points on a continuum of where they need to be at the end of the year. I know I'm not going to get all of them to the same place by the end of the year, but if I can move them along that continuum quite a bit, if I can get them to grow and see their potential, I trust that they will continue on through the process. The main thing is to have faith in them and to convey that confidence to them so they can have faith in themselves.

TOWNE: There's an old saying, "I wish I had known then what I know now." What do you wish you had known when you started teaching?

MELLOR: I wish I had known what wonderful resources older, more seasoned teachers are. In those days there were no formal mentoring programs. I, like many novice teachers, was overwhelmed by the many demands of the profession. While some teachers made it look easy, I didn't feel I could ask for help or suggestions. However, I started to take note of certain things done by teachers whom I admired. One teacher would regularly pop her head in my room and tell me what she was doing in her class that week. She would invite me to participate or offer some words of wisdom, just in chatting. After a while, I developed my own repertoire. It all became easier for me, and I made sure that I reached out to new staff whenever I could, the same way she had done for me.

TOWNE: Are there any books that you have read that helped shape and influence you as a teacher, and what did you take from them?

MELLOR: A book called *Teacher* by Sylvia Ashton-Warner. I learned how important "background knowledge and experience" are regarding what children bring to the learning situation and what they can learn easily. The book points out how much we, as teachers, need to start there and build on that if we want to scaffold what they know to what we want them to know, and to optimize learning and growth.

CHAPTER 12

Ron Poplau

2006 National Teacher of the Year Finalist
2006 Kansas Teacher of the Year
National Teachers Hall of Fame Inductee
Shawnee Mission Northwest High School
Shawnee, Kansas
Community Service: Grades 11-12

When speaking with Ron Poplau, the first word that comes to mind is passion. His unrivaled enthusiasm for teaching, learning, and community service is just as obvious today as it was 47 years ago when he began his career. Poplau never intended to become a teacher and quickly became miserable, as did his students. But he stuck with it and soon learned that the secret to success in the classroom was to focus on changing *attitudes,* as opposed to behaviors. He also mastered the art of storytelling, as nearly all of his lessons are taught through the use of fascinating real-life stories that are forever remembered.

Poplau's greatest success, and the thing he's most passionate about, is teaching the value of volunteerism. He believes that community service not only helps to rebuild communities, but also helps kids become better human beings and students. He began by incorporating small volunteer-based projects into his social studies class, but as those projects grew in popularity, Poplau decided to create a community service elective class. Thus, the Cougars Community Commitment (CCC) was born. Through the program, thousands of Poplau's students have helped people from all walks of life. On a daily basis CCC places over a hundred students into the community to assist the poor, elderly, and disadvantaged. It has been so successful that other schools around the nation are beginning to start similar classes. Poplau's book *The Doer of Good Becomes Good: A Primer on Volunteerism* describes the program in detail.

Poplau earned both his bachelor's and master's degrees from Emporia State University. In 1999, he was selected by the U.S. State Department to be a teacher-diplomat to Russia, where he shared the mechanics of CCC. Aside from winning the Kansas State Teacher of the Year award, he has also been inducted into the National Teacher's Hall of Fame and the Mid-America Education Hall of Fame.

While still teaching, Poplau also serves as the Kansas coordinator of PEP (Professional Education Program) at Ottawa University where he helps recruit and inspire future teachers. He and Linda, his wife of 41 years, live in Kansas City, Kansas.

TOWNE: You've been teaching a long time now…

POPLAU: Forty-seven years and I'm aiming for forty-seven more!

TOWNE: That's great. And you've had a tremendous amount of success in those forty-seven years.

POPLAU: I actually got into teaching on a dare. I had no experience, and what I learned after a month was to rely on the input of students. I formed an advisory group within my classes that kept me current on what they found meaningful. I have consistently used that advisory board concept throughout my many years of teaching. For instance, I had a remedial sophomore World History class once whose advice was to take some of the students to the graveyard at midnight.

TOWNE: Can you talk a little more about that advisory board? Is it all students?

POPLAU: All students. When I first started teaching I had the mentality that I could do absolutely anything. So the principal, who had known me, told me I was the man for the job. I told him no, and then he offered me a place to stay. I said no again and told him that I liked my freedom, so he then offered me an ungodly salary. I told him that money isn't everything and then he said I could use the school car as well. I said, "Now you're talking," and took the job. Exactly one month into teaching, I was ready to quit. I just couldn't do it. Then an English teacher told me that I should just go into class, sit on the edge of the desk, look at the kids and say, "How come we don't get along?" Well that was a huge insult to me. To think that I was going to admit defeat and ask these kids for their opinions was an absolute slap in the face, and I stewed about that all the way home.

The next day, I filled up the chalkboard with notes as the kids came in quietly, single file, and sat down. I'm sure they were thinking, "Same old, same old." But as I wrote the last word on the board I asked myself, "Am I happy?" Well the answer was clearly, "No." I turned around and looked at the kids and said, "How come it *appears* that we do not get along?" Every hand went up, and that turned out to be one of the best classes I've ever had. They all said to me, "We'll listen to you four times a week if you listen to us one." I agreed. Then they said, "This is a sociology class, so we need some guest speakers and field trips and community service." Again I agreed and gave them everything they wanted. From that point on, they were excited to come to class and excited to learn. They took ownership in the learning and it showed. On the very last day of school, they came down to where I was staying and carried me down the hallway. So that's how the advisory board began, and I've incorporated one ever since.

TOWNE: What about that World History class that you mentioned? Did you ever take them to that graveyard as they had suggested?

POPLAU: I sure did! Here's the story. I spent a year in Brazil as an exchange teacher, and when I came back, the only job I could get was as a substitute teacher. Guess what I had to teach? Sophomore World History for remedial students. I am no good with freshman and sophomores, so I figured I would get that advisory board going again. I asked them how they would teach the pharaohs and the mummies and so forth and how they would make it interesting. These kids didn't believe it and said, "You're asking us?" So they told me about a woman who was buried at a local cemetery and said that if you molest her grave at midnight, she would come up out of there. Well, needless to say, I thought they were full of it and asked them what that had to do with anything. They said, "Well you want us to learn about mummies and after-death and stuff, right?" They all seemed really excited by the idea, so I agreed. That Friday night, a bunch of the class actually showed up. We went out to the cemetery and were standing by the grave, and wouldn't you know it, here comes a car. And I thought, "Well, that's it. I've got all these kids with me and we're about to molest a grave. Good-bye career." Luckily, the car disappeared, and at midnight we started walking backwards around the grave shouting "Mary Butler! Mary Butler!" Then suddenly one of the kids went absolute bonkers. He ran off, jumped in my car, and locked all the doors. The other kids and I had to bang on the door to get him to open it. When we finally got in, I asked him what the problem was and he pointed up to the grave. There was a big yellow crocheted hat on it. He said, "That's hers! That's hers!" I didn't know who put that hat there, and I'm sure I never will.

The next day that kid didn't come to school and I just knew I was going to get an earful from his parents. But instead, he showed up late in the day as white as a sheet. He showed me and the class a picture of Mary Butler and she was wearing that same yellow crocheted hat. Now that was a little bit freaky. I was sure I was being had by these kids, but it didn't matter. That little escapade created a rapport with them that you wouldn't believe. Before that trip many of those students were failing, but after that, a good third of those remedial kids went up to the honors group, and every single one of them passed. Most of us are still friends to this day.

TOWNE: So it boiled down to the relationships that were created between you and them by taking that extra time and listening to what they wanted.

POPLAU: That's right. After that, they knew that I was on their side, and it made all the difference in the world. To me education is not how much you know, but the creation of an *attitude*. I got a speeding ticket two years ago on my way to school. I was going sixty-one in a forty. I knew what the speed limit was, and I had to pay $85 for that. So the point is that knowing something means very little without having the right attitude. If you create a good attitude in your classroom, the kids will come to school, and they will study and learn more than you would ever believe.

TOWNE: That's amazing and a very good point. You have said on occasion that "a student chooses what they wish to learn" and that your job as a teacher is to accept the kids as they are and make them *want* to learn. This kind of ties right into that.

POPLAU: Absolutely. Attitude is so much more important than knowledge. Students will pick and choose what they want to learn. Learning is an internalization process, not a memory game. Give the same exam two weeks later, and you'll get different results. Students want the learning to be fun and memorable. They want guest speakers, field trips, and fantastic discussions. I know when my students are learning, and there is nothing wrong with exposing them to the real world.

TOWNE: You mentioned that the "read and recite, tell and test" way of teaching has unfortunately become the norm in too many classrooms. Nowadays, more and more teachers are being forced to teach to the test. What are your thoughts on this?

POPLAU: We are stripping away the true meaning of education. No Child Left Behind is an outrage and an insult to education. Some states test 27 days out of 30. How dare we reduce education to passing an exam. Our school is a National Blue Ribbon School and has made AYP every year since community service was initiated and even here students are beginning to say their classes are nothing more than studying for exams. Experienced, professional teachers know what students need and how to teach them. I get really angry in departmental meetings when I hear what's happening to education. I used to have dozens of guest speakers per semester, but if I were to try that now, the administrators would have a heart attack. All I would hear is, "You have to start teaching to the objective." Trust me, I know what the objectives are and how to achieve them! I say it over and over again in hopes that they will hear me—it's a question of attitude. My students consistently scored higher in sociology than any other students in the district. And yet those methodical "teach to the test" changes are taking over, and now it's to the point where I no longer teach an academic subject at all.

TOWNE: How do you motivate students that aren't already motivated to learn?

POPLAU: I don't win over every student. Some students are happy to fail or just blow off a class. Ultimately, it's not what we want, but what we have to deal with. For instance, some students have no home to go to, or are worried about being pregnant, or a whole lot of other problems. Issues like those put school on the back burner for them. Teachers must get to the bottom of why that student is being defiant. A lot of times it's something that's out of our control, but we must continue to try. We must continue to be there for them so that they can talk to us. We must not be judgmental. They have to know that they can come to you for help and when they do you must help them. The truth is, sometimes I parent more than I teach, and that's okay for some students because without that emotional support they will never buy into the lessons you're trying to teach them.

TOWNE: What other teaching tools have you found to be effective?

POPLAU: Guest speakers and field trips are my favorites, also good current videos and the use of student-led discussions. Give these students an entire day or a week, and it is absolutely amazing what they will do with it. I have a student making a video right now, and previously, I had a student that produced a film Disney asked for. I simply ask myself: if I were them, what would I be interested in and how would I want to learn about it?

TOWNE: Let's talk a little about the subject you're most passionate about—community service. You teach a very popular class on community service at your school that has now garnered national attention, won you multiple awards including Teacher of the Year, and even helped put you in the National Teacher's Hall of Fame. Community service is a wonderful thing, but how does it help a student's grades?

POPLAU: Every study on community service and service-learning in regards to education comes to the same conclusion: those who are involved in community service score on average one whole grade point higher than those who are not. It is an adjunct to learning and allows students to realize why their other classes are important. It puts everything they do in perspective and gives it all meaning. The interesting thing is, strictly speaking, community service is not academic, but service-learning is. Service-learning is also episodic.

TOWNE: What's the difference between service-learning and community service?

POPLAU: Service-learning is based on an academic subject. Therefore, learning about campaigning for a candidate for public office would be an example of service-learning. It is dependent upon a specific subject taught in the classroom. Community service is not limited to a specific topic but can, and does, include almost an endless list. For instance, we just had a dinner for a five year-old boy with leukemia. We were not studying leukemia. A lot of students tutor in an elementary classroom — we are not studying teaching. In service-learning, when the unit is over, so is the "'service." There is no academic side to community service.

We started this in 1992, and prior to that, we tried twice to be a Blue-Ribbon school and never made it. In fact, we didn't even come close. We are now proudly a Blue-Ribbon school. Last year's graduating class was offered six million dollars in scholarships. We have almost the identical number of National Merit Scholars as the most elite prep school in our town.

By itself community service is not going to directly affect AYP—there are no benchmarks for community service, but it indirectly enhances all of the other skills. I've had many students tell me, after a community service project, that they now understood why various subjects are even taught. Anybody can do this. You don't have to be a rocket scientist to mow somebody's grass, bring someone food, or tutor elementary school children on reading and writing. So it will not only improve your students' grades, but it will also enhance their morale, social skills, and self-image.

TOWNE: Some principals might be interested in creating a similar community service program at their school. Do you have any suggestions for them?

POPLAU: Start off slowly so that the students can achieve small amounts of success. The kids must first experience success and then that will lead to even more. Begin with an easy but meaningful project such as helping a poor family. We began with seventeen students and one hour a day, the very last hour. Enrollment doubled the next semester and then eventually grew to over six hundred. We had to limit the amount of time students could enroll in community service because all the other electives were dying out. Word spreads very quickly once this program is up and going. I reported grades today, and many students had in excess of one hundred hours of service. The record for a two-year period is a little over 1,000 hours! The class really should be a mandatory part of the school day for kids. If it's mandatory, then it tells kids that it's as important as other subjects like math and science, and in my opinion it is.

TOWNE: Once a teacher is in place for a new community service class, how would they go about getting started?

POPLAU: They just have to look around their community. Who needs help? What nonprofits are nearby that could use a hand? Where are the poor people, the sick people, and the elderly people? Elementary schools are a great place to volunteer. Our kids go to nine different elementary schools, a community center, and two retirement homes on a regular basis. We have also helped two Alzheimer's groups and many others. There are a million things to do if you just look around your community and find out who needs help. We have the STARS program, *Students Taking Action to Reach Success,* in which our students sit with elementary kids for an hour and a half once a week and they do homework together. And guess what? Those elementary kids aren't the only ones getting better grades. My students are going from D's and F's to A's and B's. It makes a difference!

TOWNE: Can teachers of any subject matter incorporate an aspect of community service?

POPLAU: Absolutely. You don't need a separate class in community service to bring an aspect of it into your students' lives. Teachers of any subject can incorporate it to some degree. We had a family in Home Class that brought over, from the retirement home, a woman whose husband died 20 years ago and she hadn't cooked a single meal since. Well she came in here and cooked us the most delicious spaghetti and meat balls we'd ever tasted. This was uplifting to the whole class and made the woman feel alive again. Another time we had a history class go over to the retirement home and talk to residents about the depression and WWII. One of the students even videotaped the WWII veterans and then put the conversations on closed-circuit TV in the nursing home so that everyone got to know them. The Smithsonian called us after that and paid the kid $5,000 for a copy of it. Whether it's taking a field trip and getting these kids out in the community, or having guest speakers and bringing the community to them, there are always ways to make a difference, no matter the subject being taught.

TOWNE: What was the biggest obstacle you faced during your community service classes?

POPLAU: My biggest obstacle to community service was that some adults did not want high school students around them, and it took time and persistence to change their minds. I had a lady once who called and asked if we had someone who could come and clean her bathroom. I told her I'd send someone right over. She was thrilled, but then asked, "It's not some kids is it?" I said, "Yeah, it is some kids." And she got quiet for a second and said, "Well, of course, you'll be coming with them, right?" And I said, "No, I'm not coming with them." And she said, "Forget it. I'm not having some high school kids coming into my house." So there can be that hesitance among people when it comes to kids helping out. I think it's because they're just not used to kids being helpful and nice anymore, and that's a shame. Students really do care if you just give them a chance.

TOWNE: Your motto is "The Doer of Good Becomes Good." What do you mean by that?

POPLAU: Doing good is its own reward. Students, or anyone, who does community service enhance their own lives and raise their self-esteem. I polled my class yesterday and asked them to explain what it meant to them. The responses were almost identical: "It changed my life!" "It raised my self-esteem!" "I felt I was doing something of value!" "What goes around comes around!"

I remember having the school loser in my class, and she was really bad off, on drugs and everything. By the way, she called herself that, those aren't my words (*laughs*). Anyway her folks would set the alarm for every two hours and if she was in her bed, fine, and if not they would go out looking for her. She got her life together in this class by bonding with a poor family. She realized that her worst day was someone else's best day. She gradually gave up the drugs. I sent her to Washington, DC to be on a panel, and her mother went with her. After she came back she ended up being a speaker at graduation. She then went on to college and made the honor roll and now makes a six-figure salary.

Every year I have students who are depressed, confused, anxious, you name it. Then they really get their lives together in this program. I'm telling you, any school that doesn't have a formal community service program should really consider starting one. It will change these kids' lives.

TOWNE: Let's talk about the book you wrote on the subject. It's a how-to guide on setting up programs like this, right?

POPLAU: Not surprisingly the book is titled *The Doer of Good Becomes Good*. It came out in 2004 and yes, it's basically my program at Shawnee Mission Northwest. Not only does it describe the nuts and bolts of incorporating a program like this, but it also discusses the overall importance and benefits of community service for students, schools, teachers, and communities. These days, kids are so computer-savvy that they surf the internet for hours on end and their social skills are going by the wayside. I have had many students who had a low self-image and no personal skills whatsoever, and community service changed their lives. I sometimes teach at Ottawa University and we had a class called *Storytelling*. One new teacher said that she would love to take that class, but didn't want to because she didn't want to get up in front of those kids. She had very little personal skills herself, so you can imagine what her students would be like. There are a lot of teachers who are dynamite in their own classroom, but at a faculty meeting would never say anything. Well the same thing with those kids. They have all of these computer skills, but no social skills. Our problem is not long distance; our problem is short distance. Kids don't know one another. I talked to the principal at Columbine not long after the shootings there and asked him what the nature of his community service program was. He said proudly that he used community service as punishment. I was shocked and asked what he meant, and he said, "If those kids mess up at my school, they get an hour or more of community service." Well that's exactly the wrong way to use community service. How do you think those kids are going to feel about community service the rest of their lives?

TOWNE: He really used Community Service as punishment?

POPLAU: Yeah, it's terrible, and unfortunately, it happens far too often. We had a coach once that made his kids write the Declaration of Independence backwards when they were bad. He would go over that thing with a fine-toothed comb. Well you can imagine what those kids thought of the Declaration of Independence after that! Even judges sentence kids and adults to community service as some kind of punishment. It's no wonder a lot of Americans don't volunteer for community service when that's the perception of it that's being pushed on us. Community service is beautiful and should be rewarded, not used as a form of idiotic punishment.

TOWNE: You mentioned teaching a *Storytelling* class at Ottawa University. It seems to me that one of your biggest strengths as a teacher is being able to tell compelling stories that make whatever you're trying to teach more memorable.

POPLAU: When I talk to education classes I always tell new teachers to take as many speech and drama classes as they possibly can. The attention span of kids has gotten so low these days that you can't really talk that much to them. Cooperative learning is an improvement and has kids talking to each other, but even then you can see them check out after a little while. Stories, however, can last a lifetime. There are so many miracles that you can share with them that would not only get their attention, but inspire them to want to learn more. It could be stories from your own life or things that you've just read about. I use them to captivate the imagination of my students and it pays off. I would encourage all teachers to liven up their lessons by using as many stories as possible.

TOWNE: Do you have any other "tricks of the trade" that you use that may be somewhat unconventional, but that you have found to be highly effective?

POPLAU: Well I'm a big proponent of *60 Beat a Minute* music. Have you ever heard of that?

TOWNE: No, I haven't.

POPLAU: Oh, does it ever work. There's a book about it called *Super Learning* by Sheila Ostrander that's just amazing. It's basically a kind of music that, if it's playing while you're trying to learn something, will increase your learning of that subject drastically. We have a seminar period which is basically just a 95 minute study period. Well I've started playing this *60 Beat a Minute* music during this period and you wouldn't believe how much those kids' grades have improved. I'm telling you, this one girl came to me after her exam and said it was the first A she had ever gotten. The star of our basketball team also got his first A. You just play that softly in the room and magic happens. That's why I call it "magic music". I first learned about this from a workshop I had taken and part of it included this music. Then, after winning the state Teacher of the Year Award, I had to give an awful lot of speeches. But I didn't want to keep giving the same one over and over, so I would write a new one each time. Unfortunately, this meant that I had to basically memorize a different speech each time which wasn't easy. So I decided to try this *60 Beat a Minute* music. I was skeptical, of course, but I figured it couldn't hurt. I put it on as I went over my speeches, and by the time I gave the speech, I never had to look down at my notes once. This was a drastic change from what I had been doing. I went from practically reading those speeches to delivering them flawlessly as if they were in my head the whole time!

TOWNE: But how does it work?

POPLAU: Well that book talks all about it and it's very scientific. I don't know the specifics off the top of my head, but basically what it does is open up both sides of your brain. See there are more nerves going from your ears to your brain than there are from your eyes to your brain. The book covers it in much more detail. All I know is that it works.

TOWNE: What do you wish you had known when you first started teaching that you know now?

POPLAU; If there is one thing I wish I had done earlier, it would have been to have more community service, or even service learning, in my classroom. There is nothing more powerful.

TOWNE: Well, I must say, you are full of amazing insights and I thank you for your time.

POPLAU: It's my pleasure. Listen, I'm really glad I'm doing this interview because my goal is to get a community service program at every school in the country. It's not expensive to incorporate, and the rewards that schools, students and the community receive are really worth the effort. It's one thing to teach kids to memorize useless academic facts, but it's another to change their lives for the better. That's what community service will do for them and, in turn, it will make them better students, better citizens, and better human beings.

CHAPTER 13

Kimberly Oliver Burnim

2006 National Teacher of the Year
2006 Maryland Teacher of the Year
Broad Acres Elementary School
Silver Spring, Maryland
All Subjects: Grades: K-1ˢᵗ

Kimberly Oliver Burnim began her career teaching kindergarten at Broad Acres Elementary, a culturally and linguistically diverse school, where she was determined to help at-risk children succeed. When she started, the school was being considered for reconstitution by the state due to many years of declining test scores. She immediately began working with other teachers and administrators to restructure Broad Acres from the inside out. Burnim promptly became a teacher leader and is recognized as having played a major role in the educational restructuring of the school. Since her arrival, Broad Acres has had numerous successes, including having met Adequate

Yearly Progress (AYP) every year and either meeting or exceeding all requirements for No Child Left Behind.

Burnim has played many roles at Broad Acres and in the Montgomery County School system, including becoming a member of the *Teachers Leaders Network*, becoming a teacher trainer, a mentor teacher, and the Chairperson for both the Learning Walk and Staff Development committee. Always striving to improve her professional development, after only four years of teaching, Burnim earned National Board Certification as an Early Childhood Generalist. She has since helped many of her colleagues begin to achieve certification as well.

Aside from being named National Teacher of the Year, Burnim was also honored with, among many other distinguished awards, the Marion Greenblatt Excellence in Teaching Award. After completing her official term as National Teacher and educational spokesperson, Burnim returned to the classroom at Broad Acres where she now teaches first grade. She received her Bachelor's in English Arts from Hampton University and her Master's in Elementary Education from Wilmington College in Delaware. She currently resides in Silver Spring, Maryland, with her husband, Adrian.

TOWNE: You've been a big proponent of things like publicly funded 3 year-old, Pre-K, and full-day kindergarten programs. Can you talk a little bit about why these are so important?

BURNIM: It's important that we support our youngest learners. Research shows that most of the learning that occurs in our entire lives happens between birth and the age of five years old. So public education is missing a huge opportunity to engage children when they are most receptive for learning. It's also important because of the achievement gap, which is clearly evident even on a child's very first day of kindergarten. I can see clearly, even on that very first day of school, that it's really a story of the have and have-nots. The haves are those who are either "poor" enough to qualify for a quality federally funded Pre-K program or those who have parents that can afford to send them to a quality, private Pre-Kindergarten program that adequately prepares them for kindergarten. The have-nots are all of the children who cannot afford to attend a private Pre-K program or do not qualify to enter into a federally funded program. So as a kindergarten teacher for many years, I have always faced this challenge where some students are already reading, maybe even on a second grade level, and some students don't even know which way a book is held or that you're supposed to read the words and not the pictures. If that achievement gap is ever going to decrease, then we're going to have to start reaching kids at a younger age and even up the opportunities for them to be prepared for school.

TOWNE: Is the gap that obvious to teachers so early on?

BURNIM: Most definitely. A couple of years ago, my entire kindergarten class, except for one child, was composed of students who were in some type of formal Pre-K or Head Start program taught by excellent teachers. That same year, I had a student teacher working with my class and me. I have to tell you that one child, who didn't have that previous academic instruction and experience, stood out like a sore thumb. My student teacher automatically started asking if I thought the child had a learning disability or was having serious problems outside of school. It really was just that the child didn't have the same opportunities as the other kids in our class.

TOWNE: Doesn't that achievement gap discrepancy end up lasting their entire educational lives?

BURNIM: Almost always it does, and then we end up investing much more in remedial services. We end up putting students in intervention and special education. We also retain many students. I believe, if we would spend a little more money up front, we wouldn't need a lot of those things, and it would save us all a ton of money, time and resources. But most important, it will give children a fair opportunity to learn and a positive start in school.

TOWNE: They say that the first few days of school sets the tone for the rest of the year, and to many children, kindergarten is their first time ever in a classroom. What do you do those first few days of school to ensure year-long success?

BURNIM: It's critical during those first few days and weeks to establish solid routines and a community atmosphere. Young children thrive on routines and structure. Knowing what's going to happen next helps them to feel comfortable. It's important to build a community of learners who all feel at ease and have that sense of belonging. I engage my students in lessons and activities that help them get to know each other and to know me as well. It really is about establishing that community as early as possible so that students will enjoy coming to school and become risk-takers. The language that I use throughout the day supports this concept "We are all friends. This is a place where we're all going to learn and grow and even make some mistakes together." I tend to spend a lot of time on community building in the beginning of the year even though it may not look very "academic". By putting in this time up front in August and September, my students learn the expectations, learn their role in our class, and begin to work effectively, confidently, and independently.

The first few days also provide an opportunity to establish relationships with parents. Sending your child off to school for the first time can be very stressful. A lot of kindergarten programs are full day now, and even if the child had been in a half day Pre-K program, it's a big change for both them and their parents. I invite parents to stay for a portion of the day. I stay after school and come in early to talk with any parents who have questions or need reassurance. So the idea is to build good parent-teacher relationships during this early period, help them feel comfortable, and let them know essentially that I am going to be taking care of their baby.

TOWNE: What is a typical day like in your classroom?

BURNIM: When my students first come in the classroom, they have some time to get settled. This is just as important for children as it is for adults. For instance, when many adults get to work they have coffee, clear their minds of anything that may have happened at home or on the way to work, and see what their day is going to look like. I allow my students to do that as well. They eat breakfast, talk to their friends, read a book, and prepare themselves for learning. Then we meet as a whole group where I share the itinerary for the day with them. The key is to let them know exactly what to expect and what is expected of them. This helps them succeed throughout the day.

One of the most important techniques that I use is to constantly break the day up with various groupings, settings, and activities. Because I work with such young children, their attention span is not very long, especially at the beginning of the year. For instance, in my current schedule, after we have our class meeting, I like to do an opening song and dance for my kids to get their bodies moving and their brains working. Then I move right into a writer's workshop, starting with a teacher-directed mini-lesson. After this short lesson, the students work in pairs where they talk about their writing ideas with a partner and then work independently for another 20 minutes or so. But even when they're working independently, they're still sitting next to someone, which allows them to constantly get feedback from a peer. So during the first 45 minutes of school, my students have worked in a large group, a small group, and independently. They have moved from being seated on the carpet to dancing around the room to working at a designated writing spot in the classroom. This all helps to keep them engaged.

After that, we get back together as a whole class to summarize and celebrate our writing. Next, I read a book with them, and then we'll have some type of follow-up. Then they break up into small groups again and go off to work in literacy centers. This is one of my favorite times of the day, as I work with students on guided reading. Finally, after literacy centers and guided reading, we come back together as a whole group to celebrate and summarize our work. This only takes us up to lunch. But the afternoon is very similar with math and science activities. The point is that it's always a come together, go apart, come together, go apart routine. I have them sitting and doing a lesson for a little while, then follow that up with a movement activity. I really never have them doing one thing for very long, and I try to keep a good healthy balance of activities. For young children I've found that breaking up the day like this works well and really helps to keep them focused.

TOWNE: You are involved in a professional learning community as well, right?

BURNIM: One of the things I loved that my school did several years ago was to initiate study groups among the teachers. At Broad Acres, we believe that we, as teachers, owe it to our students to constantly stay up-to-date on current trends in education. So we are always studying recent education articles and reading various professional texts. Everyone is involved, including the teachers, the principal and even the paraeducators. We read these books and then determine what it means for our students and how we can apply it to what we are doing at our school to improve teaching and learning.

TOWNE: Are these teacher study groups formal or informal?

BURNIM: They started off formal. Broad Acres went through a district restructuring starting in 2001, and part of that included working late on Wednesdays to collaborate with colleagues. So we divided those Wednesdays up in a variety of ways. The first part is where we do formal planning and select the objectives that we will teach for the month. We collaboratively decide what the best way is to teach a certain concept, how we're going to pre-assess it, how we're going to assess it, what we're going to do for those students who already know it, and what to do about those students who make it through the unit and still don't get it. The second part of Wednesdays includes opportunities to plan vertically and to be involved in activities such as the book study group. Over the years they have become less formal, but still have an incredible impact on what we do as educators.

TOWNE: What does educational equity mean to you, and how do you maintain it in your classroom?

BURNIM: Educational equity is about giving every child exactly what he/she needs to be successful and to steadily progress to higher levels. That may mean a child could need intervention to get up to the expected level; or if he or she is already at that expected level, then we want to progress them on to the next level. In my class, I first assess where my students are at the beginning of the year so that I have some baseline data on their academic achievement levels. I do this by talking to the real experts, their parents, about where their children are academically and socially and what their strengths, passions, and needs are. I also use formal assessments, informal assessments, and observations as well. I then determine a plan on how best to use this information to help the student, especially in the areas where growth is needed.

I must always consider the various learning styles my students have so that I can plan my lessons accordingly. It's also important to find out what each of their interests are in order to keep them motivated. For instance, if they like a certain character or a certain animal, I actively seek to find books that incorporate those things so that I can keep the engagement level high. Finally, it's important to really differentiate instruction accordingly for each student. That might mean that even though we're all working on the same project and using the same materials, the kids will be working at different individual skill levels. Kids don't learn at the same pace, and instruction should reflect their differences.

TOWNE: I definitely agree with that. Frequently, I hear teachers talk about differentiated instruction, but many just seem to break them into groups.

BURNIM: There are various levels of differentiation, but it really is one of the hardest things to do in the classroom. Grouping is at the very basic level and is what many people talk about. I think that is the expected and should be the norm with small reading and math groups. But differentiation is also important within the work that they're doing. We must provide children an opportunity to work at their appropriate individual skill level. For instance, I have a new student right now who is reading at a very early kindergarten level in first grade, yet in the same class I have two kids who are reading at a high second grade level. So the work that they're doing independently can be quite different than what goes on in the whole-class instruction. We all have high expectations for our kids, and that can be difficult, especially for those reading below their required or expected levels. It's okay to have those high expectations, but the work given to them needs to be skill-level appropriate, and it's best to help them reach those expectations in small increments so that they can experience ongoing success.

TOWNE: You're a big proponent of reduced class sizes in order for teachers to better focus on individual students. You are in a wonderful position of having only 15 students in your class, but what if you had 30? What would you do to compensate for having so many children and still try to keep that level of individual instruction and close relationships?

BURNIM: I've been very fortunate that I've had smaller classes because that's not the reality for most teachers. My school district has taken the idea of equity to heart and really tried to keep the numbers down in its Title 1 schools. But if I were working in my same school district in another school, I would probably have closer to 30 kids per class. In fact, with the economic times that we're having right now, I could very well have 30 kids in the future anyway.

That being said, even if I do ultimately end up with 30 students, I would still be true to my teaching style, which is heavily centered on relationships. I would still strive to get to know each of my students as an individual. I would still strive to incorporate their families into the learning process and use them as an asset to help me get my job done. It would all certainly take a lot more time, but I don't think my style of teaching would change much. Things would become a little larger. Instead of having a group of four, I might have a group of six or seven, but I think potentially it's still the same style that I have grown accustomed to. Although it would be harder, I would keep the same principles that have allowed me to succeed thus far.

TOWNE: Can you talk a little about the formal sessions you and the other teachers had when you got together and examined students' work?

BURNIM: Keep in mind we started this almost a decade ago and it has really evolved over the years. This is important, in and of itself, because if professional development becomes stagnant, then your teaching and the progress that your students are making will become stagnant as well. We started off with what's called the Tuning Protocol, which included a detailed outline about what we were to do, with clear restrictions on how and when things were supposed to happen. A designated teacher would bring student work and have a certain amount of time to describe the work and pose a guiding question. That teacher would ask about something specific such as, "What can I do to help this student move to the next level in reading?" The group would then review the student's work and give feedback and/or advice on whatever the issue was.

That's how we started, and it provided us with good feedback on helping individual students that a teacher was struggling with. But one of the things we realized was that it was a little too restrictive for us. We didn't really like being bound by the time restrictions, so we began modifying it a little each year. It eventually moved to the point where we examined student work in various ways, by groupings, grade level, individual students, etc. I think we've become much more effective, and it helps us benchmark where we are and where we need to be. It has worked out well and provides excellent feedback from colleagues with whom we otherwise may not have had an opportunity to talk.

TOWNE: You have learning walks as well, right? What are they like?

BURNIM: When we started the learning walks about eight years ago, they were still pretty new. Now they're much more common, but ours was a bit different as we didn't want them to be a top-down process and given by the administration. Central office staff and principals coordinate most learning walks. They walk through teachers' classrooms, observe what's going on and then come to certain conclusions. We didn't like that idea and instead wanted the walks to be coordinated and given by teachers in more of a bottom-up approach. We wanted teachers to be in complete control of the learning walks; setting them up, implementing them, gathering our own data, and then coming to our own conclusions about where we needed to be. We wanted it to be one of the vehicles we used to drive our professional development.

These learning walks turned out to be real enlightening experiences because teaching can be extraordinarily isolating. We as teachers don't typically have the opportunity to go to other classrooms and see what our peers are doing because we're too busy teaching our own class. But these learning walks gave every teacher in the building an opportunity to get out of their own classroom and to see what was happening around them. It helped with school culture and helped to build a sense of trust among colleagues. It helped teachers to see how interconnected the work we do really is. So even though I may be a kindergarten teacher and don't give those important state tests in third, fourth, and fifth grade, I can now see my role in that learning continuum that our students progress through in order to be prepared for those tests. Furthermore, it helped us identify some key areas that we had mastered as a staff and some key areas that we needed growth in.

One of the problems that we had with our learning walks when we first started was that we did too much patting ourselves on the back about things that we were doing right. It took us awhile to get to the point where we started to look critically at ourselves and point out things that we weren't doing so well and we needed improvement on. It's so important to be honest and have those critical conversations.

TOWNE: How long do you typically stay in each classroom?

BURNIM: Less than five minutes. But it's enough to provide just the snippet we need to really get the feel and general commonalities among the classrooms. It also helps take the pressure off of teachers as well, as they know it's never just about them, but rather about what we're doing as a staff collectively.

TOWNE: Classroom management is often a big hurdle for teachers, and one of the biggest worries for young teachers. I've talked to a lot of middle and high school teachers about discipline, but it's different for very young children. How do you handle this issue?

BURNIM: Oh yes, it's a whole different ballgame at this level. There are several things to keep in mind. First, it's so important to set and follow routines. Young children thrive on structure and need to know what to expect and what's expected of them. Building in these routines is one of the most effective ways to help them consistently work to their fullest potential.

Second, it's important to be extremely prepared before class begins. This will help take away the chance of having those management issues, because for any teacher, whether in their first year or thirtieth year, if you're not prepared and you're dealing with five- and six-year-olds, then things can go downhill pretty fast. The minute you turn away from students or go to your desk to get what you need, anything can happen, and the kids will form their own agenda that probably isn't the same as yours.

It's also important to keep young children constantly engaged. Find out what they like and put it in the classroom. Technology plays a role for me. I have a Promethean Board in my classroom now, which is an instant attention-getter. I also have the companion Activotes, and I allow the kids to give and get immediate feedback by voting. For instance, I can write any question on the Promethean Board with multiple-choice answers. My students will then use the Activotes to select one of the answers. With the click of a button, my students and I can see the results and know what percentage of the class gets it and what percentage of the class is not getting the concept being taught. Now my students are always asking if they can vote on things. It's like they're begging me to assess them. Sometimes it's things I am not ready to assess them on, yet they still want to vote on it because they're so into that process. It's what they like to do.

Another thing I do is give kids plenty of responsibility, especially those who have a difficult time sitting still or focusing. I give them a job such as sharpening all of the pencils when they first get in the classroom. Then that child doesn't have time to get off-task and has a personal investment in our classroom community. Last, it's important to make learning purposeful for the students. They don't like to do things just for the sake of doing it, but if it's purposeful for them, even at this young age, then they will buy into it a lot more.

TOWNE: How can a kindergarten or first grade teacher get their students to sit still and pay attention?

BURNIM: Well you don't expect them to sit still for very long; they're only five or six years old. Teachers have to be realistic in their expectations and must keep that in mind when planning. Maybe teachers can have a mini-lesson that's not going to be any longer than ten minutes because the kids need to get up and move after that. If I keep them on a lesson for twenty or thirty minutes and then expect them to sit down and be quiet, then shame on me. That's not going to happen. Also, as I mentioned, it's important to mix the day up. At the beginning of the year in kindergarten, a typical lesson might be only five minutes, but then you gradually increase the time, so that by the end of the year a single lesson can be maybe fifteen minutes long. That's my suggestion. But if you think they are going to sit still and be quiet for an hour then you're kidding yourself. It's not age-appropriate, and it's not realistic.

TOWNE: Since becoming National Board Certified, you have helped many of your colleagues also start on that path. How much of a difference did board certification make on your abilities as a teacher?

BURNIM: I started National Board Certification when I was in my fourth year of teaching, so I was still a relatively new teacher. It really helped me become a better teacher and refined my practice. One of the things that it did was help me reflect on precisely what it was that my kids needed and what they did not need. Sometimes that meant questioning the curriculum that I had been given to work with, and that's not an easy thing to do, especially for a new teacher. But if the curriculum is not relevant or is ineffective, then we are wasting valuable teaching and learning time. Likewise, the process made me analyze my teaching and the lessons and activities that I created for my students. It forced me to cut out the "fluff." The National Board Certification process helped give me the confidence to become an advocate for my students, both inside and outside of the classroom. I would encourage any teacher who is ready and willing to take an in-depth look at his/ her practice to try National Board. It is a very rigorous process but one of the best forms of professional development that one can find. Students reap all the benefits.

TOWNE: And your district actually aligned its teacher evaluation system with the five core propositions of the National Board, right?

BURNIM: Yes it did. Our school district is a big proponent of the National Board for Professional Teaching Standards and believes that the five core propositions are essential for every teacher. So by having that outlined and knowing that our evaluation system is based on that, it really takes out the guesswork for teachers about what's important and what they should be focusing on, as well as how they should be developing as professionals. It promotes a common baseline for all teachers, and I think it works great, especially in large school systems like ours.

TOWNE: Mrs. Chandler, your daycare teacher, has always had a huge influence on you. What was it about her that stayed with you all of these years and made you want to emulate her as a teacher?

BURNIM: Mrs. Chandler did more than just teach me. It was all about the relationship that she had established with me and with my family. She always took the time to nurture me instead of just trying to fill me up with information. She urged me to develop into the person that she felt I was destined to be. So it was really that idea of establishing and maintaining meaningful relationships with students that I took from her and that I try to apply within my own teaching. I constantly strive to build those relationships and continuously nurture my students as much as possible. In fact, I don't just see them as "students" at all, but as unique individuals and human beings with feelings and valid ideas and thoughts. Ultimately it's not about them learning one particular piece of information, but it's about them feeling that sense of belonging and importance, about making them feel like they are part of a community, and being able to learn how to think for themselves. Creating that sense of high self-esteem and confidence in young children is critical to their development later in life.

Being a teacher is so much more than just teaching what the curriculum says you're supposed to be teaching. This is especially true in this day and age when there is so much focus on teaching to "the test" and accumulating "the data" and what it shows. Sometimes I think we might be missing the boat here, as there is so much more to these children that we don't see reflected in "the data." These children are human beings, not bits of data. I worry that we're starting to forget that and not realizing how important it is to really take the time to nurture these kids. That's what Mrs. Chandler did for me, and that's what I always strive to do with every child in my classroom.

CHAPTER 14

Tamara Steen

2005 National Teacher of the Year Finalist
2005 Washington Teacher of the Year
Mabton Junior/Senior High School
Mabton, Washington
English/Art: Grades 9-12

Current Position: Director of Student Learning,
Mabton School District

Tamara Steen was raised on a farm in Washington State. She grew up wanting to see the world, but also wanting to teach the children of poverty who live in different cultures. Her dream came true, but not in the way she had imagined. After leaving home for college, she spent her junior year as an exchange student in Germany. It was there that she came to understand what it means to be a struggling student—not from a lack of intelligence, but rather from a lack of academic understanding. This proved to be excellent training, as several years later she became a teacher in a high-poverty, high-minority school district.

Having now taught for 27 years, Steen continues to believe that teaching children of poverty is her life's work. She calls it, "An avocation, not a vocation. A passion, not a job." She has a firm grasp of working with ELL students. Half of her school is composed of English Language Learners with nearly 90% of them on free or reduced-cost meals. Steen, however, doesn't let language issues become a barrier to her students' success. Her classroom is organized around the principles of "to-with-by," which has proven to be highly effective in helping students attain independence in learning. She also keeps her lessons fun and engaging, often letting students form teams to create specialized documentaries. But Steen insists that there's a lot more to it than that. "High standards and creativity will not by themselves produce the results I want. Students need to feel connected." Developing relationships with her students is her primary focus, and she often becomes a surrogate parent to many of them. This high level of personal attention has helped increase her students' test scores dramatically and has had other benefits as well. The need for discipline has become virtually non-existent, as Steen has had to send only one student to the office in the past 20 years.

Ever the lover of diversity, Steen spent time as an exchange teacher in Australia and has hosted six foreign exchange students from all over the world. She is currently writing a fantasy novel with her 14-year-old grandson, working on her Doctorate in Educational Leadership, and serving her district as the Director of Student Learning. She lives in Grandview, Washington, with her husband, Roger.

TOWNE: What attributes do you think contributed most to the success you've had as a teacher?

STEEN: I give my students unconditional love even when their behavior is difficult. I believe in their potential even when they cannot see it, and I develop my lessons around their learning styles and instructional needs. I engage them as partners in their learning by actively soliciting their feedback about how well my strategies work or do not work for them—and I let them know when I adjust my strategies according to that reflection. I teach my hobbies—reading and writing—which means I bring to my students a passion for English, a passion for teaching it, and a passion for sharing it with them.

TOWNE: What pedagogy or formal methods of teaching have you incorporated that you have found most effective in your instruction?

STEEN: I have implemented concepts garnered from the Gates Foundation with the assistance of Dr. Tony Wagner of Harvard: the "to-with-by" approach to lesson planning and the need for intellectually rigorous and relevant work. *Understanding by Design* has also formed part of the framework for my instruction. After my training in SIOP (*Sheltered Instructional Observation Protocol*), I became more intentional about meeting the needs of ELL students.

TOWNE: It's been stated that you are known for using innovative and engaging teaching strategies to get your students' attention. Can you talk about what some of these strategies are?

STEEN: There have been many over the years, so I will mention only a few of my favorites. First of all, most high school students hate poetry. When I implemented the Poetry Coffeehouse, I found I had to spend a whole quarter teaching poetry because of the demand. The students were divided into teams, and each team was assigned one Friday during the quarter to bring refreshments. During the week, I taught poetical terms and analysis through hands-on activities. For example, I taught meter through the use of a cheer during which students had to stand up and use hand gestures to demonstrate iambic pentameter or whatever I called out. Several days would also be spent with the teams looking through numerous poetry books or on the Internet for a suitable poem they would like to analyze and present to the class. On Friday, each team (and each member was required to have a part) would read its chosen poem and analyze its components, including the use of poetical terms and theme. The tables would be set with white tablecloths, the lights would be turned off and candles lit, and we ate the refreshments as we listened to the poems from each team. My students read and analyzed far more poetry than they ever had through more traditional methods. And my students loved the activity.

Another highly successful activity happened after the Advanced Placements exams in early May. Juniors and seniors are mentally done with school by then, so to keep them going in a meaningful way, I let them form teams. Then I gave them the assignment of creating a documentary connecting our small town with some global issue. The documentaries had to be professionally done and worthy of being aired on television. On alternate years, I had the students in their teams create parodies of a popular movie of their choice. Then I provided my students with a real audience—their families and friends—during the last week of school. Over the years the event grew so big that we had to move out of my classroom and into the small gym to accommodate everyone who wanted to see the videos.

TOWNE: What was the biggest change you've made during your career that made your teaching more effective?

STEEN: I changed my attitude. I decided I would no longer think of my students as being "lazy and unmotivated." Instead, I would own my students' learning, assuming full responsibility for whatever happened in my classroom. I thought only about those things over which I had control—namely, my instruction. Whenever my instruction did not produce the results I wanted, I analyzed it and changed it.

TOWNE: How were you able to do that?

STEEN: I'll give you an example. I used to give an assignment and maybe only five or so got turned in on the due day. I then asked myself, "How do I inspire my students to complete their assignments on time?" Then I made an assumption, "Students are complicated beings with complicated lives. Therefore, there are many reasons they do not finish their work, including not being sure how to successfully complete the assignment. All humans want to feel successful, but they also want work that is meaningful. I contemplated it for awhile and came up with a solution. Prepare lessons as if the students are all ADHD, ELL, tactile-kinesthetic learners, left-brain oriented, and male.

TOWNE: Wow, that was specific.

STEEN: Well, these are individuals most likely not to do well in English. The rest of the students are likely to achieve even if I lecture.

TOWNE: I see.

STEEN: So I varied my instructional strategies to include such things as peer collaboration, hands-on activities (e.g. use clickers that resemble television remote controls to choose responses to multiple-choice questions instead of giving students a handout), and reflection. For instance, I would ask students for feedback about the selected strategies at the end of each period. And I would always phrase the question so that they would understand that they were not evaluating me, but rather the strategy. I wanted them to feel free to be honest about how well something worked or didn't work for them. Then I made sure to adjust my instruction according to that feedback and let the students know how valuable their insights were in helping me improve as their teacher.

TOWNE: So you are constantly changing and improving your instruction based on their feedback?

STEEN: That's right and it works great. You also have to keep the students focused on learning, learning, learning every minute of every period. I never assigned anything that wasn't important for them to know or be able to do.

TOWNE: What happened after you made these changes?

STEEN: Within a month, late or incomplete assignments became a non-issue. Once the students had partnered with me in their own learning, it all changed for the better.

TOWNE: When educating children of poverty, what "extra" is needed that may not be needed when educating other students?

STEEN: Usually, the children of poverty do not have the vocabulary or schema taken for granted by the teachers who work with middle or upper class students. When I taught such works as Shakespeare's Julius Caesar, for example, the students did not even know where Rome was, much less be able to grasp the significance of Caesar's ambition. I had to teach the historical background and a little politics first before we began the play. Vocabulary is also a huge barrier. They often cannot understand even a contemporary work because so many words are unfamiliar. I had to do a lot of work with prefixes, suffixes, and root words to give them the means to increase their vocabulary beyond just a weekly list of words.

TOWNE: You talked in a previous interview about how important it is to develop relationships with the students. How are you able to develop relationships with, and build the trust of, defiant students? How about apathetic students?

STEEN: Humans are highly complex and complicated in their motives for behavior. Therefore, simplistic solutions do not exist. However, one class of resistant struggling learners taught me the importance of building relationships among even the most defiant and apathetic. They were a class from educational hell until a cold January day when they finally did something well, and I told them, "You have been my best class today." Nobody heard the word "today."

TOWNE: They only heard that they were the best class.

STEEN: Yep, that's all they heard (*laughs*). So I have found that I had to spend ten valuable minutes of instructional time at the beginning of each period to speak to each student, and if I was busy helping one of them, those with whom I had not spoken would follow me around the room until I acknowledged their existence through some positive comment. Once I had done that, they would settle down to learn what I wanted to teach. By the end of the year, they had transformed into my favorite class. Four years later, when it was time to graduate, they were still asking me if they were my favorite class. Twenty years later, a student from that class saw me, hugged me, and then asked, "Are we still your favorite class, Mrs. Steen?"

TOWNE: They remembered that 20 years later? That's amazing.

STEEN: Building a relationship means letting a child know that I SEE him or her, separately, distinctly from all the rest—that I will miss him/her if absent, and that I value that child's contribution to my life. How do I do this? By making sure that there is approval in my eyes whenever I look at them, that I smile with joy for having them present, that I laugh with them and cry with them, that I know their interests and concerns. It's not magic, but it feels like it sometimes because the better I've gotten at building relationships, the faster the process works. Within the past year, while coaching teachers with management issues at the elementary level, I have been able to bring a class under control within two sessions and after that, the children are very excited to see me and very cooperative. We all want to be loved for ourselves. This is the greatest gift any teacher can give a student.

TOWNE: Parental involvement is a huge part of educating a child. Unfortunately, some parents are either too busy or just not around to help in the process. How are you able to compensate for that lack of involvement within your classroom?

STEEN: In the school where I work, teachers must be willing to serve as surrogate parents—and I have certainly done my share. It's outside the classroom where a lot of the parenting occurs. In fact, I have been told by various counselors that my name comes up a lot as someone students trust enough to talk to if there is a problem, and those problems are such that they require after-school hours. I make my telephone number and home address available to students, I've driven them places, I've invited them over to swim in my pool or to eat dinner, I've attended their games, I've gone to their birthday parties and other major events in their lives, I've found scholarships for them, and I've even bought clothes for them.

TOWNE: How do you encourage busy or apathetic parents to become more involved? Do you use specific ways of reaching out?

STEEN: I have a slight advantage. I have now taught for so long in this community that many current parents were former students. I have also taught brothers, sisters, and cousins, which makes my connection to parents even stronger. In addition, my family and I were Mabton residents for many years until my children graduated from the school and we no longer needed five acres of land for their FFA projects. We moved to a neighboring town because that was where we were able to find the house we needed, but we are still only ten minutes away from my school.

The parents of my students tend to see me as a member of the community—and in a culture of poverty few teachers ever live here, which sets me apart. Furthermore, I speak a little Spanish and always begin conversations with Spanish-speaking parents in their language. When they realize I am willing to make a fool out of myself in Spanish, they laugh and relax. I really like the parents of my students, they know it, and I think that helps to get them more involved.

TOWNE: What is your philosophy on discipline in the classroom and how do you implement it?

STEEN: The purpose of discipline is to change negative behaviors into socially acceptable ones. Twenty years ago, I discovered that kicking students out of my class for misbehavior never changed that behavior; indeed, it seemed to reward it by giving them a vacation from my class. I also discovered that lecturing students on their behavior never had an impact on them the next day. Not being stupid, I decided to cease using ineffective methods of control. Through trial and error, I discovered that nearly all discipline problems can be eliminated through two things: (a) a warm, nurturing environment where students can feel safe to try and even to fail without being humiliated by the teacher or other students, and (b) instruction that has a real-world application, is intellectually challenging, and engages students' interest. Ever since I discovered these two basic principles twenty years ago, I have had to send only one student to the office. I remember once when a student (who had spent time in jail, by the way) was disrespectful during class. None of my usual strategies worked to bring him under control, so I finally turned to him and said firmly but respectfully, "Look, I treat you with respect, so I expect to get that same respect back from you." Several of the other students chorused, "She's right. So shut up and behave yourself." Peer pressure worked beautifully because the boy looked at me, nodded, and apologized. He was never disrespectful again.

TOWNE: What techniques do you use to help ELL students meet state achievement standards? Can you give specific examples of what you have found works best?

STEEN: Strategies that work well with ELL work well with everyone else, too, actually. Recent research shows that students learn best through the *To-With-By* model: TO: The teacher models (briefly) the expected outcome for a task (e.g. how to write an introduction, how to find examples of metaphors, how to punctuate introductory phrases and clauses) so that the students are clear about the expectations, WITH: the students work collaboratively with a partner or with a team to achieve the same outcome, and BY: after sufficient practice, the students accomplish the task independently. Through this process, ELL students have multiple meaningful opportunities to hear, read, and speak using academic vocabulary, thus increasing their learning without dumbing down the curriculum's content. I also have had to learn to speak slower, sometimes translating my usual vocabulary into simpler words, and use visual aids so that ELL students can understand my instructional content. Furthermore, I frequently offer tutoring after school for those who need extra help in a specific area of grammar, reading comprehension, or essay construction. My goal is not that students meet state standards, by the way; my goal is that they be prepared for college when they graduate. If they are college-ready, they will pass the state exams along the way.

TOWNE: Being an ELL teacher gives you greater insight in dealing with children from different cultures and backgrounds. In your opinion, where is the line between maintaining diversity and the need for cultural assimilation?

STEEN: About ninety-five percent of my students speak Spanish. I absolutely love diversity! It's the reason I've lived overseas twice and I've been happily married for thirty-eight years to a man with whom I have nothing in common except two children. As for my students, I love sharing their culture, especially the food and the music. As for the line between maintaining diversity and cultural assimilation, the assimilation will happen anyway, sooner or later. My ancestors, for example, came here 300 years ago from Germany, but I don't consider myself German and I don't celebrate German holidays unless I happen to be in Germany. Nobody in my family even speaks German, except for me, because I decided to get a major in that language when I went to college. I find my second and third generation students don't tend to speak Spanish, either.

As for signs being in Spanish in this area, I've traveled enough to know that I am very grateful for signs being printed in English when I travel to Europe and Asia. Why not return the favor for foreigners here? I don't seem to draw any lines until it comes to selecting texts for my English classes. I tried for a couple of years to avoid the "Great White Fathers" of literature as much as possible in order to present my students with an international buffet, only to discover they would look at me blankly and say, "Geez, what was the point of that?" Every year when I surveyed my students, the top favorites were Hamlet, Romeo and Juliet, Beowulf, and Oedipus Rex. I've even had males walk into my room on the first day of school demanding to know how soon we'd be reading Beowulf because they'd heard it was a great story (it's all that action, blood, and gore that they love). Therefore, I abandoned cultural diversity in literature so that I could focus on finding just plain great tales that would grip my students' imaginations. Along the way, with help from some of those students, I discovered great pieces by Isabel Allende, Luis Rodriguez, and Yann Martel, just to mention a few.

TOWNE: What do you wish you had known when you first started teaching that you now know?

STEEN: I wish I had known how to separate the critical, foundational content from the rest. Our state standards are so numerous; teachers really must condense their instruction down to what will leverage the most student achievement. I also think I spent too much time with frivolous activities that really didn't move students as far as something else would have done. I wish I would have known how to organize a lesson according to "to-with-by" and been more adept at understanding how to use formative assessments to measure student progress. Knowing what I know now, I often feel compelled to apologize to former students because I wasn't able to get them as far as I should have. It always seems strange to me that they don't see my instruction the same way I do. In fact, one of those little hellions from my first year at Mabton told me a month ago that she thought it was tragic that I had recently decided to give up teaching in favor of being an administrator. "Gifted teachers," she said, "are really rare in this district. I feel sorry for all those students who will not have you as a teacher." I think the fact that I loved them so much has clouded their judgment of my instruction.

TOWNE: What were the greatest challenges you have experienced while teaching and how were you able to overcome them?

STEEN: My greatest challenge was learning not only how to survive, but also to thrive in a high-poverty, high-minority culture. Back when I first entered teaching, my college professors had absolutely no clue what teaching in a high-poverty, high-minority environment meant, and their courses proved worthless. My colleagues were no help either. They were perfectly content to operate in isolation and let me drown in a sea of despair and confusion. I quit after my first year of teaching in an African-American elementary school in the Los Angeles urban sprawl.

Twelve years later, I got tired of teaching Hamlet to my living room furniture and acknowledged that I was not meant to spend the rest of my life as a housewife, no matter how much I loved my children. By that time, my husband and I had moved to Washington State, where I was hired to substitute for a junior high teacher who resigned five weeks before the end of the school year. I walked into a hell inhabited by twelve- and thirteen-year-old demons. After a few days I decided life was too short to put up with that and vowed to resign at the end of the last period. As I said good-bye for what I thought would be the last time to the last class, a darling seventh grade girl hugged me fiercely and exclaimed, "I love you, Mrs. Steen." In that moment I knew it was possible to make a difference in the life of a child and not even know it. So I thought to myself, "Well, I guess I could come back tomorrow." I never dreamed I would be coming back tomorrow for the next twenty-five years, but I lost my heart to these children and they won't give it back.

CHAPTER 15

Sharon M. Draper

1997 National Teacher of the Year
1997 Ohio Teacher of the Year
Walnut Hills High School
Cincinnati, Ohio
English/Language Arts: Grades 7-12

Current Position: Educational Speaker/Author

Sharon M. Draper is one of the most respected educators in America. As a teacher and as an author, she has reached levels of success which few can rival. Aside from winning the National Teacher of the Year Award, Draper is also a five-time winner of the Coretta Scott King Literary Award, and has won dozens of other teaching and writing honors. A *New York Times* best-selling author, she recently was chosen as one of only four writers in the country to speak at the National Book Festival Gala in Washington D.C.

Before becoming a full-time author and distinguished educational speaker, Draper spent 30 years in the classroom teaching children to read and write. Refusing to be locked into structured routines, she was extremely flexible with her lessons and focused on giving individual students what they needed, when they needed it. "Flexibility is key," she states. Draper also set high expectations for her students and invited them to participate in many aspects of the decision-making process, from creating rules to choosing assignments. She helped her students love reading by letting them act out various parts of a story or even turning it into a play, thus transforming the material into something relevant and meaningful to them.

On the writing side, Draper is the author of over two dozen books that have helped transform classrooms all over the country. Two of her nonfiction books, *Teaching From the Heart* and *Not Quite Burned Out, But Crispy Around the Edges*, were designed to help teachers adjust to various classroom issues. At the same time, teachers frequently seek out Draper's award-winning fictional books, which have become required readings in many classrooms.

Draper received her bachelor's degree from Pepperdine University and her master's from Miami University of Ohio. After becoming one of the first teachers in the nation to achieve National Board Certification in English/Language Arts, Draper was later elected to the Board of Directors of the National Board for Professional Teaching Standards. She is currently on the Board of the National Commission on Teaching and America's Future.

Draper travels extensively around the world and has been a guest on television and radio programs, discussing issues of literature, reading, and education. She lives in Cincinnati, Ohio, with her husband, Larry, and their golden retriever, Honey.

TOWNE: What was a major challenge you faced while teaching and how were you able to overcome it?

DRAPER: All professions offer challenges. Teaching stresses one's time, energy, and the capacity to encompass it all— the responsibility, time management, and need. I wanted *all* of my students to write well, to love books and to embrace learning with a passion. Of course, we never manage to grab them all, but the success stories make it all worthwhile.

I overcome problems with the same energy and positive attitude with which I approach the problems. If a child couldn't master a skill, I had to find a way to give them success. If I got tired because I had four kids, two dogs, a hundred and sixty students, and a car that needed a new transmission, then I had to figure out a way to refresh myself so that I could approach each need one at a time. I enjoyed my time as a teacher and saw a lot more positives than negatives.

TOWNE: You have won numerous high-profile teaching awards over the years. What would you consider to be the "secret" of your success as a teacher?

DRAPER: I have no secret. I have passion and energy and creativity. I love what I do. I'm a positive person who believes in praise and recognition as opposed to criticism and disapprobation.

TOWNE: What formal pedagogy and systems did you use in your classroom and how specifically did you apply them?

DRAPER: Although I studied all the educational theories in various classes over the years, I never set out to teach with one codified approach. I probably used all of the "systems" that are or were in vogue among the pedagogical academics, but I gave no name to them. If putting kids in groups to read books was successful, then I used that long before someone came up with the term "Literature Circles." My classroom was a living being, not a stagnant pool. I didn't bother with names of theories. I used what worked and what was needed for that particular group of students.

TOWNE: What unusual methods did you incorporate in your classroom that may be different than most teachers use, but that you have found to be effective?

DRAPER: Whatever worked. If you're stuck on the idea that "I must play a game today," or "We must have a spelling test because it's Tuesday," you won't be successful. It's so important to be flexible. Give your students what they need when they need it.

Kids today live in a noisy, frenetic world of instant gratification and electronic satisfaction. Information they need can be instantly downloaded from their computers to their printers without having to pass through their brain for thought or digestion of ideas. Their worlds are hurried, pushed, and scheduled. They go to soccer practice, ballet lessons, and gymnastics. They heat their dinner in the microwave, watch television while they pay cursory attention to their homework, and then fall asleep in exhaustion to start the routine again the next day. They are computer-literate and were seemingly born knowing how to multi-task. Join them. Let them teach you while you teach them.

TOWNE: I'd like to ask you about your professional book *Teaching from the Heart*. Can you give us a few of the more unique gems from that book that teachers could incorporate?

DRAPER: *Don't be afraid to smile.* If it's clear that you like what you're doing and you know your material, then smile and share that with your class. Smiles are infectious. Let the kids know that you like them. Talk to them at lunch, after school, between classes. Find out what they like, what they think, who they really are. Remember, you don't teach a subject, you teach young people.

Have fun! If you present a lesson that seems boring to you, then I guarantee that it will be boring to your students. Let's say you have to teach a lesson on the Civil War. You can have them memorize dates and battles and generals and they will learn very little. Or you can have them research uniforms and living conditions and medical treatment and have them act out battles, role-play decisions, and participate actively in the fabric of the times. They will never forget it and neither will you.

Praise them. Young people respond so much better to praise than to criticism. Find something good about even the most difficult student and praise him publicly and honestly. You will find that he becomes a little less hard to handle. Let your students have some input whenever you can and let them think they are giving input when you can't.

Listen to them. Many of them live in a world that is very unlike the world that many of you are familiar with. That old slogan about walking in another man's shoes begins with listening to the story of the paths he walks upon.

Share with them. When the last bell rings at the end of the day, you'll be tired, drained, and ready to collapse. But don't be in a hurry to rush off. Volunteering with after-school clubs is not only educational for you, but it also shows the students another dimension of your personality. They realize that you are really human and you'll learn the same about them. Stick around for play rehearsal or cheerleader practice or a baseball game. Kids will remember that you took the time to share your life with theirs.

TOWNE: Another one of your professional books is called *Not Quite Burned Out, But Crispy Around the Edges.* What's the message there that may help discouraged teachers consider staying in the profession?

DRAPER: Sometimes it's hard to see the big picture—how we figure in the vastness of educational goals and curriculum concepts. How can one teacher, working in one small school, in one district, in one state, ever claim to make a difference in the millions of students that march toward us each September and leave us, sometimes having marched over us, the following June? How do we know if it matters? Sometimes it takes a gentle encounter like this one:

A young woman approaches you as you reach your car. "Hi! Remember me?" she says cheerfully. You do, but only vaguely. You remember the face when it was longer, more innocent, thinner. Strangely, you somehow remember her handwriting—how she dotted all her I's with little hearts. But you can't remember her name. Nevertheless, you smile broadly and say, "Yes! How are you? What are you doing now?" She seems to understand that you need a memory push so she tells you her name and how many years ago you had her in class. It all comes back—that class, that year, that student. You remember doodles and drawings on the sides of all her papers. You remember she had sad eyes. She tells you she is an artist working for a large greeting card company and happily doing work she loves. Her eyes are no longer sad.

She says, "I just wanted to let you know that you changed my life. I was an unhappy child and coming to your class was always fun. Of all my teachers you were the only one who made me laugh, took the time to talk to me, and gave me encouragement. Because of you, I didn't give up. Because of you, I made it through. I'm so glad you're still here and still teaching. I wonder if your students today know how lucky they are to have you as their teacher."

You are stunned, almost speechless. Here is a young woman you had forgotten. A faint blip on your memory screen, but in her mind, *you* were the dominant memory. You were the reason she made it as a human being. She hugs you, thanks you, gets back into her car, and drives away.

You stand there in the almost empty parking lot, a little overwhelmed. You glance at the building, take a deep breath, and smile. You hurry home because you have much to do. Tomorrow is another day and you get to do it all over again. You can't wait.

TOWNE: One of the biggest problems for beginning teachers is classroom management. Teachers are often afraid to let the students get out of their seats for fear of losing control. How did you handle classroom management?

DRAPER: It all starts with the first day of school. Classroom behavior and rules should be established from the beginning and not all of them should be decided by the teacher. Try letting students take part in determining classroom protocol. They are often more strict on themselves than you'd expect. If you post the classroom rules that they had a part in creating, they are less likely to rebel against them. Another requirement is routine. They should know what to expect. For example, first we write in journals, then we review homework, then we break into groups, then we discuss, then we clean up—or whatever works for you. If they know the routine, they know the expectations.

TOWNE: An English teacher from a disadvantaged high school comes to you for advice. Her students can read the words well enough, but their comprehension of literary works is awful. She wants to know some specific techniques that you used that helped students better comprehend literature. What are your suggestions to her?

DRAPER: Kids today live in a world of video and action. Let them act out parts of stories. Let them turn a novel into a reality show or a quiz show. Let them create a video game from the text. Meaning must be meaningful. Lots of times kids don't comprehend the words because they don't choose to do so. It's boring, so why try. Make it real to them, and you'll be surprised how much comprehension increases.

TOWNE: You were one of the first teachers in the nation to receive National Board Certification in English/Language Arts. Can you talk a little about what is learned during National Board Certification that would benefit veteran teachers who think they might not need it?

DRAPER: The process of National Board Certification turned out to be probably the most rewarding experience of my professional life. Not only was there much-needed introspection into my teaching, but I also got to interact with other teachers who were also undergoing this unprecedented process. We shared ideas and methods and tales about former students. We also discussed teaching techniques and curricular issues. It was both stimulating and refreshing to be in a room with not just teachers, but the best teachers in the area. It was noticeable and it was wonderful.

Working through the components of the portfolio, writing the commentaries as I completed each section, taking the Assessment Center exercises—none of this was the piece of cake that I had envisioned. It was sometimes painful and tedious, but it was also rewarding and exciting. It was a learning experience that benefited all of my teaching that year. I learned more about myself and my strengths and weaknesses as a teacher than I ever have in twenty-plus years of teaching. But most important, I've learned. I've learned that the best teacher is a learner, and I've learned that teachers are indeed professionals. If we wish to produce new quality teachers, we must use only the very best and most qualified master instructors to guide and nurture quality in the next generation of teachers.

TOWNE: What books have you read that have helped shape you as a teacher?

DRAPER: I read three hundred books a year—mostly on airplanes and waiting in airports—mystery novels, biographies, historical fiction, poetry. Each one shapes me in some way. I learn from all I read and all that I do. It's always been that way. I was the little girl who checked out ten books every week from our local library. I was the child who read late at night with a flashlight. I majored in English so I could read more. I taught English so I could share that love of reading and books with the next generation.

TOWNE: I'd like to ask a few questions that you cover more in depth on your website (www.sharondraper.com), but ones I think would be beneficial to talk about here as well. What is your definition of a good teacher?

DRAPER: I once asked a class of fourth graders that exact same question and posted their answers on my website. If we could all live up to this simple list, we'd be successful teachers. Here are some of their responses: a good teacher is soft enough to hug, but too hard to punch; a good teacher knows lots of dirty jokes, but only tells the clean ones that make you laugh; a good teacher is not scared of thunder and lightning and knows what to do when the lights go out; a good teacher never makes fun of you when you do dumb stuff like throw up or forget the answer; a good teacher would be fun to have at your house for dinner, but you'd never want him to come for real; a good teacher knows a little bit about a lot of stuff, and a whole lot about things you need to know; a good teacher makes you have so much fun you don't realize you're learning, and then when you've learned it, you realize it wasn't hard at all; a good teacher never has bad breath; a good teacher loves you and you know it.

TOWNE: For new teachers that have been given their first teaching assignment, what are some things they can do to maximize the experience?

DRAPER: There are several things that should be done before you ever start your first day of class. I would drive by the school and see what it looks like on the outside. What neighborhood is it in? What businesses or homes surround it? I would go early in the morning as school begins and watch the children enter. Do most of them walk to school? (Meaning most of them are neighborhood children.) Or do they arrive on buses? (Meaning most of them do not live in the neighborhood where the school is located.) Do many parents drive their children to school? (A possible sign of parental interest, lack of buses, or both.) What does the school yard look like? Do the children wait outside before a bell? Are teachers monitoring them? If so, that will surely be assigned to you at some point.

I would also go after school and watch the dismissal routine. Do students leave right away or are numerous children left in the school yard after hours? Do students use the school area as a play space? Are organized after-school activities apparent? How soon does the teacher parking area empty of cars?

Finally, I would visit the school during school hours. How does the school "feel"? Do the students seem secure and adjusted to school routines? Do the teachers seem relaxed and confident?

TOWNE: So you're getting a real glimpse of your future before ever setting foot in a classroom.

DRAPER: Right. Another important thing is talking to your cooperating teacher. Find out his or her expectations as well as fears, and share your own. Set up a time for planning lessons and classroom transition. Find out how much your cooperating teacher will want you to follow his or her lesson plans. Every cooperating teacher is different. Some want you to follow their lesson plans and others encourage you to come up with your own. Find this out early.

Have you ever written on a chalkboard? Can you write legibly and not make the chalk squeak? Do you know how to use the new whiteboard that many schools now use? What about technology like overheard projectors or projection screens? Make sure you practice these things before you try to use them with students.

In your practicum classes you probably designed lots of lessons and classroom activities and games. Collect those, and put them in a large binder. You never know when one of those will be useful. As you develop more lessons, add to your binder as a record of success as well as specificity.

Prepare an introductory letter to send parents. In it you want to introduce yourself, ease their fears, and exude confidence. Plan to make direct parental contact for each of your students as soon as possible.

TOWNE: What should teachers keep in mind while creating effective lesson plans?

DRAPER: A new teacher once showed me her carefully planned vocabulary lesson for a seventh-grade class. The words were on their reading level, covered a variety of word roots and vocabulary skills, and were neatly typed on a worksheet. The lesson was an absolute failure. The students dutifully looked the words up in the glossary, copied the definitions, and the knowledge was transferred from dictionary to ditto sheet without ever having to pass through the brains of the children at all. They remembered none of the words the next day; they barely remembered the activity. After discussing with her how she could adjust and make this activity a meaningful learning experience, she tried again. This time, the students generated their own vocabulary list by finding the words from newspaper and magazine articles. They defined the words initially using context clues, and then challenged each other to find the correct definitions. Then they made up sentences that used their own names and information from their own lives, using each of the vocabulary words. Not only did the students respond with excitement and enthusiasm, they remembered all of the words the next day, the next week, and the next month. And they begged to do that activity again.

The teacher enjoyed the lesson, as did the students, and learning occurred for both. Learning should be fun and painless, not hard and laborious. If the teacher is enthusiastic and creative, the students will follow.

TOWNE: You have been very successful with your books for young adults and middle-grade readers. How did you get started as an author?

DRAPER: I'm a writer because I'm a teacher. My students, some of whom didn't like to read the assigned texts, were my inspirations. I wanted to write something that young people could read that would be contemporary and exciting, yet have a solid literary base for teachers to use. I had been working on a novel for young people, so I decided to see if I could get it published. *Tears of a Tiger* is written for high school students – on their level, in their style, about their world. I sent it to 25 publishing companies and got 24 rejection notices. The very last letter I almost threw away (rejection can be depressing!), but I opened it and enclosed was a letter of acceptance from Simon and Schuster. My students walked with me through the entire publication process – the edits and rewrites and corrections. We learned together how a book gets from idea to draft to bookstore. It was a monumental experience for all of us.

Tears of a Tiger had so much success that I was asked to write a sequel. That led to *Forged by Fire*, and later to the third book, *Darkness before Dawn*. When I started, I had no idea I was going to write a trilogy, but students and teachers demanded to know more about the characters. As they grew and developed, I guess I did too. I write for young people—teenagers. I try to deal with topics that are both current and topical. I also hope that by reading these books young people can perhaps apply some of the messages to their own lives. Abuse and death are topics that need to be discussed by young people. They are not pleasant, but by talking about the difficult realities of life, perhaps someone can be made stronger. I write about these things because, unfortunately, those are the realities of life for many teenagers today. I hope to say something that will change their lives for the better.

TOWNE: That's great. And as successful as those books were, you didn't stop there, right? What came after that trilogy and why?

DRAPER: Young people are accosted with decisions every day—most of them much more dangerous and serious than anything I'm able to put in a book. Not only do they have to decide what to do, they have to make those decisions under the grim, watchful scrutiny of their peers who show no mercy to those who dare to break with the norm. It is critical that they are given a platform to discuss options and choices and the consequences of making those choices. I tried to open the doors of thoughtful discussion through the characters in the next trilogy. The first is called *The Battle of Jericho*, the sequel is *November Blues*, and the third one is called *Just Another Hero*.

TOWNE: Why should students read books other than the "classics"?

DRAPER: I've read most of the "classics" as well as hundreds of less "literary" works. Each has its place. We can learn much from the old masters—the attention to detail and characterization and plot structure in the days before television and movies is exquisite. However, I don't think we should read *only* those works. We need to balance our reading with contemporary authors, those whose books, after the test of time, might one day be considered classics in their own right. In order to get our students to read, perhaps we can start with something they want to read, then move to something they need to read for college.

TOWNE: How can teachers implement your books into their classrooms?

DRAPER: I'm blessed. I've just finished my twenty-seventh book. I have provided in-depth study materials for every single book and made them available for teachers, free of charge, on my website. The teacher in me knows that students need to not just understand the plot, but should also be able to analyze a novel for theme, character, and purpose. So I've provided study questions, writing assignments, research projects, and, thoughtful discussion topics. *Copper Sun*, the historical fiction novel, has all that plus timelines, maps, photographs, websites, and tons of historical research information.

I am a teacher. It is not a job description, but a definition of who I am. I teach wherever I go—whether I'm talking at a school, or a convention, or to a group of teenagers at the mall. My entire essence revolves around "explaining" so that others can see—transferring the pictures and ideas in my mind into someone else's consciousness. I think that philosophy transfers to my writing. I'm blessed to be able to create words on paper that produce images in the minds of others—images that make them think, or wonder, or feel the need to talk. I visit dozens of conferences and schools every year, and the joy on the faces of the students I meet, their fascination with the characters and their lives, and their excitement about reading more are the things that keep me going. I'm writing as fast as I can – trying to write stories that young people can enjoy. I get hundreds of letters from kids who tell me how the books have touched them, made them think, or made them want to read more. It's wonderful as well as humbling.

TOWNE: What do you wish you had known when you started teaching that you know now?

DRAPER: Wear comfortable shoes!

CHAPTER 16

Betsy Rogers

2003 National Teacher of the Year
2003 Alabama Teacher of the Year
Leeds Elementary School
Birmingham, Alabama
All Subjects: Grades 1-2 (Looping)

Current Position: Improvement Specialist,
Brighton Elementary School

Not many teachers can claim to have had an actual day named after them, yet in 2003, Governor Bob Riley declared a "Betsy Rogers Day" in Alabama. This sums up the respect and admiration Dr. Betsy Rogers has earned over her 28-year teaching career. She always knew she wanted to become a teacher and has devoted her entire life to educating the disadvantaged, doing everything possible to help close the achievement gap.

After 20 years of classroom experience, Rogers felt it was time for an academic tune-up and returned to Samford University, her *Alma Mater*, to continue her education. Within five years she earned both a Master's and an Educational Specialist Degree in Elementary Education, as well as a Doctorate Degree in Educational Leadership. She topped it all off by earning National Board Certification, one of the highest teacher credentials available. "Teacher training should be never-ending," says Rogers, "All children deserve the most highly-skilled teachers possible."

Inside the classroom, Rogers has a reputation for nurturing and focusing on the whole child. Her class was known as "The Nurturing Class," and students were often handpicked for it based on their need for extra stability and attention. Rogers relied on the learner-centered model, but kept her lessons memorable by incorporating art, music, cooking, and literature into the curriculum. She is also an advocate of "looping", becoming the first teacher at her school to successfully incorporate it.

Her in-class accomplishments and work with at-risk schools has gotten Rogers featured in several national magazines and news media. She has won a multitude of awards and has been placed in various educational leadership positions. Rogers recently completed her fourth year at Brighton Elementary School as the School Improvement Specialist. She has chronicled this journey in a blog (Brighton's Hope) for *Education Week* and the *Teacher Leaders Network*.

Aside from her current duties at Brighton, Rogers also serves as the Chair of the Governor's Commission on Teaching Quality, is on the Executive Committee of the National Board for Professional Teaching Standards, serves on the Board for the Center for Teaching Quality in Chapel Hill, North Carolina, and is the president of the Alabama Conference of Teachers. She lives in her hometown of Birmingham, Alabama.

TOWNE: I would like to start with a general open-ended question that I often ask. What was the biggest challenge you have faced in your teaching career?

ROGERS: Probably the greatest challenge I had was trying to meet the needs of all the children and figuring out how to help them all be successful. I remember being very frustrated when that did not happen for every child every year. This was especially true when I first started teaching and it had a huge impact on me. It was usually a child who was having problems or had some special needs or issues and I just couldn't determine how to successfully meet their needs day in and day out.

TOWNE: How were you able to overcome that?

ROGERS: As the years went on, I think I've gotten much better at handling it, but it's an ongoing challenge that you never totally overcome. It's really about continuously trying to improve your practice and trying to get extra time in to help and support those children so that they can all be successful. It's something that I always strive to do.

TOWNE: I read your teaching philosophy in your Teacher of the Year application and was hoping you could share that here.

ROGERS: It basically says that all children learn differently and at a different pace. It's my job as a teacher to find the best methods and materials for each child to master needed skills as well as aid in social and emotional development.

TOWNE: That fits right in with the idea of teaching the "whole child" versus just the academic side, which I think is so important and is often ignored.

ROGERS: It is, and it's too bad that students these days are often thought of as the sum of their test scores because they are so much more than that. In the parent handbook that I gave to all my students' parents the first line reads, "Children, like rosebuds, bloom at different times. However, the last bloom is just as pretty as the first." My first grade teacher said that and it's stayed with me ever since.

TOWNE: I want to talk a little bit about the methods used in your classroom. I understand that you used the Learner-centered model as well as a variety of other methods that made a big impact on your students. Can you talk about a few of those methods?

ROGERS: Well, my job was to teach these young children to read. In order to do that, I used many different methods. I worked diligently to make the daily lessons memorable by incorporating art, music, cooking, and drama. As far as the reading methods go, I adjusted instruction according to the students' needs. My main reading program was phonetic-based, but when I had a student struggling with this approach, I would try the *Sight Word Approach, Language Experience,* or *Recorded Books.* But no matter what, I would first conference with the parent and give them the materials and methods they needed to implement the program at home. Then I would have the student attend a before-school tutoring program. I used various computer programs that often helped a lot. And then, of course, there's the theme-based approach that I used.

TOWNE: I wanted to talk a little about that theme-based approach. How did that work?

ROGERS: I often used a theme-based curriculum that followed the state guidelines. I basically wrapped the lesson around a theme such as a Middle East/Desert theme or something. This was a very important method for me and was constantly a part of my practice. There's always a population of students that need to have things flow. They need to have connections between events and that's where the theme-based approach comes in. When teaching kids to read, it really helps to bring science, social studies, and math into your literature. This allows them to better see those connections and makes it easier for them to understand the various subjects better than if they were separated. That's why I incorporated themes. I take whatever standards I'm teaching and pull out all the resources I can find to connect it with all the other content areas. This takes a lot of prep time, but the results are worth it. This is especially important within the population of students that I've always worked with, ones who are considered at-risk. Often their lives outside of the classroom are scattered, so it's critical that they have a very connected day in the classroom and know just what to expect.

TOWNE: You are also a big proponent of looping and even wrote a proposal for it that allowed you to successfully implement it at your school. What is looping and why does it work?

ROGERS: Looping is basically teaching the same class of kids for more than one year in a row. For instance, I was a first grade and second grade teacher with the same children. In order to loop, teachers have to learn two years of curriculum and I personally enjoyed this challenge. It also helps to have another strong teacher who will do this with you, so that you can flip-flop years with them. I had a teacher who was willing to do that in my school and we had several classes that we handled like that and shared resources. It was great. Whenever new kids came in, we told the parents up front about the system, and at the end of the first year, each of us could option out of it. So if the parents felt like their child would do better somewhere else, or if you felt like that child would do better with another teacher, you both have the choice to option-out.

The reason that I think this is such a nice structure is because it adds time and that second year is very powerful. They estimate that it saves about 6-8 weeks of time because you don't go through all that preliminary stuff when you start teaching that second year. Also, the summer between the first and second year would be valuable as I would have class meetings in the community library, and they would bring in work and stuff. That way the relationships continued to grow. So it's really about that added time for learning, and time is critical, especially when dealing with students in poverty. It's a way to extend the year and add to the time that it takes to build those critical relationships.

TOWNE: It sounds like a great idea. Is there any downside to it?

ROGERS: I have had teachers say, "I wouldn't want those same bad kids for two years." Well, by the second year, you know exactly what works with each child, and by then, you have very few discipline problems. But the only problem I really had with it was that it was difficult for the students that were leaving me after that second year, and for me. But the benefits far outweigh the negatives in my opinion. I would encourage all educators that teach young children to look into it.

TOWNE: After winning the state Teacher of the Year Award, you traveled around and visited a lot of failing schools. What did you see that was a common problem at these schools and what could similar schools do today to start improving?

ROGERS: That's when my life really changed. My travels that year took me to some of the poorest areas in the entire state of Alabama. I would spend every other week at one of the lower-performing schools and then about one day a week, on average, at the school I'm in now, which was the lowest-performing school in my district. At these low-performing schools I saw the same two major problems: Poor teacher quality and poor leadership. It was very disturbing. It wasn't the kids that were failing; it was the schools that were failing the kids. There were so many important things that were overlooked in those schools. Proper books weren't available in the library, classes didn't start on time, there was a lack of any kind of effective structure, etc. It was terrible. These are the sorts of things that happen in high poverty areas where you don't have parents complaining every day like you do in upper-class schools. I realized something that was hard for me to admit; some of those teachers and principals simply didn't care about these kids. Some seemed to think that children of color and children of poverty don't need to go anywhere anyway and that attitude came across as clear as could be. Fixing their schools was definitely not a priority for them.

Ever since then, I have become convinced that we have to have our strongest teachers in our most needy schools, which is why I came to the most needy school in our district. Unfortunately, that's not the norm with teachers, but it should be. That should be the obvious choice for strong teachers, but many are afraid of that challenge and shy away. Students are only as good as the educators that teach them. One pet peeve I have with other teachers is the statement that, "I taught them; they just didn't get it." That's unacceptable. Our role as teachers is to find out why "they didn't get it." Improve the school leadership, improve the teachers, and I promise you that you'll improve the quality of learning in these schools.

TOWNE: So it really boiled down to teacher quality and leadership? Do you think a real focus on those two issues could virtually fix most failing schools?

ROGERS: Absolutely! The very first thing these schools need are the best leaders the system can provide. Low-performing schools must have strong, proven principals and a critical mass of Master Teachers. The school calendar in these schools should also be adapted to allow for extra academic time through after-school and summer programs. The curriculum must match the needs and learning styles of the students, and the teachers need additional training to teach such a curriculum. Those are the basic points, in my opinion, and from what we've done so far at my school, it really works. The first year my principal and I were there, our test scores... and I know test scores aren't everything but that's what we have to go on... our test scores went from 38% to 88%. The next year, they went from 88% to 100%. We've been AYP every year since. Now being AYP doesn't make us a great school, but it's a rung on the ladder to greatness and it's a major improvement. However, the challenge is about more than just fixing schools—it's about creating schools where success can be sustained.

TOWNE: One of the areas you're most passionate about is figuring out ways to help close the gap when it comes to equitable educational funding. What have you found that works?

ROGERS: In Alabama, we fund schools through sales tax, so if the economy is not well, then we're not doing well. It's all about local money, but if you live in a poor rural community, then there is no local money. So the inequity is there, but how to overcome it is the big question. Some parts of my state had 'Reading First' money and other grants that helped them along, but it never really closed that huge equity gap. The school I'm in right now was in School Improvement for years and we were just able to come out of it two years ago. When you're in School Improvement, you get a lot of federal dollars that help, but as soon as you get out of School Improvement, the money is gone. There definitely needs to be more federal funding because with only state funding, those inequitable situations can really hurt schools in poor areas, especially during an economic downturn.

The federal, state, and local governments along with educators, parents, and citizens all need to become stakeholders in our schools. One way we've been able to start closing the gap at my school is through the use of a corporate sponsor which helps pay for field trips and resources that other schools take for granted. We also have a partnership with a local university that has helped a lot. So those are two other things I think schools should consider in order to help close that gap.

TOWNE: What about parental involvement? It's such a big part of being able to educate the whole child. How do you increase parental involvement in low-performing schools?

ROGERS: There's this perception that if you're in a Title 1 school, the parents aren't going to give you the support that others might, but I've found that to be completely opposite. From what I've seen, parents in Title 1 schools very much want to know what to do about their children's education. A lot of times they didn't have a very good experience in their own schooling, which makes them somewhat reluctant to trust us, and that's something we, as teachers, have to overcome. That can be done by going that extra mile and really reaching out to the parents: making weekly contact with them, having them in the classroom for conferences, and giving them tips that might help at home. I used to send home weekly reading tips to parents that showed them exactly what their child needed to work on. It's important that you include parents in the learning process. Do I ever get 100% of my parents to help? No, but the majority of them are very receptive as long as you reach out to them. Don't expect them to come banging your door down. It's your job as a teacher to make them feel like they're a part of a team. Whatever you do, don't assume a parent doesn't care because of their lack of involvement. Many parents are themselves just trying to survive and when you're struggling to feed your child, then English grammar or math are certainly not priorities. You've got to get to know parents and talk to them on a regular basis about everything that their children are doing, both good and bad.

TOWNE: It's always nice to get a call from a teacher just to say how great your child is doing.

ROGERS: I would always send out holiday cards and thank you cards to the parents because I wanted them to know that I care and that we are on the same team. I also scheduled multiple conferences per year with parents even though it was not required by the school.

TOWNE: You have an extraordinary talent to take students who are typically at-risk and raise their confidence and motivate them to *want* to learn. How does one go about doing this?

ROGERS: You really need to have the heart and passion for children, especially those that are in high-need schools. It's not easy and there will be times when it seems impossible. Your passion for them will carry you through those times and make the impossible, possible. However, there will be other times that you will need help. A good teacher is never afraid to ask for help. They're never afraid to seek out advice of the experts, especially when it comes to helping at-risk children. These children depend on you, and you owe it to them to do whatever is needed to better their lives. Not just their academic side and test scores, but the whole child. It's really about reaching out beyond your classroom door and not being afraid to say, "I don't know what to do about this. Can you help me?" Sometimes teachers don't like to admit that. No matter how long you've been teaching, you should constantly be searching out new things and trying to improve your craft.

TOWNE: Speaking of improving their craft, many of the Teachers of the Year I've talked with have graduate degrees in education. Research has shown that the number-one way to improve schools is to improve teachers. How important is continuous professional development to teachers, including becoming National Board Certified?

ROGERS: Being a lifelong learner is absolutely critical for teachers. No matter how good a teacher you are, you could be better, and you owe it to your students to become better. I waited 24 years before going back and completing my master's degree. I'm not proud of it taking so long, but I waited until my youngest son graduated from high school. I went back when I was in my 40's to get that master's and then my doctorate by age 50. The point is that it's never too late to learn and you can never know enough. Going back to school renewed me as a teacher. It opened my eyes to what new research was telling us and how trends were affecting education inside the classroom, and education as a whole. Understanding these things and how they change over time is so important for teachers.

Becoming National Board Certified was the same thing. It's a challenging process, but it took my teaching to a whole new level. When you've been teaching for many years, you often think that you know everything you need to know, but that's a fallacy. Our world is forever changing, and learning is not a static thing. Research shows that after ten years of teaching, your impact as a teacher starts declining. If you don't go back and get that ongoing professional development, you are doing yourself and your students a massive disservice. As I came toward the end of the National Board process, the standards just became embedded in me, and I felt like I was no longer just a teacher, but rather a professional educator.

TOWNE: Sounds like every teacher should aim for National Board Certification.

ROGERS: That certainly would be ideal. At Brighton, my current school, we recently received a grant from the National Board of Professional Teaching Standards that makes us a THNI (Targeted High Need Initiative) site. Nearly our entire school, including our principal, has agreed to attempt the TAKE ONE program within THNI. In this program teachers prepare and submit one pre-selected video portfolio entry from any of the current certificate areas of National Board Certification. Then a teacher can later transfer the score if he or she pursues National Board candidacy. This makes it possible for teachers not officially seeking National Board Certification to complete one of the Board's assessment entries. The idea is to expose teachers to the standards and propositions that the National Board believes define accomplished teaching. This is really great professional development for our teachers, and we hope a lot of them will go on to pursue certification.

I really believe that National Board standards are the standards to which all teachers should subscribe. These are the standards that will reform education.

TOWNE: Another common thread among the teachers I've been talking to is a study of Educational Leadership. Is it important for teachers to be leaders outside of the classroom?

ROGERS: Absolutely. What we're doing in school today is really much more complicated than when I first started teaching. Teacher accountability has become a major issue, and I welcome it and consider it very important. For this to happen, teachers have to step up to the plate as service leaders. If we're not producing for our students, then there's something wrong. I always push for teachers to fill that role; step up and become leaders, not just with your students, but with your colleagues as well. This includes other teachers, administrators, and even policy makers. I've been lucky enough to have always had principals who respect me enough to allow me to create various opportunities. Early on, I worked with teachers to write our own curriculum that was based on the needs of our students. No principal or administrator knows your students' needs better than you do. So if you're allowed to do that type of work and be that kind of leader, it can make a big difference. Teachers need to take every opportunity that they can to be leaders. I don't mean just being a committee person, but actually working with other teachers throughout the school on designing and implementing best practices. Don't wait for positive change—create it.

TOWNE: One of the biggest challenges for teacher recruitment and retention is the notoriously low pay teachers receive. In 2007, you worked with 17 other award-winning teachers to come up with a performance-pay plan for teachers. Can you tell us briefly what that plan encompassed?

ROGERS: Well, it revolved around ten core concepts. One is to get the base pay system right. There must be a career ladder that would allow teachers to advance their careers as well as their pay. Two is to supplement the base-pay system with a performance-pay system that's open to all teachers. Basically you don't want to put a cap on the number of teachers that are eligible for performance incentives, nor do you want to limit it to teachers who only teach certain subjects. Three is to reward teachers who help their students make significant academic gains. These gains should be measured over time, not with just a single standardized test score. Four is to provide additional pay for additional degrees and professional development, but only if the training is relevant. Professional development for teachers should be rewarded just as it is in other professions. Five is to allow local flexibility. All localities are different and performance pay should not be decided at the national level. Six is to encourage collaboration. All the great teachers know the importance of teamwork to a child's education, yet highly competitive compensation plans discourage this and that's got to change. Seven is to offer incentives to qualified teachers who want to teach in high-need, low-performing schools. Eight is to reward leadership, not seniority. It's not the "highly qualified" teachers that should be rewarded so much as the "highly effective" teachers. Nine is to be brave and be bold. Risk must be taken for any great change to happen, and education is no different. And finally, ten is to make sure to include accomplished teachers in any efforts to overhaul teacher compensation plans. Teachers need to be at the table, not just policy makers.

TOWNE: That's good stuff. Where can we learn more of the details?

ROGERS: The report is called *Performance Pay for Teachers* and you can find both the entire report and an executive summary of it online at www.teachingquality.org.

TOWNE: My final question concerns teacher accountability, which you touched on a few minutes ago. Most of the interviewees I've talked to believe that teachers should be held accountable for the success of their students, just as you said earlier. That being said, should they be held accountable based solely on standardized test scores?

ROGERS: On any given day, anything could happen to a kid taking a test. Things occur in their lives that affect test scores, but there's no footnote on the test stating that, so it becomes all about the numbers. We have these little portfolios of our kids that we look at that have all their reading data, math data, absences, behavior, everything about them we can find. And we look at this stuff regularly to find out what things may be going on that are hindering them from maximizing their learning. Looking at things like this is critical, and we do it in a team-based way, not only with their teacher, but also with other teachers at the school as well. Teams are often much more effective than any one teacher could be and we all know the kids and take a collective responsibility for them.

That being said, I truly believe that teachers should be held accountable for the success, or lack thereof, of their students. I hear so many teachers whining that "It's these kids!" No, it's not "these kids"; it's us. Standardized test or no standardized test, we must find ways to educate these children properly through the use of best practices. It's our obligation as teachers. Don't be afraid to go against the grain and challenge policies and rules that aren't working. Yes, it may be risky, but priority number one as a teacher should be the students and nothing else, including a flawed administration or government policy. I'm not suggesting anyone break the law, but find ways within the law to create positive change for your kids. Sometimes it's difficult for me to balance being kind to my profession and fighting for kids, but when it comes down to it, I will always fight for kids first.

CHAPTER 17

Jason Kamras

2005 National Teacher of the Year
2005 Washington, DC Teacher of the Year
John Philip Sousa Middle School
District of Columbia Public Schools
Math: Grades 7-8

Current Position: Director of Human Capital Strategies,
DC Public Schools

"Every child, regardless of background or circumstance, deserves an excellent education. This is a civil rights issue." That commitment to educational equity, combined with an innovative teaching style and dramatic student achievement gains in one of Washington, DC's lowest income schools, led to Jason Kamras receiving the National Teacher of the Year Award in only 8 years.

Kamras graduated *summa cum laude* from Princeton and received his master's degree from Harvard. With credentials like these, he could have done just about anything, but he wanted to teach. Therefore, he joined *Teach For America*, which placed him in Washington, DC, at John Philip Sousa Middle School, one of the Capital's lowest income schools. The District of Columbia has historically been one of the lowest-performing school systems in the country, but, in a short time, Kamras was able to achieve significant gains with his students. He established high expectations right away and used data-driven instruction to keep his students on track.

While at Sousa, Kamras worked to maximize his students' achievement and engagement in math. He helped administrators reorganize the school schedule to provide every student with two math classes per day. In addition, to get his students more excited about the content, he used his own passion, photography, as an entry point, putting key math concepts into an engaging context. His classroom innovations, combined with his curricular improvements, helped the percentage of students scoring Below Basic on the Stanford 9 to fall from 80 percent to 40 percent in just one year. Additionally, Kamras co-founded the EXPOSE photography program, which empowered Sousa students to develop their own creative voice through digital photography. His leadership of the program earned him the Mayor's Art Award, the highest arts honor bestowed by the District of Columbia.

More recently, Kamras served as a volunteer education policy advisor to the Barack Obama presidential campaign. He now serves as a senior advisor to Chancellor Michelle Rhee in the District of Columbia Public Schools. He and his wife, Miwa, also a *Teach For America* alum, live in Washington, DC, and are expecting their first child.

TOWNE: What's one of the biggest challenges you've faced while teaching, and how were you able to overcome it?

KAMRAS: I think one of the most significant challenges I faced was the culture of low expectations that had become the norm for so many of my students. As is the case in so many low-income communities across America, society did not expect much of my students and, as a result, achievement levels were alarmingly low. This was so painful to see because, although over ninety percent of my students lived below the poverty line, they were every bit as capable and every bit as bright as any other children I had ever met.

Let me share with you a story about one of my students that illustrates the culture of low expectations. When Erika first came to my class, she was fearful of math. She never had much success with the subject and, as a result, came to dislike it intensely. My colleagues and I worked diligently with her over the course of two years to build her confidence and instill in her the idea that she was perfectly capable of excelling in math. Over time, she became one of my most enthusiastic students. She even applied to a high school that focused on the math-heavy fields of business and finance. When I spoke to her in October of her freshman year, though, I was startled to learn that she wasn't taking any math. When I asked her why, she said: "The school counselor said she couldn't fit it in the schedule, and that I'd take math next year so it didn't matter." I was stunned. This would have never happened in a more affluent part of the city. It reflected a failure on the part of this city to create a school system that truly holds all students to the highest of expectations. I'm fortunate that I now have the opportunity in my current role to help change that.

Turning back to my classroom, to help combat the culture of low expectations, I did three things. First, I made it clear from the very first day that I expected every single one of my students to achieve at the highest levels. As a class, we set ambitious goals for student learning and diligently worked our way towards those goals throughout the school year. I firmly believe – and experience has borne this out – that students will rise to the expectations we set for them. Second, I explicitly taught the theory of malleable intelligence, investing my students in the idea that achievement was a function of effort, not innate ability. This was critical as so many of my students had come to believe that they simply weren't capable of success in school. Third, I used achievement data to strategically differentiate my instruction in an effort to ensure that every one of my students was adequately challenged. I built this process of data analysis into my long-term and weekly lesson planning. I was able to take this a step further when I managed to obtain a wonderful piece of technology that allowed me to quickly assess individual student learning right in the middle of a lesson. This enabled me to adapt my teaching in real-time to ensure that I was efficiently moving every single student towards our ambitious achievement goals.

TOWNE: How were you able to make math so interesting for your students?

KAMRAS: I love math and always wanted my students to feel the same way. But I know that many children, particularly those who haven't had a lot of success in school, fear math. So I started thinking about ways to embed the key concepts into a context that was more accessible to middle school students. One evening, while I was at a photography class at the Corcoran Museum of Art here in Washington, DC, it suddenly hit me: I could create a photography curriculum as the basis for some of my math instruction. I know this sounds a bit unusual, but it worked. My students loved learning about photography and created beautiful and moving photo essays about their lives. At the same time, they learned so many critical math concepts. Let me give you a few examples. When you zoom in and out on a camera, you're just changing the angle of view. That's a great way to start talking about basic geometric concepts. To fully understand exposure settings, you need a strong foundation in fractional comparison. You need to know, for example, that 1/1000 of a second is less than 1/500 of a second. And, if you're working with digital photography (as we were in my later years of teaching), you need to understand ratios, the foundation of digital resolution. I could give you literally hundreds more examples. Photography is just one of the real-world contexts that I used to engage my students. The key, I learned, is to make the concepts jump off the page by showing how they're relevant to students' lives.

TOWNE: You are consistently able to make math fun for inner-city, middle school kids that have a history of being ignored. How are you able to establish enough trust, with kids that are entering your class for the first time, in order to get them to buy-in?

KAMRAS: I don't think there's a magic bullet here. What I've found is that children come to trust you once they see how hard you're working, how high your expectations are, and how much you care about them personally.

To illustrate, let me tell you a story about a student of mine named Wendall. Wendall was in my very first sixth grade class, and he definitely didn't trust me at the beginning. He frequently disrupted my class, challenged me all the time, and rarely followed my class rules. I'm not ashamed to admit that I was struggling those first few weeks, and it was in no small part due to Wendall. I also knew that he was getting involved in some activities outside of school that were taking him down a decidedly negative path.

Fortunately, I was smart enough to know that I needed some help. So one day after school, I dropped by Wendall's apartment, sat down with his mother, and explained the situation. That afternoon, Mrs. Jefferson gave me some of the best educational advice I've ever received. She said: "Mr. Kamras, I want you to do two things. First, I want you to be tough with Wendall. And if that means you have to give him detention every single day from now until June, go ahead. You have my blessing. Second, I want you to reach out to him – make a connection with him – so that he knows you're being tough not because you're mean, but because you actually care."

I was deeply appreciative for Mrs. Jefferson's advice, but wasn't exactly sure how to make the kind of connection she talked about. When I told her this, she asked me if I played chess. I told her that I did, but that I wasn't particularly skilled. She told me that, even though Wendall's grades and behavior had been erratic, he always loved playing chess. So she suggested I invite him to play a few matches after school. That's exactly what I did.

One Wednesday after school, we sat down to play five matches. I didn't want to embarrass Wendall, so I took it easy on him. After fifteen minutes, he had defeated me. I upped my game a bit for the second match. This time, it took him only ten minutes. For the third match, I brought everything I had, and it took him only five minutes. By the fifth match, he knocked me out in three *moves*.

To make matters even more interesting, we had made a wager that day. If I won three out of five matches, Wendall would have to come see me for after-school math work for a month. If he won three out of five – let alone all five out of five – I would have to admit defeat in front of the entire class the following day. So this is what he made me say: "Wendall is a chess *beast*. He beat me five times in a row."

I figured that this small embarrassment was worth the reward of having made even the smallest of connections with one of my students. From that moment on, Wendall and I had something of an understanding with each other. He knew I was committed to seeing him succeed, and I knew he was committed to meeting me halfway. Things weren't always easy. We had moments of triumph, and moments of despair. But, we persevered–together. Over time, he became a class leader, and his achievement soared.

Even after he left my sixth grade class, we would meet in the afternoons to play chess, go over math assignments, or just talk about music, movies, or politics. His focus improved, his grades rose even higher, and when 8th grade graduation finally arrived, Wendall walked across our auditorium stage as class Valedictorian. He went on to Banneker Senior High School, one of Washington, DC's flagship academic academies.

TOWNE: Wow, that's a great story. Any idea what became of Wendall after he left your school?

KAMRAS: Well, attending Banneker was a transformative experience for Wendall. Surrounded by extremely industrious students in a magnet school setting, he began to realize that his innate abilities would only carry him so far. The messages that both his mother and I had been sending him about diligence and consistency suddenly had new resonance. He asked me for additional assistance, and I enthusiastically accepted. We worked on geometry, chemistry, and English. We read and analyzed novels, and we explored museums across the city.

By his sophomore year, Wendall was progressing quite rapidly. Then, suddenly, he called me and told me he was leaving Banneker and transferring to his neighborhood high school. After speaking with him further, I found that he transferred not because the work was too difficult or the competition too fierce, but because his younger brother, a freshman at the neighborhood high school, had begun to stray from his family, and needed closer attention. Out of a deep sense of loyalty for his brother, Wendall gave up his spot at Banneker, and, in doing so, gave up a nearly guaranteed path to college admission.

I was deeply moved by this, particularly because I have two brothers myself. I'm in the middle, so I know what it's like to look over my younger brother, and to be looked over by my older brother.

After the transfer, Wendall's mother was concerned that *he* might lose his focus. She asked me to develop an SAT preparation course for him to ensure that he would be prepared for the college application process. His family could not afford Princeton Review or Kaplan. I happily agreed and immediately ran off to Barnes and Noble and purchased every SAT prep book I could find. We worked every afternoon for ten weeks, first on reading and then on math. The work paid off. Wendall scored in the mid-1300s (on the old 1600 scale) and the college acceptances poured in.

I've continued to keep in touch with Wendall, and I'm proud to report that he now has an electrical engineering degree from Temple University and is working on his master's. Not only that, but he's also working at one of the premier engineering companies in the DC region making three times what I was paid when I taught him!

The only reason I was able to play a small part in Wendall's success was that he came to trust me. And that trust came from three things: working hard, holding the bar high, and showing him how much his success meant to me.

TOWNE: One of the qualities I've noticed in top teachers is their refusal to accept the status quo of things that are obviously not working. You're a good example of this as you came in and pretty much redesigned the math curriculum. Can you tell us what the curriculum was like before you got there and what you did to improve it?

KAMRAS: Originally, there wasn't much of a curriculum at all. There was a textbook, but not much else. So I basically created a course from scratch, using the content standards. In doing so, I realized that there simply wasn't enough time in the day to cover all the standards, particularly given the fact that so many of my students were already three or more grade levels behind. So I convinced my principal to double the amount of time for math instruction. I also added a zero period class for students with higher-level skills to ensure that they were being challenged sufficiently. All told, the amount of math instruction per day increased from 45 minutes to 120 minutes.

As I mentioned before, I also developed a number of photography-based units. To get the program off the ground, I needed a lot of equipment, including digital cameras, printers, computers, software, memory cards, and lots of consumables like ink, paper, and batteries. Our school couldn't afford any of these things, so I started writing grants. All told, we were able to raise about $65,000.

TOWNE: So you were able to use these grants successfully to fund the teaching methods you thought would work best, but the school could not afford?

KAMRAS: That's right. I was able to secure a small amount of money in the beginning, which enabled us to get things off the ground. Then the *Washington Post* did a small story on the program, and suddenly we had legitimacy. That helped us secure even larger grants. When the program was honored with the Mayor's Arts Award – the highest arts honor bestowed in DC – things really took off.

TOWNE: You're not the first teacher I've interviewed to stress the importance of learning how to write grants.

KAMRAS: Given the resource constraints that so many teachers face, it's a critical skill. I believe that educators need to find a way to be successful for their students despite the challenges – resources or otherwise – they face.

TOWNE: How do you establish authority in your classroom, and what methods of discipline do you use?

KAMRAS: I think it comes down to five things: setting very clear expectations; establishing equally clear consequences for failing to meet those expectations; consistently applying the consequences; taking every possible opportunity to highlight positive behavior choices; and having really great lessons. Let me say a few words about each of these. First, though it sounds obvious, it's incredibly important to set clear guidelines for how you expect your students to comport themselves in your class. I've found that a lot of new teachers assume their students know what's expected of them. In reality, many do not.

Second, and just as important, is clearly laying out the consequences for failing to meet the expectations you set. I've found that students, particularly in middle school, actually crave boundaries. They need to know what's going to happen if they come late to class, speak with disrespect, etc. Given this, I actually taught my expectations and consequences as an academic unit.

Third, consistency is key. If you say you're going to make a phone call, do so – every single time.

Fourth, highlighting positive behavior is always more effective than highlighting negative behavior. Children – like adults – crave positive recognition. I had all sorts of simple methods for highlighting positive behavior choices. For example, when a student who traditionally struggled with my class rules had a great day, I'd make a positive phone call home right in the middle of class. Many parents were astounded and delighted to get such a call. I also make certificates and small thank you cards to recognize students who demonstrated leadership when it came to behavior. I know these certificates and cards had an impact because I'd see them posted prominently on the walls of my students' apartments when I made home visits.

Finally, one of the best ways to promote order in your classroom is to have a wonderfully engaging lesson. No systems or routines can replace the power of a lesson that captivates students' minds.

TOWNE: So you used more positive reinforcement than punishment or negative reinforcement?

KAMRAS: Yes, I did – because it worked. For instance, suppose you're trying to line up thirty students for lunch. I guarantee you that you'll be more successful if you start publicly thanking the students already in line than publicly reprimanding those who are not. We all crave positive recognition; it's human nature.

TOWNE: What about defiant children? How do you handle a defiant child who refuses to learn?

KAMRAS: Sometimes the basics aren't enough. In those cases, I've found that it comes down to relationships. It's about taking the time to really get to know a student and develop a meaningful connection. This can be challenging, particularly in a secondary environment where you may have over 100 students. But it's essential. Wendall proved that to me early on.

TOWNE: How about motivating an apathetic student?

KAMRAS: Here, too, I think it's about relationships and about taking the time to understand what motivates a student. Every child is interested in *something*. It's our responsibility as educators to find out what that is and capitalize on it. I also think it's critical to be as creative as possible with your teaching every single day. Learning should be exciting, not monotonous.

TOWNE: How do you deal with unruly, uncooperative, or just uninvolved parents?

KAMRAS: Every parent I've ever met really wants the best for her or his children. But some face so many challenges in their own lives – and those challenges are only increasing in today's declining economy – that they may be too exhausted or overwhelmed to effectively support their children's learning. Also, many parents in low-income communities did not, themselves, have positive experiences in school. As a result, many are reluctant to engage with teachers and administrators about their children's education. So we've got to do more to meet our students' families half way. That means being flexible when we schedule conferences; it means making home visits; and it means creating welcoming classrooms for our students' families. It was critical for me to take these steps in order to build positive and productive relationships with their parents and families.

I'm not suggesting that parents don't have an important role to play. Of course, they do. They need to make sure that the television is turned off, that homework is done, and that children get to school on time. But when that's not happening, we, as educators, can't give up. We need to do whatever it takes to help our students succeed.

TOWNE: What are your thoughts on the debate related to social promotion and retention? Both are thought to be unappealing options. Are there any other options that could be considered?

KAMRAS: I believe we need to err on the side of maintaining high standards and holding students accountable for those standards. Simply moving children along because of their age, with little regard to their achievement, is tantamount to giving up on them. That's the manifestation of low expectations that I spoke about before. At the same time, nobody wants to be in the seventh grade at sixteen years old. Middle school is already awkward enough as it is. So we need to create non-traditional educational environments for over-age children. In short, we need to be smarter about how we meet every child's needs while still holding them to high standards.

TOWNE: What do you think is the biggest problem facing the education system right now, and do you have any suggestions on how to fix it?

KAMRAS: I believe that the greatest injustice in education right now is our nation's collective failure to ensure that low-income and minority children have access to outstanding public schools. As a result of this inequity, we see enormous and alarming gaps in achievement among our children. I believe that we have the responsibility to close these gaps and I further believe that the first step towards this goal is ensuring that every low-income classroom is staffed with an outstanding teacher. An overwhelming body of research confirms that great teachers can erase the achievement gaps in their schools.

So how do we ensure that every child, regardless of background, has access to an excellent teacher? I think it comes down to five things. First, we need to ensure that low-income schools have great principals. High-performing teachers look for great leadership above all else. Second, we need to provide far better support to educators serving in low-income communities. The work is extraordinarily challenging, and most professional development programs simply aren't up to the task. More often than not, they lack both rigor and relevance. Third, after we've given teachers additional support and opportunities for improvement, we need to do a better job of transitioning those who are consistently low-performing. I recognize that this is controversial, but I believe it's necessary if we're going to close the achievement gap in America. High-performing teachers – just like high-performers in all professions – want to work with similarly capable colleagues. Fourth, we need to give high-performers more opportunities to take on additional leadership roles – to be mentors or curriculum specialists, for example – without pulling them from the classroom. Finally, we need to pay high-performing educators serving in low-income schools significantly more. Of course, teachers don't choose this profession to become wealthy, but they certainly deserve to be. We need to target our resources towards educators who demonstrate that they can increase student achievement in the most challenging circumstances. Such educators should be making in excess of $120,000 early in their careers.

TOWNE: Tell me your thoughts on No Child Left Behind. What do you like about it and what don't you like about it?

KAMRAS: I know I'm in the minority of educators on this, but I think NCLB has been incredibly positive for public education for a couple of reasons. First, it has created incredibly high standards for *all* children and, in doing so, forced school systems to pay closer attention to the achievement of low-income children. Let me tell you a story to illustrate this. When I was Teacher of the Year, I met a principal in Virginia who told me the following: "I used to use any 'warm body' to teach my remedial math classes, which were mostly my poor and minority students. But now with NCLB, I have to put my most effective teachers in those classes, or we won't meet Adequate Yearly Progress." This is an example of how NCLB has forced schools to maintain high expectations and produce significant results for *all* students – not just some of them. If that's all that NCLB did, I think we should call it a success.

Second, NCLB has pushed the data-driven instruction movement forward by requiring standardized testing in grades four through eight and in the tenth. Of course, standardized tests aren't perfect. They often don't assess higher order schools and are typically limited to English and math. But these deficiencies can be rectified. The key here is that we now have data in every state that we can use to more strategically guide our instruction.

Though I'm a supporter of NCLB, I also believe it has some problems. First, although it required testing in every state, it didn't establish a clear set of national standards or an accompanying national assessment. As a result, every state assesses student progress differently, making it incredibly difficult to make meaningful comparisons. Second, the law required that every teacher be highly *qualified* when it should have required that every teacher be highly *effective*. I'm hoping that both of these issues will be addressed in the upcoming reauthorization of the law.

TOWNE: Teacher turnover rate is high, especially in the high-poverty schools and among teachers in their first couple of years on the job. What words of advice do you have for future and new teachers that might be interested in teaching in these schools, but are afraid of failure?

KAMRAS: I think it's important to be honest. Teaching in a low-income school is extraordinarily challenging – the hardest work I'll ever do in my life. But it's also critical. Therefore, I tell college students, and people who are thinking about switching careers, to spend some time tutoring in a low-income school to get a sense of both the challenges and the joys of teaching in such an environment. If it feels right and you're having some success, then you should jump in. You just can't be afraid of failure. I teach my students to take risks and to push themselves beyond what they believe are their limits. We have an obligation to ask the same of ourselves.

CHAPTER 18

Tamra Tiong

2007 National Teacher of the Year Finalist
2007 New Mexico Teacher of the Year
Dulce Elementary School
Dulce, New Mexico
Special Education: K-3ʳᵈ

Tamra Tiong (better known as "Miss Tammy") is a guitar-playing, star-gazing, garden-growing, Frisbee-throwing, bird-watching, book-reading, bike-riding lover of life. She grew up in a trailer park in South Lake Tahoe, where she would pick jarfuls of pine nuts and create imaginary worlds in forested lots with her cousins. She graduated from Santa Clara University in 1998, with a degree in English and a minor in Environmental Studies, but also dabbled in other subjects that interested her, such as anthropology, sociology, watercolor painting, geology, botany, philosophy, and ballroom dancing. She later went on to receive her Special Education Teaching license through the alternative licensure program at Northern New Mexico College in Española, New Mexico.

After graduation, Tiong rode thousands of miles by bicycle throughout the western United States just to hear people's stories. She then taught 6th grade science at a middle school in Santa Cruz, California, through an AmeriCorps program (often referred to as the domestic Peace Corps), and implemented a schoolyard garden using curriculum focused on Sustainable Agriculture and Ecological Design. When funding for this program ran dry, she spent 3 years as a teacher-naturalist at the Hidden Villa Environmental Education Program in the Los Altos Hills. This job allowed her to do interactive presentations in diverse schools all over the Bay Area and bring kids (PreK through 6th grade) out to a 1,600-acre wilderness preserve, farm, and organic garden for educational field trips that made connections to what they were learning in the classroom.

Through her travels, Tiong later fell in love with the majestic landscapes of the southwest, where she began working (and playing) as a Special Education teacher for kindergarten through 3rd grade at Dulce Elementary School on the Jicarilla Apache Indian Reservation in Northern New Mexico, a position she has held for 7 years. She currently resides in Dulce, New Mexico, with her trusty rez dog, Peyote.

TOWNE: What were some of the biggest challenges you have faced as a teacher and how were you able to overcome them?

TIONG: The biggest challenges I have faced as a teacher were not static, one-time hurdles that could be jumped over and left behind. The biggest challenges are dynamic monsters that need to be faced continually, that are ongoing battles, conflicts to be overcome on a daily basis.

One of the biggest challenges I face as a teacher mirrors what I find to be one of the ultimate challenges in life—namely, how to find the balancing point between optimism and reality, sanity and frustration, hope and rage. I have often felt that in order to be "successful"—however we choose to define this word—a person needs to be able to constantly seek out that balancing point between living sanely in the world that exists and purposefully working to improve it. As a teacher, I am faced daily with living bundles of curiosity, creative little beings eager to grow and learn and explore. At the same time I have felt the impacts of an educational system that seems to be growing more and more standardized, mechanized, and homogenized. I realize that in order to remain sane in the profession, I need to put some of my energy toward educational reform (which includes severely challenging the test-and-punish mandates of No Child Left Behind) while maintaining a positive presence in the classroom.

I agree with the late Asa Hilliard, who said that "to establish the standards of output without having standards of input is a travesty." We often hear the line that teachers are the most important factor in determining the success of a child, yet to ignore the reality of unequal opportunities and resources that exist in society is to adopt a "hard bigotry of indifference" (to borrow a phrase from Gerald Coles). I think it's criminal to expect schools to solve all the problems of society, as this relieves governments of their responsibility to address the pervasive social inequities that exist in areas such as housing, income, nutrition, health care, safety, literacy-rich environments, and opportunity. As teachers, we can hold high expectations for all students, but as teacher-citizens, we can demand that governments do all they can to address the inequities outside of school, closing the gaps that do—let's face it—affect children.

In addition, I believe that all students need to be able to see themselves reflected in a curriculum in order to feel a connection to it, in order to feel that school is not an isolated abstract thing which has no relevance to their home or to the real world that is their life. But what happens is that public schools, particularly those labeled "in need of improvement" according to No Child

Left Behind, tend to adopt curricula based on whether they are "scientifically research-based," rather than on whether they will reflect the individual students in their own classrooms. I think that nationwide curricula (and tests, for that matter) still tend to mostly address white, middle-class students, and that teachers in low-income, working-class urban neighborhoods, or on Indian Reservations in rural America, are forced to look elsewhere for books and materials that will be relevant and interesting to the faces and lives in front of them.

The challenge, for me, is to remain angry enough to fuel a passion for justice and to work for change in an unjust society and educational system, but not so angry that I become bitter and want to throw in the towel. The challenge is to remain positive enough to share the joy and love of learning with the kids I get to work with, but not so optimistic that I become complacent in an educational system that's in need of a major overhaul. I overcome this challenge constantly because I am inspired every day by the sheer tenacity of kids. I am inspired by their sincerity, their directness, their ways of keeping things real and living in the present moment. I am inspired by their infinite curiosity and imagination, their determination and resilience, the purity of their laughter and their tears. I am inspired by their stories, their excitement and energy, and even, I'll admit, by the moments when they refuse to conform.

TOWNE: What was the best teaching advice ever given to you and how have you worked to incorporate it into your teaching?

TIONG: Some of the best teaching advice I've taken has come from the writings of naturalists. They might be giving advice about writing, or about appreciating nature, or about living life in general, but lots of their words hold very true for teachers specifically. Barry Lopez, for example, talks in an interview about a Nunamiut

Eskimo man he once met and asked, "When you go to a place you've never been, what do you do?" The man had replied very simply, "I listen." Lopez also says that the first rule of everything is to pay attention, and that "to do this you've got to be curious all the time."

To listen, to pay attention, to be curious—what simple yet sound advice, a reminder to constantly check in with myself and decide if I am being present with the young people in front of me. Most kids have far more to say than we give them opportunities for in any given school day, so I make it a point to try and listen as much as I can to the funny and bizarre and scary and touching stories they have to share. I have to set aside time when I can listen with an active heart, not with one eye on the clock or on the next assignment. The act of listening validates children, builds relationships and trust, helps me gauge a student's emotions, helps me know how to approach a particular lesson or day. It also seems the more we listen to kids, the more likely they will listen to us when it's our turn to talk.

The concept of paying attention and being curious all the time is a piece of advice I try to carry everywhere; it's a philosophy that can help anyone become more aware, and, in turn, more empathetic and proactive in dealing with life in general, with teaching in specific. Becoming aware and observant takes conscious practice, especially in today's fast-paced world of information overload.

Here is an exercise to try right now: if you are sitting at home as you read this book, try to imagine your classroom, the place where you likely spend the majority of your life's hours. Picture each wall and either describe to someone or write down what is on each wall, how your chairs, desks, and tables are set up, which students sit where. Try to remember something each student said to you over the course of the last week. If you are reading this book from somewhere other than your home, try to imagine the outside and inside of your abode. Which side of the door is your doorknob on? What color is your carpet, what hangs from each wall, how is your kitchen set up? Later, when you look, notice all the things you missed. We often get so busy that it's impossible to notice everything, all the time. But I find that practicing paying attention in various settings helps me be able to "read" my students' emotions and better predict (or change the course of) their behavior.

Finally, being constantly curious (e.g., trying or learning new things, exploring new places) is a way to stay actively engaged in life, which is one of the best ways to remain an interesting and dynamic teacher. My students love it when I share stories or pictures from my summer in Alaska (where the sun doesn't set!) or my Christmas vacation in Baja (on a surfboard!) or the snowy hike with my dog just down the road from my house (how he loves to fetch snowballs!). We know that yawning can be contagious; so can enthusiasm.

TOWNE: What unusual methods or strategies do you incorporate in your classroom that may be different than many teachers, but that you have found to be highly effective?

TIONG: I was an Environmental Education teacher for years before I decided to go into the classroom and work specifically with students who had special needs. Throughout my years as an environmental educator, I filled up a large tool bag full of tricks, songs, games, skits, interactive lessons, and snazzy ways of getting and keeping kids' attention. When I later went back to school to get my Special Education Teaching license, I filled up many new bags full of knowledge about how to teach diverse learners to read and write and do math, but I always held on to some of the strategies I had picked up while teaching outdoors.

I have a science lesson I do, for example, in which I bring a grocery bag full of various fruits and vegetables into a first grade class that's learning about the different parts of plants. There's a song that I've already taught them called "The Six Plant Parts," whose chorus engrains in their brains the plant parts they're learning about (roots, stems, leaves, flowers, fruits, and seeds), and whose verses describe the function of each plant part. The song also provides an example of each of the plant parts that is something people eat (i.e., carrots are roots, celery is a stem, lettuce is a leaf, broccoli is a flower, an apple is a fruit, a peanut is a seed). The grocery bag contains all sorts of edible things that the kids take turns categorizing by placing the food on a desk with that label, and then writing the name of the food (or placing an index card with the word already written) on a chart. I love this lesson because it addresses several New Mexico standards and benchmarks while incorporating all eight of the multiple intelligences.

I've also had my students plant carrots, lettuce, radishes, and beans in box beds by the window. Starting from seed, they create a Grow Journal in which they draw pictures and write about what they think each plant will look like as it grows. They water and measure their plants each day, and draw pictures to scale. They use math, learn new vocabulary, practice writing using past, present, and future tenses, and get to eat their final product.

One of my favorite things is using songs that incorporate movement. I have songs that teach color names, days of the week, months of the year, planets, continents, opposites, verbs, nouns, adjectives, coin values. I use jump-rope rhymes to teach and practice skip-counting. I have had the fortune of working with a great speech therapist who also writes songs and teaches the sign language to go with them. After the kids learn to sing the songs (which they learn very quickly), I eventually begin putting up transparencies with the words printed out, and point to each word as they sing the songs they know so well. This helps reinforce the print/speech connection, and I've seen children's reading vocabulary increase greatly through these songs.

I use puppets and various voices at times just to spice things up, or to link a visual and tactile memory to whatever I am teaching at the time. I march around the room with kids while reading a story to emphasize the jobs of punctuation marks (we stop in our tracks when there's a period, pause, and swing our hips at a comma, and jump excitedly at an exclamation point). I've found that anything that incorporates music, movement, and laughter will generally reinforce the skill or lesson to be taught—and as a bonus, will brighten up the day.

TOWNE: What was it about Mrs. Thoren, your 5th and 6th grade teacher, that made you want to be like her? How can teachers become a Mrs. Thoren to their students?

TIONG: When I graduated from high school, I wrote and delivered a six-page hand-written letter to Mrs. Thoren, who had been my teacher in 5th and 6th grade (she taught a mixed-grade class). I wanted her to know how much she had meant to me, and that I remembered all the things we had done in her class. I recalled the "book reports" we used to do after reading books of our choice, and all the creativity that was allowed and encouraged with these "reports." I almost never chose to do the standard written report, but rather chose a different product from her "menu" of options each time. I made a greeting card from one character to another after reading *Brian's Song*; a garbage can containing items that one central character would have had after reading *Charlotte's Web*; a board game with trivia questions and answers after reading a biography of Lew Alcindor (better known as Kareem Abdul-Jabbar). I remembered hollowing out eggs and using glue, yarn, markers, and fabric, creating an entire egg family about which I wrote countless poems. I remembered creating funny Picture Dictionaries to learn new vocabulary words. I remembered learning about killer whales and then deciding as a class to adopt one. I remembered getting to write in a journal every morning and rate our feelings on a scale from 1 to 10, and then explain why we felt that way (and it was partly through these journal entries that I came to deal with my parents' divorce). I remembered having auctions using paper money that a student designed and which we had opportunities to earn each day. I remembered her using students' names in each dictation sentence we had to write, which helped us relate, made us laugh, and made each one of us feel like we were noticed. I remembered working on a gift book during the holiday season. We would work on it for a month or more… it included poems and stories we would write, recipes, drawings, coupons, and photos. I made one in particular for my Auntie Rachel (72 years old at the time), who several years later passed away. I remember thinking when she died that at least I had no regrets, for I had expressed all of my feelings for her in that Christmas gift book I had made in Mrs. Thoren's class.

I especially remembered the many creative-writing assignments from Mrs. Thoren's class that would begin with a simple starting point or central idea but leave miles and miles of room for endless possibilities. She loved and appreciated outside-the-box thinking, so I thrived on approaching every assignment from a different angle; I remember wanting to surprise her with an even *more* creative story each time, something she could never predict. In the letter I wrote to her after graduating high school, I told Mrs. Thoren, "I absolutely loved filling up page after page with my ideas, and the fact that you almost always read my stories to the class gave me such a feeling of pride. The other kids seemed to enjoy hearing you read my stories; they weren't envious or resentful as I at first thought they might be. Instead they simply enjoyed the tales, and the more they did, the more delight I took in preparing them. You may not have realized it, but by reading my stories to the class, you gave me confidence, and you sparked my desire to write and to entertain."

Mrs. Thoren had a genuine love of children. I can still feel her warm hugs, hear her caring voice, and see her interested, sympathetic eyes that twinkled with delight at her "job." I put that word in quotation marks because she made us feel like there was nothing she would rather be doing than hanging out with us kids all day; we couldn't help but enjoy ourselves when she was having such a great time. She managed to create a safe and embracing environment in which *everyone* enjoyed the journey of learning, whether they were traditionally "low-performing," "gifted," or simply "too cool for school." She had a beautiful ability to find every child's strengths and interests, and build a strong classroom community based around this knowledge.

In addition, Mrs. Thoren never teased or embarrassed me for being too quiet or shy, as most teachers had in the past. I knew that there was more to me than that quiet, bookish kid that most teachers couldn't see beyond—a side that was zany and passionate and creative and wild. But it becomes difficult, if not impossible, to show people something that they refuse to see because they've already labeled you. I learned early on how easy it is to become what we are labeled. But Mrs. Thoren wouldn't let that happen. I thought she was a sort of superhero whose gift was a pair of magic glasses that enabled her to see what others couldn't: she could see, in every child, what we wanted and hoped somebody would find in us.

It wasn't so much that I wanted to *be* like Mrs. Thoren; it was that she made me feel that it was okay to be fully myself. What I did want to do, however, was to bring out the best in children the way she had done with so many. You ask me how can teachers become a Mrs. Thoren to their students? I say: become fully yourself. Do what you love and love what you do. Remember what it is like to be a kid, but don't imagine every kid has the same thoughts, strengths, and weaknesses that you did.

Try to discover all you can about each student and find a way to sincerely value each individual. Have fun, and don't be afraid to wear your heart on your sleeve once in a while. Understand and believe that kids are not just in your class rehearsing for their future; they are living life NOW, and it matters.

TOWNE: What have been the most successful methods you have found in implementing differentiated instruction into your lessons?

TIONG: I remember being in high school and having a teacher give a writing assignment that I was initially excited about. I also remember that excitement being squashed when the teacher explained that before we began writing, we would have to create and turn in an outline, modeled after the given example. I loved to write, but, as much as I tried, I could not make my ideas stand still and organized in the stifling form of an outline. I found that when I did create an outline to fulfill the teacher's request, my actual writing lacked the creativity and passion I had initially wanted to infuse the paper with. I understand that this teacher was trying to get us to practice an important pre-writing skill, but remember thinking, "If I can write a better paper without creating an outline, with just pre-writing and letting my ideas flow out first, why can't I do that?" Without knowing it, I was essentially wishing the teacher would differentiate instruction by allowing us different processes and pathways to the same goal: a well-organized yet creative and thoughtful paper.

I share this story to explain why, as a teacher, one of the most successful ways I've found to differentiate instruction is to allow students multiple pathways to a common destination, particularly when it comes to writing. For example, when a piece of creative writing is the goal, I will give kids a number of choices on how to begin. Some kids choose to use one of the magazine pictures I have on file as a starting point for their story. Some kids choose to use pattern blocks on the floor to create a scene or character that becomes the focus of their story. Some kids choose to use a "squiggle," literally a scribble I have made on paper with a black marker which they extend into a picture their imagination creates, and write a story based on the original picture they have drawn. Yet other kids can begin by using a flip-book that gives them a silly sentence around which to create their story.

I also find that graphic organizers are a great way to differentiate the ways that kids are allowed to learn and study things such as important concepts from a story, or vocabulary definitions (there are a zillion free printables on the internet, or some great ideas from Dinah Zike's books). While some kids may benefit from copying definitions or notes off the board, others spend such an inordinate amount of time copying that they never get around to finishing, or their copying skills are so laborious that they don't learn a thing from the process. If the goal is to know and understand key concepts or vocabulary words, kids should be allowed various methods to master them. Picture Dictionaries (which I learned from Mrs. Thoren!), charades, matching games, and story boards are all strategies I have found to be successful in helping kids master key concepts and vocabulary.

One of the most successful methods of differentiating instruction I've implemented (and also one of the most fulfilling and gratifying to observe) is utilizing mixed-age study buddies. The first time I ever used this strategy in the classroom was not exactly planned; it actually grew out of what I like to call a "situational necessity." My particular situation involved having second graders help kindergarteners with their handwriting, or math, or letter recognition. I have also had second and third graders pair up with kindergarteners to read to them. I recall one second grader with a learning disability (I'll call her "Maria") who was shy about reading in front of her classmates, but who shined when given the task of being "teacher" to some kindergarteners. "Sit down," I heard Maria tell a group of kindergarteners, doing her best teacher impersonation. "Criss-cross, applesauce," she instructed. She proceeded to read to them while showing the pictures, holding the book exactly as I always did, mimicking my gestures and even questions. "What do you think will happen next?" she asked, making them raise their hands and take turns. As fun as this was for me to watch, it provided much more than just entertainment for me. I have found using mixed-age study buddies to be beneficial for everyone involved. The second or third graders get the opportunity to practice their own academic and language skills, and gain self-confidence, while the kindergarteners enjoy the novelty of being taught by someone only a foot taller than they are.

I have seen a variation of this strategy used in classrooms, where students can post "ads" on a bulletin board. On one side of the board, kids post index cards listing things they consider their strengths, that they would be willing to help other students with. On the other side, kids post index cards listing things they need help with. When a student needs help with something, he must first check the bulletin board to see if a particular student can help before he goes to the teacher. This helps foster interdependence, frees up the teacher's time to work with individuals or small groups, and offers students different ways to both acquire and apply academic skills.

TOWNE: What is your method for classroom management and handling discipline issues?

TIONG: Keep kids engaged! Okay, there's a little more to it than that... I try to set up an environment that is fun and engaging, yet predictable and structured. I clearly state and post my own expectations, make sure kids understand a few of my basic classroom rules (and consequences for not following them), and explain *why* I have these rules. They are then invited to add additional rules they think would help make the classroom a good and safe place to learn. I give my students opportunities to practice procedures daily until they become automatic routines. I hold kids accountable for their actions, and let them know that they are in control of choosing their actions. I try to have materials organized and accessible. I treat students fairly and with sincere respect, and keep them actively involved in meaningful work. I try to always model cooperation, good manners, and responsibility.

I write students' names on index cards, and each gets to take a turn (in a predictable rotation) being the "Big Cheese." The "Big Cheese" for the day gets to hold the foam block of cheese I have with a bean-bag mouse that serves as an eraser for the dry-erase boards. The student who is the "Big Cheese" gets to erase the boards, be the line-leader, and put the books away. I began this routine because when I first started teaching in the classroom, kids would all argue over who got to do these basic jobs, and pout if they didn't get to help or be the line-leader. I quickly found that having a predictably rotating "Big Cheese" solved most of these problems, especially if they knew that the privilege could be taken away.

I feel that anticipation and adjustment are key ingredients to managing a classroom. By that I mean we need to constantly pay attention and be aware of how students are feeling and responding to a particular lesson or situation, and if we see hints of boredom or sleepiness or frustration, change it up! Have the students stand up, do an exercise, shift gears. I play with voices a lot, using different accents, or just getting really quiet if students are getting loud. I notice that they often adjust their volume to match mine.

Perhaps most importantly, I tell students that it's always okay to *feel* angry, or sad, or frustrated, but that it's what we *do* with those feelings that can either be acceptable or not. Kids (as well as adults) need to know that their feelings are valid and acceptable, and that they have choices of how they deal with those feelings. I have games and puppet role-plays that demonstrate appropriate and inappropriate ways of dealing with all sorts of potential situations. It's important for them to understand that if they do face consequences (which should naturally and reasonably match the behavior), that it is because of the behavior they chose, not because of the feeling (anger, frustration) itself.

TOWNE: Many teachers with a "problem student" may be inclined to label them as "special-ed" and have them removed from their classroom. What do you tell teachers who are considering this? What specifically can they do to determine whether or not that is the best method to take?

TIONG: I don't think the issue is as simple as teachers wanting to label "problem students" and have them removed from the classroom. It may appear this way at times, due to an over-abundance of referrals to Special Education, but I don't blame teachers for this problem. If anything, teachers feel more and more pressure, particularly in schools that have been labeled "In Need of Improvement" according to No Child Left Behind, to ensure that every student is proficient on their state or district's standardized tests. Most teachers I know *do* have high expectations for their students, and try to meet the needs of all of them, but feel they are in an unforgiving system that doesn't allow room for students who work at a different pace, or learn in a different way. Many teachers feel that after exhausting all the strategies they know, their only options are to refer to special-ed or to retain the student (because they are not allowed to send students on to the next grade if they have not met the previous grade's benchmarks).

When teachers talk of a "problem student," it can mean one (or more) of many things. It can be a student whose academic skills are below that of his peers, who acts out because he'd rather appear "bad" than "dumb." It can be a student whose intellect is worlds beyond what is happening in the classroom, who is bored to tears. It can be a classroom that lacks the specific structure or routines or consistency that this "problem student" needs. It can be a student who learns best through hands-on strategies while most of the curriculum is being delivered auditorily or visually (or vice versa). It can be a student who is going through crazy tough times at home and wants any kind of attention she can get. It could be a personality clash between student and teacher. In short, there are an infinite number of reasons why a student may be perceived as a "problem student," but ultimately the decision of whether a student needs special education services is not a choice to be made by a teacher alone.

Most schools have a Student Assistance Team (SAT), which might be called different things in different places, but serves essentially the same purpose. As a member of my school's SAT, I participate in weekly meetings comprised of a committee of teachers who are dedicated to helping teachers intervene with students who are struggling in any way in the classroom. Teachers can refer a student to SAT, and then be prepared to answer loads of questions about that student. Observations are done, strategies are recommended, interventions need to be implemented and documented, parents are involved, etc. When done right, it is a very thorough process (which goes beyond the scope of this book) that helps to rule out or narrow down the reasons that a particular student might be giving his teacher a headache. Pulling a student out of the classroom might take the headache away, but won't help the child. We owe it to all students to give them a fair shot in the classroom by doing the detective work it takes to understand why something's not working for them.

TOWNE: Many teachers are very concerned that they won't be able to handle special-ed students being "mainstreamed" into their classrooms. How can teachers best prepare for this and alleviate their worries?

TIONG: Although it's not the *only* factor, attitude is definitely a crucial component when it comes to mainstreaming. Let me give you an example. I used to lead field trips for an Environmental Education Program. Before the day began, a classroom teacher would give me an index card with the names of the kids who would be in my group for the day. Sometimes the teacher would tell me that she had put an asterisk next to the names of students I should keep a close eye on, who were "behavior problems." Unless I knew that there were true medical or safety issues involved, I would generally put the index card in my pocket without even looking at it. I would play games to learn the kids' names, and then spend a whole day with them hiking in the woods, doing gardening projects and farm animal chores, teaching about watersheds and ecology and connections. When the day was over, out of pure curiosity, I would sometimes pull out the index card and find that the kids who had been blacklisted by their teacher had been the ones who were most inquisitive, helpful, or engaged. I sometimes wondered if I would have subconsciously treated those children differently had I taken note of the asterisks.

It's true that in schools we *do* have to take note of the asterisks; that is, we can't just stuff students' IEPs in our pockets and look at them out of curiosity when the year is over, hoping they did okay. However, if students with special needs are going to be mainstreamed successfully, teachers need to adopt accepting attitudes, hold high expectations, and truly value all students as contributing members of a learning community. If you are intimidated or feel unprepared to work with students who have disabilities, do some research about the disability: read books and articles, search the internet, watch DVDs, attend workshops, talk to experts, talk to the parents, and listen. Get inspired by the success stories of others. Know and understand and believe the mantra, "Fair doesn't mean everyone gets the same thing. Fair means everyone gets what they need."

Finally, mainstreaming can't work if students with special needs are just "dumped" into general education classrooms with wishes of "Good luck!" and "Try your best!" Working with students with disabilities needs to become a larger and more essential component of teacher prep programs. Successful mainstreaming also requires that the general education teacher is not left alone without adequate support from the special education teacher and related service providers as necessary. Responsibility for ensuring that students with special needs are receiving a fair and appropriate education does not rest solely on the shoulders of general education teachers. However, it *is* the classroom teacher's responsibility to do all she can to ensure that students with special needs feel as valued, necessary, and capable as every other student in the room.

TOWNE: What are some of the most effective inclusive education practices you have found, especially those related to "full inclusion"? What can administrators do to help ensure that special-ed inclusion at their schools is successful?

TIONG: First, I think it's important to mention that even "full inclusion" doesn't necessarily mean that students aren't pulled out of the regular classroom at all, ever. Multi-disciplinary teams (or IEP teams) will still determine student placement on an individual basis, even in a school that embraces a "full inclusion" model. "Inclusion" is not just about placement of students receiving special education services; it is a word that implies acceptance and validation of *all* students in a classroom, school, local, and global community. When I talk of inclusion, I am referring not so much to a place as to a philosophy.

One strategy I have found to be very effective with regard to inclusive education is when teachers have deliberate and on-going discussions with their students about differences and similarities among people in general. A student should not have to be ashamed of her disability, nor should a teacher feel he has to "hide" a student's disability, or pretend it doesn't exist. Essentially, the more differentiated activities are allowed and encouraged in a classroom, the less a particular disability or accommodation will stand out as being unusual or unfair. A classroom that celebrates differences and individuality while acknowledging and valuing the common humanity we all share is an inclusive classroom.

One year I was fortunate enough to be able to work as a co-teacher in an inclusive first grade classroom that had five students with IEPs, only fifteen students altogether. At certain times in the day, we had an educational assistant as well, and were able to create three flexible, heterogeneous groups of five kids each that would rotate among the three of us. With such a low student-to-teacher ratio, we were really able to target individual needs, and easily identify and work with students' strengths and gaps. We held high expectations for all students, provided multiple pathways for students to attain and demonstrate concept mastery, and showcased and utilized every student's strengths. As co-teachers, we were able to model or demonstrate concepts in fun and amusing ways, with one acting as teacher and the other acting as student, so the kids could see exactly what was expected of them. I remember our district superintendent visiting the class and later talking to the school board about her experience. She challenged any one of the board members to come into our class and see if they could distinguish the students who had special needs from the ones who didn't. *She* couldn't do it; she didn't think *they* could do it; and *that*, she said, was an inclusive classroom.

Administrators have the power to make inclusion either sink or soar. In order for inclusion to be successful, they need to ensure that general educators are sufficiently trained and prepared to work with students of varying abilities. They need to incorporate time for teachers to plan and collaborate with colleagues, including special educators, relevant paraprofessionals, and grade-level or same-subject peers. They need to ensure that teachers have access to appropriate materials and resources to support the students with special needs in their classes. In some cases, inclusion might require a major reorganization of a school's infrastructure and ideologies. Also, administrators might need to help create school-wide schedules that take into consideration students with special needs, and design ways for inclusive classrooms to have the support of a special educator and relevant paraprofessionals as needed. One of the biggest obstacles that prevents successful inclusion efforts is when one special education teacher has fifteen kids on her caseload, spread out among ten different classrooms, and cannot physically be everywhere at once. I once proposed that, as outrageous as it might sound, schools might need to provide funding to place a regular *and* a special education co-teacher in every classroom that had students with special needs. Either that, or create manageable schedules that allow special educators to co-teach in various classrooms throughout the day where he is needed most. There *are* schools that are currently implementing inclusive education successfully; administrators struggling to make it work in their own schools would do well to visit these successful schools, take detailed notes, and try to adapt the systems to match their own schools' unique needs.

Research (and common sense) has shown that well-designed inclusive classrooms benefit *all* students. "It takes all sorts to make a world," says the badger in Kenneth Grahame's classic tale *The Wind in the Willows*. It is our job as both educators and administrators to ensure that *all* children are exposed to the rich diversity of which real life is composed. We can no longer accept loose justifications for segregation, and should feel morally obligated to give *all* students a full opportunity to blossom, shine, and be truly valued in this interdependent and eclectic world we share.

TOWNE: Being a special education teacher, you have witnessed various teaching techniques in a wide variety of areas. What are the best practices you have found for both multi-sensory activities that reach all learners, and brain-integration techniques?

TIONG: I think it's safe to say that multi-sensory activities are *always* a good idea, even for those who learn easily through any modality. The more ways we learn or experience something (visually, auditorily, kinesthetically) the more likely we are to remember it in the long term. Physically acting something out, for example, stores a memory in the body as well as in the brain.

For teaching phonics, phonemic awareness, letter recognition, spelling, and other beginning language arts skills, I love using aspects of *Zoo-phonics* and *Lindamood-Bell*. I don't generally endorse specific products, but it's really the strategies and techniques I support more than the products themselves. I've seen kids really learn their letter sounds through *Zoo-phonics*, which first introduces animals (to whom kids can more easily relate than abstract symbols) in the shapes of lowercase letters. They learn to say the animal's name (which incorporates the letter sound) and do a movement to go along with each letter. I also often incorporate aspects of *Lindamood-Bell*, which helps kids to focus on what their mouths are doing as they produce each sound. They look in little mirrors and watch and feel what their tongue, lips, and teeth are doing as they produce the /d/ sound, or its quiet brother, the /t/ sound. They become aware that their tongue is tapping the roof of their mouth, and call it a "tongue-tapper." The /b/ and /p/ sounds become noisy and quiet "lip poppers," as the kids watch and feel their lips coming together and popping open to make that sound (and so on).

I like using colored felt squares to represent sounds as kids are learning to blend phonemes together to make words. I like to play games such as *Pictionary* or charades to reinforce vocabulary words in visual and bodily-kinesthetic ways. I like to create origami animals with kids to help them understand concepts of symmetry, vertical and horizontal lines, two- and three-dimensional objects. I demonstrate the folds myself first using verbal cues, and then have the students watch and mimic what I do with no auditory input.

Again, using more of the strategy than the actual product, I have found great success using the multi-sensory components of *TouchMath* to teach number recognition, adding, subtracting, and counting coin combinations. Beginning with concrete objects (plastic lady bugs, beads, marshmallows), I teach kids to recognize numbers and connect a numeral with its quantity by placing the objects on specific "touchpoints" on the numeral. They can learn to add and subtract pretty quickly by manipulating the concrete objects that are placed on or taken off the numerals. Later, these objects are replaced by symbolic dots which are touched and counted out loud, and eventually, the kids either simply imagine the dots as they add and subtract, or gain automaticity of facts through successful practice of the multi-sensory approach.

As far as brain-integration techniques, I often draw upon strategies from *Brain Gym* (originally developed by Paul and Gail Dennison), which is comprised of 26 targeted body movements designed to activate specific aspects of cognitive function by developing the brain's neural pathways, integrating all parts of the brain. Most school-based activities require all parts of the brain for optimal achievement. Reading, for example, requires students to recognize symbols (a left-brain function) as well as understand what they read (a right-brain function). Writing requires forming letters (left-brain) while composing thoughts (right-brain). Math requires calculating numbers (left-brain) as well as understanding reasons and applications behind it (right-brain). Success in these activities depends on the integration of both sides of the brain. Some of the exercises I do take only a couple minutes, but truly help to integrate both sides of the brain by crossing the midline of the body (e.g., drawing "lazy eights" in the air with our arms, or doing "cross-crawls" in which opposite hands touch opposite knees). Other specific stretching and movement exercises from *Brain Gym* help students focus, attend, remember, or organize by connecting neural pathways between the front half of the brain and the back, or between the top and bottom.

In short, the brain affects the body, and the body affects the brain. Knowing specific exercises to maximize student learning has been greatly beneficial to my teaching.

TOWNE: Is there anything you wish you had known your first year of teaching that you now know?

TIONG: I wish I had known that my job would soon seep into all aspects of my life. I wish I had known that I would worry about a certain first grade boy while eating my oatmeal in the morning, hoping he got a good night's sleep and that his parents didn't fight all night long. Or that I would frequently wonder, while brushing my teeth at night, about a second grade girl who moved to a different community...I wondered if she would be accepted, if her new teachers would be able to see past her disability to the brilliant and creative girl I knew she was. I wish I had known that I would shed tears of pride when my first group of kindergarteners completed fifth grade and moved on to middle school. I wish I had known that I would spend many weekends and nights dreaming and scheming and coming up with new ways to reach the supposedly unreachable child, that I would grow accustomed to the scent of markers and find solace in the texture of construction paper. I wish I had known that even if I wasn't taking home lesson plans to create or projects to grade or IEPs to write, I would spend a sunny Saturday hike composing a song in my head about adjectives. I wish I had known how passionate I would become about wanting the students I encountered to become adults who would find enjoyment in life, who would read and wonder and critically analyze their world, who would become active protagonists rather than mere spectators. I wish I had known that I would come to care so fiercely about my students that my heart would burst with joy at their accomplishments and shatter with despair at their tragedies.

If I had known then what an emotional roller-coaster ride this teaching stuff would entail, would I have signed up? Would I do it all over again?

You bet. I wouldn't trade this experience for the world.

25 Teacher Recommended Books

The following books have been recommended by the teachers interviewed in this book. Each teacher was asked to name one or two books that had a substantial influence on their teaching methods or philosophies. A few of these books were recommended by more than one teacher.

36 Children	Herbert Kohl
A Framework for Understanding Poverty	Ruby Payne
A Whole New Mind	Daniel Pink
Death at an Early Age	Jonathan Kozol
Enhancing Teaching	Madeline Hunter
Experience and Education	John Dewey
Freedom Writers Diary	Erin Gruwell
Getting Started	Rick DuFour
I Read It But I Don't Get It	Cris Tovani
Innovation Nation	John Kao
Man's Search for Meaning	Viktor Frankl
Molder of Dreams	Guy Dowd
Out of Our Minds	Ken Robinson
Pedagogy of the Oppressed	Paolo Freire

Reading Don't Fix No Chevys	Michael W. Smith
Savage Inequalities	Jonathan Kozol
Sometimes a Shining Moment	Eliot Wigginton
Super-Learning	Sheila Ostrander
Teacher	Sylvia Ashton-Warner
Teaching With the Brain In Mind	Eric Jensen
The First Days of School	Harry Wong
The Quality School Teacher	William Glasser
The Skillful Teacher	Jon Saphier
The Water is Wide	Pat Conroy
Tough Choices or Tough Times	The NCEE

Index

CPSIA information can be obtained
at www.ICGtesting.com
Printed in the USA
LVHW011316010822
724880LV00001B/58